M000205880

Dear Reader:

The book you are about to read is the latest bestseller from St. Martin's True Crime Library, the imprint *The New York Times* calls "the leader in true crime!" Each month, we offer you a fascinating account of the latest, most sensational crime that has captured the national attention. *The Milwaukee Murders* delves into the twisted world of Jeffrey Dahmer, one of the most savage serial killers of our time; *Lethal Lolita* gives you the real scoop on the deadly love affair between Amy Fisher and Joey Buttafuoco; *Whoever Fights Monsters* takes you inside the special FBI team that tracks serial killers; *Garden of Graves* reveals how police uncovered the bloody human harvest of mass murderer Joel Rifkin; *Unanswered Cries* is the story of a detective who tracked a killer for a year, only to discover it was someone he knew and trusted; *Bad Blood* is the story of the notorious Menendez brothers and their sensational trials; *Sins of the Mother* details the sad account of Susan Smith and her two drowned children; *Fallen Hero* details the riveting tragedy of O. J. Simpson and the case that stunned a nation.

St. Martin's True Crime Library gives you the stories *behind* the headlines. Our authors take you right to the scene of the crime and into the minds of the most notorious murderers to show you what really makes them tick. St. Martin's True Crime Library paperbacks are better than the most terrifying thriller, because it's all true! The next time you want a crackling good read, make sure it's got the St. Martin's True Crime Library logo on the spine—you'll be up all night!

Charles E. Spicer, Jr.
Executive Editor, St. Martin's True Crime Library

PRAISE FOR *A SCREAM ON THE WATER*

"Vivid...skillfully told...A detailed and engrossing account of a sensational murder case."

—The Patriot Ledger

"Engrossing."

—The Standard Times

"A fascinating account of what happened in the spring and summer of 1991 on Salem's waterfront... [this] is one of those books you cannot put down."

—North Shore Magazine

"Press...keenly illuminates the people and places surrounding the tragedy of a woman whose compassion led to her downfall."

—Library Journal

A SCREAM ON THE WATER

A TRUE STORY OF MURDER IN SALEM

MARGARET PRESS

WITH JOAN NOBLE PINKHAM

Published in trade paperback as *COUNTERPOINT*

St. Martin's Paperbacks

The author gratefully acknowledges permission from the following to reprint material in their control:

"Be My Anchor Tonight" by Julie Dougherty
© 1994 by Julie Dougherty. All Rights Reserved. Used by Permission.

"Close to Murder" by Kitty Babakian
© 1993 by Kitty Babakian. All Rights Reserved. Used by Permission.

"Under the Willows," and "I But a Little Girl" by Bob Franke
© 1987 by Telephone Pole Music Publishing Co. (BMI) All Rights Reserved. Used by Permission.

"My Ballad to Martha" by W.H. Goodwin III © 1993 by JPT Music. All Rights Reserved. Used by Permission.

Published in trade paperback as *Counterpoint*

Published by arrangement with Addicus Books, Inc.

A SCREAM ON THE WATER

Copyright © 1996 by Margaret L. Press.

Cover photograph of Tom Maimoni courtesy of Salem Police Department. North Shore map by Dan Carsten.

Library of Congress Catalog Card Number: 96-4989

ISBN: 978-1-250-09298-4

Addicus Books trade paperback published in 1996
St. Martin's Paperbacks edition / June 1997

St. Martin's Paperbacks are published by St. Martin's Press, 175 Fifth Avenue, New York, NY 10010.

P1

In Memory of
Martha Conant Brailsford
(1954-1991)

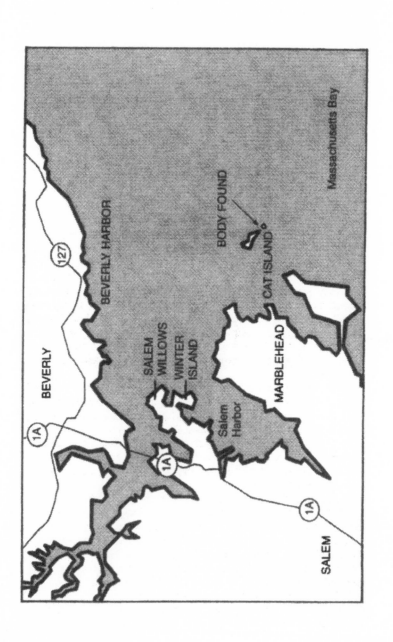

Acknowledgments

W ithout the help and encouragement of Detective Sergeant Conrad Prosniewski of the Salem Police Department, we never could have written this book. Much of it is his story, and we thank him for sharing it. We also express our deep appreciation for members of Martha's family who, despite their pain, shared whatever they could. Many, many other people also helped make this work possible with their insights, their memories, and their support. We are particularly grateful to those who set aside fear, grief, and privacy to talk with us—including those who, for one reason or another, prefer not to be identified.

From the Salem Police Department we thank Chief Robert St. Pierre, Detective Sergeant Richard Urbanowicz, Lieutenant Mary Butler, Detective James Page, Detective William Jennings, Detective James Gauthier, Officer Frank Baccari, Sergeant Karen Pooler, Captain Paul Murphy, and Captain Paul Tucker. In addition, we thank from the Essex County District Attorney's Office Assistant District Attorney Kevin Mitchell and Victim/Witness Advocate Sandra Clark.

We also thank Paul DeJoie, Superintendent, Essex County Correctional Facility at Middleton; Robert Pino, Commonwealth of Massachusetts Crime Lab; Gerald Feigin, M.D., forensic pathologist; Attorney Jeffrey Denner; Dr. Harold Bursztajn; Rosemary Farmer; Roxcy Platte; Tucker Goodman; Dr. Raymond Mount; Charlene Colella; Hooper Goodwin III; Julie Michaud Prosniewski; David Panka; William Connolly; June Chappell; Kitty Babakian; Robert Corcoran; Attorney Edward N. Garno; Bette Greeley Rantz; Dr. Benjamin Polan; Laney Roberts, Wharf Rat Productions; Mark Wile; Dorothy Chainey; Ian Chainey; Laurie

Cabot, High Priestess of Witchcraft; Dean Hartling; Peter Boyce; Mark Steele; Carmen Labrecque; Mary Norman, and Scott Clark.

We wish to extend our appreciation to Ann Green, Kaye Gordon, Richard Adamo, and Katie Hezekiah, from the Essex County Superior Courthouse.

For legal, technical, editorial, and other assistance we thank Margaret Leighton, Sara Press, Stan Anderson, Michael Johnson, Michael Gosselin, Robert Cusolito, Caleb Hanson, L. Allen Brown, Laura Driscoll, Carl Dawson, MaryEllen Zani-Nicolopoulos, Nelson and Jane Dionne, William Press, Bobbie Bush, Jody Ray Goodwin, Joan Kendall, Priscilla Willhite, Paul Briand, *The Salem Evening News*, and Attorneys Howard Zaharoff, Elizabeth Ritvo, and Frank McElroy. For assistance in procuring photographs, we thank Jonathan Whitmore of *The Salem Evening News*. For their guidance, commitment, and abiding support, we thank our agent Susan Crawford and Rod Colvin of Addicus Books. For their endurance and encouragement, we thank our families.

We are deeply indebted to them all.

Author's Notes

I was drawn to this story from the moment in July 1991 when missing-person posters showed up on the Salem waterfront and a local police detective appeared on TV asking for viewers' help. The missing woman—a lovely, compassionate, young artist named Martha Brailsford—happened to be from my neighborhood. So was the man with whom she was last seen—a senior product engineer with Parker Brothers Games and member of a nearby yacht club.

I have a particular abiding interest in writing about Salem. The city fascinates me without end, with its mixture of crusty maritime history, its modern-day witch population, and its three-hundred year struggle with guilt. However, my genre has been mystery fiction, often based on interviews with detectives from the Salem Police. Crossing over into nonfiction meant embracing risks I wasn't sure I wanted to embrace, particularly when the people involved lived just down my street.

Nevertheless, I followed with growing passion the investigation with its surprising twists, the arraignments, pretrial hearings, and ultimately the two-week trial. By the time the verdict was handed down I knew I wanted to tell this story. It was now part of Salem's history. With encouragement from the lead investigator and many others, I found the courage needed to tell it.

The entire community was fueled by shock, sadness, anger, and a need for resolution as this case progressed. But the fascinating glimpse into the complexity of human motivation is what fueled me personally. Things are not always what they seem, we learn again and again in this story. The reasons often lie locked in the human mind and heart.

In the course of the research and writing, I was gifted at every turn with countless lessons in psychology, law, linguistics, philosophy, and the human condition. A window on the mind, a window on life. And provoking questions along the way: Should I now learn to be less trusting, and more fearful? Where is the line between normal and sociopathic behavior? What's acceptable risk? What's reasonable doubt? What would I have done—on the boat? In the jury box? The reader now faces these same tough questions.

The names and places in this book are real, with a small number of exceptions. *Jennifer Eccleston* and "*B.C.*" are fictitious names. The first name of Martha's husband has been changed at his request, as was the street where they lived. A couple of minor events have been told out of sequence when the actual chronology would otherwise confuse or disrupt the flow of the story. Wherever possible, dialogue has been taken from transcripts, or from the recollections of those interviewed. In some places conversations or scenes have been partially recreated, but always in conformity with known facts, and only where it was reasonable to assume they occurred.

Nearly 2500 pages of trial transcripts and hundreds more from pretrial hearings were reviewed. We also studied the case files, motions and affidavits, press clippings and numerous other sources to help shape this story. Above all, Detective Sergeant Conrad Prosniewski's unselfish granting of his time allowed focusing on the unique perspective of the investigator, his frustrations, his challenges, the skills he had to call upon, and the effects on his private life.

From copious correspondence and a half dozen interviews with him, I gained a richer understanding of how the man accused of killing Martha constructs and views his world. Close to sixty other people were also interviewed for this book. A very small number of those we approached declined to talk, preferring not to resurrect painful memories, or because the appeal was still pending, or out of fear of getting involved. Living in this town has resulted in innumerable other chance encounters with individuals who would share some memory, some irony or insight. Martha touched many lives with her generous spirit. In this story we came to know her through the remembrances of those she touched and those who were moved enough to share her with strangers.

One of my greatest rewards during interviewing was witnessing relief and closure for some who had long needed to talk about the experience. In a number of instances I was thanked, and humbled, since it was I who was the more indebted. I was grateful for the affirmation that this undertaking had been worthwhile.

I am a mystery writer. I write about death because it's a good way to understand life. As is often the case, it is pathology which illuminates the most. Whether in fiction or non-fiction, writers have an obligation to pursue truth, to shun safe routes and easy answers. Distrust absolutes. Question the obvious. Things are not always what they seem. In examining the pathology in this particular case, I hope I can fulfill these obligations.

M.P.

A SCREAM
ON THE WATER

PROLOGUE

The town of Salem took its name in 1630 from the Hebrew word *shalom,* meaning "peace." But around the world, Salem is associated to this day not with peace but with witches. The town, which hugs the Atlantic coastline of Massachusetts some fifteen miles north of Boston, forever earned its place in history in 1692 by condemning to death twenty people, falsely accused of witchcraft. Witches may or may not have thrived here in the seventeenth century, but in the twentieth century, self-proclaimed witches are here, alive and well.

On a summer morning in July 1991, Laurie Cabot donned a black floor-length caftan and strolled into her living room, her cat trailing behind her. Silver strands capped her long black hair and framed her face. Her eyes were made up with heavy black liner, mascara, and shadow to honor her goddess.

Against the eastern wall was her altar, crowded with candles and objects filled with meaning and magic to her. She drew close, lit a candle, then stood for awhile, letting her spirit mingle with the universe. Sixty-year-old Laurie Cabot, High Priestess of Witchcraft, once named the "official" witch of Salem, cast a spell to the rising sun asking for balance and for clarity of mind.

After the meditation with which she greeted each new day, Laurie fixed herself a cup of tea and faced the jarring sound of the telephone. Bright and early, people rose in every time zone and called in need of spiritual guidance with life issues. One of the first calls this day came from Captain Paul Murphy, a local friend of hers in the Salem Police Department. He called unofficially to ask for Laurie's help in a search for the body of a missing woman. The case had frustrated police for days.

"They're taking a helicopter up over Gloucester Harbor," the captain told her. Gloucester was several miles up the coast. "It's a big area. Anything you can do?"

The witch resided a few houses from the waters of Salem Harbor. From her first floor condo, she overlooked a small backyard and a street crowded with three-deckers. She couldn't see the water, but in her mind she could see the universe with all its multiple paths. Laurie closed her eyes and counted silently, taking herself into an "alpha" state within four seconds.

Laurie touched her heavily ringed fingers to her forehead and took a hard look at her mental screen. "You're wasting your time, Captain Murphy," she said after a moment. "You won't find her anywhere near Gloucester."

"Where is she?"

"Near an island...off Marblehead." Just south of Salem and miles away from the search area. There were several islands off Marblehead, so Laurie probed further. "The island...is to the right of a lighthouse. There's a dark colored rock..."

The wire mesh corner of a lobster trap broke through the water's glassy surface and banged against the wooden gunwale of the *Nadine S.* As the thirty-six-foot lobster boat moved steadily southeast, Hooper Goodwin's hydraulic hauler pulled the trawl line in at the same speed. This kept an even tension on all 600 feet of line from one end buoy to the other. Hooper's rig was a one-man operation. All he had to do was to hook the first buoy with his gaff—a long pole with a hook on one end—and to slip the line between the plates of the hauler. Then the rest of the line would come up by itself.

Between the buoys on this particular trawl line were strung six traps. Each was attached to the line by a ganget, a short length of rope that allowed each trap to pass by the open block and tackle and through the plates without interruption. Hooper unlatched his first trap as it swung up to him, removed a pair of lobsters, threw in some fresh bait from the bucket by his feet, closed it up again, and stacked it on the deck behind him. As the hauler continued to drone, he quickly measured his prey. One was too small. Hooper threw it back. He banded the second one and dropped it into a tub with the rest of the day's catch.

Hooper's trawl line was one of five he had set out the week before on the back side of Cat Island, a scant mile from the Chandler Hovey Lighthouse at Marblehead, Massachusetts. On shore, the mid-July temperature was reaching ninety-nine degrees. Already by mid-morning the lean, muscular thirty-year-old was working bare-chested. His tan pants hung low around his hips, spilling down onto his rubber boots. A row of gold chains dangled around his neck. A rust-colored Chesapeake Bay retriever named Zeke, his unpaid stern man, sat at his feet. Together they tackled the next three traps on this string.

The fifth trap pierced the surface in a shower of water, barely audible over the slow chug of the engine. Hooper was lucky again and pulled out another two lobsters. The bowl-shaped ocean floor in the area between Cat Island and dark-colored Cormorant Rock off its southern tip was one of Hooper's hot spots. He could count on a good catch here. With Zeke's close supervision, the lobsterman reached over to measure and band. They waited for the sixth and final trap to come up.

Suddenly the low drone of the hauler rose to a whine. Somehow, the final trap must have jammed. Hooper turned around. As he glanced toward the block and tackle, he saw something like an old anchor that prevented the ganget from proceeding further. The angular metal was lodged in the wire mesh of his trap. A length of green and white nylon rope was tangled around both the ganget and the anchor. One taut end disappeared down into the water. Hooper dropped the lobster he was banding, kicked off the hydraulic engine, threw the boat into neutral, and leaned over to free the trap.

At first, all he saw was the reflection of his own curly blond head, peppered with water droplets falling from the mesh above. But then his eyes focused just below the sparkling surface. When he realized what he was staring at, the horror took his breath away. Then he swore aloud. Hooper Goodwin swallowed back the faint bitter taste rising in his throat. He reached for his radio with one hand and his gaff with the other.

PART I

There's a sailboat on the ocean,
The sun's surrendering its light
Faded ripples on the water
Say the sea is calm tonight
But no one knows the depths I've seen,
Keeping solid ground in sight.

Julie Dougherty

1

"Oh, a corgi!" The auburn-haired jogger had slowed to a walk and couldn't resist bending down to stroke the butterscotch fur. It was late spring of 1991. Roxcy Platte, a psychiatric social worker—divorced, attractive, mother of two boys—regularly jogged in Fort Sewall, a park overlooking the ocean in Marblehead. At the other end of the leash was a man in his forties, quite tall, balding on top, distinguished looking. A soft smile.

Roxcy had recently lost her own dog and was still dealing with the sadness. Welcoming a rest, she joined the stranger on the bench. The man told Roxcy that he too had suffered a recent loss. "My wife died not too long ago. Fifteen months, to be exact." He was still having a tough time with it. "Ovarian cancer," he explained sadly. "I'm pretty much an expert on it now. By the way, my name's Tom. Tom Maimoni."

After learning that Roxcy lived in Marblehead, Maimoni remarked, "I used to live here too. I live in Salem now. Sailed down this morning." He told her he owned a thirty-foot Cal sailboat and two coveted moorings in Marblehead harbor. Also a slip in Beverly, across the sound. It turned out Roxcy enjoyed sailing. "Like to see my boat?" he asked her.

Since she was heading that way, Roxcy followed Tom to the public landing a block away where his sloop *Counterpoint* was docked. The two climbed aboard. Tom suggested they take her around the harbor a bit, and he let Roxcy take the helm. She was surprised at his trust. "I could tell by the way you got on the boat that you knew what you were doing," he explained. He also complimented her on her unpainted nails and lack of hair spray. So many of the women who boarded *Counterpoint* were long of nail and short of sailing experience, he complained.

They chatted about classical music, which they also shared in common. Tom popped some Mozart into the onboard tape player, then served up some cheese and crackers and something to drink. He was courteous, his behavior impeccable. When they returned to the dock, he asked if she'd like to sail again the following week.

They sailed four or five more times during the next few weeks, always on weekdays. A couple of times Tom canceled or failed to show up. And Tom talked more about his dead wife. When Roxcy asked if he had resumed a social life, Tom replied that he was confining himself to affairs with married women. He wished to avoid commitments.

Tom seemed to enjoy his conversations with Roxcy. Whatever she was interested in, or had dabbled in, he had done, too. Only better. Roxcy was working as a real estate agent while completing her postgraduate courses in social work. Tom had been in real estate and had earned a doctorate. Roxcy painted. Tom painted. In fact, he was having a show up in Rockport soon. He was a pilot. He had been in the air force. Tom Maimoni was an accomplished man.

On the fifth sail, in early July, Tom's behavior changed. The two had anchored somewhere off Magnolia, up the coast from Marblehead, and were sitting in the cockpit eating sandwiches. Tom started in on the women with long fingernails and hair spray again, but he then suddenly switched to the sexual appetites of some of his visitors. One woman was a sex-crazed former nun who wanted to give him blow jobs "all over the boat," he told Roxcy.

They pulled up anchor and sailed east toward Gloucester for a while. Suddenly Tom announced, "I think I'll sail naked. You don't mind, do you?" Before she could respond, he had dropped his pants. Roxcy refused his invitation to do likewise. Roxcy answered lightly that if he didn't put his pants back on, she would have to avert her glance all day and risk a stiff neck. To this, Tom responded by trotting up to the bow of the boat, grabbing the roller furler, and swinging around to face her with a splayed hand covering his face. Roxcy endured the rest of the sail by keeping conversation light, physical contact minimal, and by averting her gaze as much as possible. She wasn't able to avoid noticing his erection, however. After a while, Tom settled in beside her as they sailed in silence, his arm loosely around her shoulder. Once or twice he leaned over and softly kissed the top of her head. She felt it was a sad kiss from a sad man who was trying to connect and protect himself at the same time. A little sneaky contact which kept commitments at bay.

Finally, they turned back. The captain pulled his shorts back on, and they sailed into port without further incident. On the dock Tom said to her, "Let's not make a big deal of this. You don't have to tell anybody." Roxcy had received her first indication that this man was not as free as he had claimed.

As they parted, Tom discussed the possibility of going ballroom dancing at the Wonderland Ballroom in Revere on July 10. Tom also told Roxcy that he was on vacation for two weeks and wanted to do some extended sailing during that time, perhaps even go on a cruise.

The following week the dancing date was canceled. Tom called at the last moment to say that he was "flying to Dallas" on a short business trip. However, he suggested that they go sailing when he got back on July 12.

By now, Roxcy had grown more and more suspicious that Tom was in fact married, or otherwise involved with someone else. The abrupt cancellations, his unavailability on weekends. She decided to find out first before going on any long sails with him. Roxcy located Tom Maimoni in the Salem phone book, called his house, and hung up in surprise when a woman answered. She resolved to ask Tom about her on July 12.

2

Tom Maimoni had failed to tell Roxcy Platte that he did have a wife, one very much alive. Patti Maimoni was a special education teacher in the Salem school system. During the week of July 12, 1991, however, Tom was alone. Patti had gone to visit her sister in Kansas to help out while the family moved.

The Maimonis' freezer was stocked with enough dinners to see Tom through his wife's two-week trip. Patti had even baked brownies. The painful deprivation of her companionship during their first long separation perhaps would be assuaged by the snacks she had left behind. Brownies brightened up with walnuts and one or more phone calls a day would hopefully provide Tom the necessary nourishment for both body and soul. She also had asked a close friend from school to check on him.

Tom met Patti in the summer of 1987 at Scarborough Beach in Rhode Island, where her family lived. Tom also had grown up in Rhode Island. He frequently visited his parents, who still lived there. Patti had been divorced about two years, had no kids, and was teaching in the area. On a summer day, Tom strolled by, sat down beside her, and struck up a conversation. Tom told her that he was a mechanical engineer and that his wife had recently died of cancer. He also told her that he had a doctorate in education, a master of architecture degree, and a bachelor's degree in mechanical engineering. He further related that he was a veteran military pilot who had seen some harrowing experiences in Vietnam in the service of his country. In 1987 Tom said he was working for Arthur D. Little in Cambridge, Massachusetts, as a consultant.

Patti liked to scuba dive, as did Tom. He liked classical music. She played the piano, and was classically trained. The two had much in common. To Patti, Tom seemed a superstar. They began dating.

Tom also loved to sail. A few months later he and Patti purchased a Cal 28 sailboat, which he named *Counterpoint*. Tom had owned boats before and had been a member of the local Palmer's Cove Yacht Club in Salem since 1981. After several years on the waiting list, he had finally secured a coveted slip there for his latest pleasure craft. Proudly, he was one of the few boat owners who kept his vessel in the water year-round.

About a year after they met, Tom and Patti were married. For their honeymoon they took *Counterpoint* on a two-week sail to Newport, Rhode Island.

The couple moved into an apartment on Federal Street in Salem, on the outskirts of the historic district. A short distance down the street, a neighbor's house would later gain national attention when it underwent remodeling during a series of episodes for *This Old House* on PBS.

In early 1990 Tom Maimoni was laid off from Arthur D. Little. He picked up contract work for a time. By December of that year, he had finally landed a job as an engineer with Parker Brothers Games, based in Salem. The Maimonis then decided to buy a house.

Tom and Patti found their first home on a peninsula separating Salem and Beverly Harbors. The peninsula is known locally as Salem Willows, named for the park at its easternmost tip. On the northern shore leading to the park is a cluster of townhouses lining a private road called Settlers Way. The ten-year-old condominiums overlook Collins Cove, an inlet off Beverly Harbor to the north, and to the south, the stacks of the New England power plant. The Maimonis moved into 2 Settlers Way at the end of 1990.

The couple's new condo enjoyed a good view of the water and the onion-shaped top of the Russian Orthodox church on Webb Street to the west. With two bedrooms upstairs, a living room, small dining room, and kitchen downstairs, one and a half baths, and a full walkout basement, their particular floor plan was known as the "Conant" model. The name evoked the rich history that had shaped the town. It was Roger Conant who had founded

Salem in 1626 along with a handful of Puritans searching for religious freedom. The town began as a cluster of crude huts along the bank of the North River a few blocks from Collins Cove. Known then as Naumkeag, the colony endured harsh, killing winters, surviving largely with the aid of Conant's own leadership and perseverance. A statue of the stern-faced Conant with tall hat and flowing robes today stands watch over the Common and divides the square in front of the Salem Witch Museum.

As they moved in, Tom and Patti acquired a Welsh corgi and named her Salli. Tom walked the puppy every morning and evening and frequently took her aboard *Counterpoint*. Salli was given her own tiny life jacket and embroidered collar. Unfortunately, with his expanded family, yacht club fees, two cars, and condo and boat payments falling due with increasing size and regularity, Tom Maimoni was suddenly laid off six months after he had started with the Salem toy company. While she finished up the school year, Patti helped her husband put together new résumés and begin the painful task of looking for a job—again.

3

Kitty Babakian met Tom Maimoni in the early spring of 1991. It was cool at the time—cool enough to be huddled inside a leather jacket. The slender woman sat on the grass near the wharf behind the Collins Cove condos on Settlers Way in Salem. It was evening. The gate to the pier was locked. Private Property—No Trespassing, read the sign. She suspected even the lawn belonged to the condo association, and so she huddled deeper and hoped she wouldn't be seen. Kitty decided to risk a joint.

As she lit up, a soft, deep voice broke the stillness behind her. Kitty was startled and turned around. It was a man with a dog—the man as tall as the dog was short. They conversed for awhile, after Kitty discretely crushed the roach beneath her foot and spent a few ingratiating moments warding off her imminent arrest for trespassing. But he turned out to be no threat. A resident of one of the condos, he was well dressed, straight out of an L.L.Bean catalog. He looked like a pillar of his community, and she in contrast felt vaguely criminal. The stranger was polite, attentive, and allowed his adorable little dog to do most of the flirting. For her part Kitty Babakian had, like other women Tom Maimoni gravitated toward, a straightforward, independent manner and an unfussy outdoors appearance—naturally attractive and devoid of makeup, with intelligent eyes capable of conveying bemusement even in the waning light. A woman neither coy nor self-indulgent. Her few strands of ash-colored hair among the black suggested experience rather than age.

They didn't talk about much. He had bought the dog because he was lonely, he told her. Both were irrevocably drawn to the water. Tom had purchased the seaside condo six months earlier, after having lived in Salem a couple of years. Kitty had moved to town in 1989. At that time she had just left a job in downtown Boston as night manager of a bookstore cafe. While looking for new work in Salem, she had taken to walking about the city each day, incorporating Collins Cove in her circuit. She mentioned to Tom that when she first came to Salem, several unsold units in his complex had been temporarily rented out. One was occupied by a six-member rhythm and blues band that rehearsed in the condo for a time. Tom said that he wouldn't have liked it much if they had stayed on. The more affluent, settled population of the now exclusively owner-occupied development was much more to his taste. Kitty had befriended the group as an ardent fan of good rhythm and blues and kindred souls. Tom probably now pegged her as a "rock and roll bimbo," she speculated.

Sailing didn't come up. Nor boats, nor wives, nor jobs, nor wars. Just a little warm conversation on a cool spring evening. It blew in on the breeze and left with the tide.

About a month later, Kitty had a dream about her grandmother. In the dream she remembered Gramma Mishkin saying to her, "He asked me to go for a boat ride, but I told him I was too busy." Kitty had no clue who her grandmother was referring to, but she recalled how distinct the words were and how out of character. Mishkin Babakian was fun-loving and would certainly have gone on a boat. The dream made no particular sense to Kitty and seemed out of the blue. Until she met Tom Maimoni again three weeks later.

Summer had finally come, with the warm weather and longer sunlight that Kitty craved. She found herself one afternoon on the path behind the condos, a route she frequently took to get from one small beach to the next. As she passed behind Unit 2, Tom Maimoni pulled open the glass door and trotted out to intercept her. Kitty was slightly taken aback.

"Hi," he shouted out in recognition. "Come have a cold drink!"

The woman demurred. However, her interceptor persisted. Eventually she agreed and followed him into his townhouse through the walk-in basement. The man had said he was lonely.

She assumed he was a bachelor. But as they made their way through the basement, she noticed a stack of board games. *Monopoly*. Stuff married couples buy.

Tom led her upstairs. In the kitchen he swung open the refrigerator door, revealing well-stocked shelves. "Hi-C Orange, or Pepsi?" he asked Kitty.

Hi-C? Pepsi? She had expected something more along the lines of "Michelob or Becks?" The full arrangement on the refrigerator shelf somehow didn't spell *bachelor* either. Hi-C certainly didn't spell *bachelor*. "Pepsi," she answered.

The two settled into the living room. White walls, beige rug, bland surroundings, non-committal appointments suggested the compromise and accommodation of housemates, spouse or otherwise. Kitty lowered herself into a recliner chair, yet another icon of Till Death Do Us Part. The finishing touches, she concluded, were decidedly feminine. Embroidered collar on the dog, a hefty sculpture of a corgi on the side table. This was a family, and the dog was their child.

Tom noticed her studying the statue and read her mind. "That—that was something my brother sent me. Shipped it to me," he said with a dismissive gesture.

Kitty looked at him with surprise. "Shipped it?" It just so happened she had worked in shipping. She glanced back at the statue. It was massive. Not the sort of item anyone in their right mind would try to ship.

Tom became evasive and shifted to talking about his work. He had been an engineer at Parker Brothers, the Salem-based game company, until the axe fell on the entire division. Presently he did consulting, which required a lot of traveling. "Whenever I'm on trips, I can't wait to get off those airplanes and get back to Collins Cove," he said dreamily. Back to the sea. And the quiet condos.

The conversation drifted to sailing. Tom had a boat. "How would you like to go for a sail?" he asked her. Tom Maimoni would never call it a boat ride.

The corgi, whose name was Sallí, approached Kitty's chair and climbed up into her lap. It was an affectionate gesture. *I like you*, the Corgi seemed to suggest. *He's a bit scattered. But I will protect you.*

Kitty was still processing his question. "What?" she asked, looking up.

"Would you like to crew for me? We could go early some morning."

Kitty thought of Gramma Mishkin. "Actually, I don't think so. I work mornings." She wove her sinewy, dark fingers into Salli's butterscotch fur and drew the dog into a hug. She suppressed a shudder and added, "Anyway, I'm...busy."

Tom chatted a bit about corgis and how they were the favorite breed of British royalty. Kitty sipped the rest of her Pepsi, then eventually took her leave.

She saw Tom Maimoni on a third occasion—this time in early July. Kitty was on one of her daily walks. Along Collins Cove she had taken to leaving the path and climbing down to wade in the shallow water as she made her way around the condos, hoping in the back of her mind that she might avoid another encounter with Tom. His attentiveness was mildly flattering but discomforting. Yet on this morning she saw him, high up on the path. He didn't seem to notice her. He was walking with a woman who was blonde and slim and "smiling like an angel." The two were deep in animated conversation. Salli was tugging at her leash. Kitty Babakian felt a sense of relief and continued on her way.

4

The long Fourth of July weekend was the high point of summer for many of the residents of Salem Willows. Late in the morning, as it had for many years, a parade of costumed revelers and floats wound its way through the neighborhood. Strollers, wheelbarrows, and festooned pickup trucks all competed for the coveted awards. The holiday tradition continued with hot dogs, contests, and games for the kids on the beach, plus block parties up and down the street that would continue well into the night. One neighbor celebrated by firing a small cannon in his backyard over Salem Harbor, every hour on the hour.

Meanwhile an old-fashioned, wood-paneled station wagon looped its way around the Willows carrying the esteemed judges of the house decorations. The vehicle paused every few yards so that the houses could be fairly and impartially judged. The group circled a second time, hunched over in the high seats of the station wagon in the sweltering heat. They were having difficulty deciding between a house decorated with stars and stripes on Columbus Avenue and a residence on Cove Avenue draped with T-shirts. Most of the neighbors were standing on their front steps, waving and shouting to the woody as it passed by. A few ran up and tossed bribes of candy through the car's windows, particularly if their houses were short on bunting. Enthusiasm compensated for inadequate ornamentation.

As dusk approached, the parked cars stretched from the Willows beach almost to Settlers Way. Local families were still flocking to the park and amusement arcade. All evening they smelled the popcorn and saltwater taffy at Hobbs' Ice Cream Stand. Dogs wound themselves around feet. The lights came on in the harbor on all sides. Gradually it got too dark to tell the pigeons and seagulls apart, or the Harley Davidsons from aluminum lawn chairs parked by the Men's Cottage. The band's music coming from the small cement stage played in exuberant counterpoint to the melodies wafting from the arcade.

The Maimonis spent the day out of town, picnicking on *Counterpoint* in Boston Harbor with family and friends. This was their last weekend together before Patti was to leave for Kansas. They sailed down to view the annual turnaround of the USS *Constitution*, accompanied by music, fanfare, guns, displays, salutes, and climaxed by fireworks in the evening. They clowned with the camcorder. Salli was tucked inside her doggie life jacket. Tom showed off his expertise in sailing, history, and as master of ceremonies. He was the captain of all he could see. He was told off camera that he should be on the evening news.

Then there were those who had to work during the holiday. Hooper Goodwin III, a Marblehead lobsterman, was trying to make up for lost time. Hooper's ancestors on both sides had been among a group of renegades from Salem who had founded neighboring Marblehead before the Revolutionary War. Heaving lobster pots since he was a kid, Hooper was a Marbleheader through and through. His left biceps sported a tattoo depicting a schooner. Marblehead Forever, it read. A scrimshaw earring dangled from his left ear.

During the winter, when lobstering was slow, Hooper (known on the Marblehead waterfront as "Hoop,") signed on to merchant ships for work as a merchant marine. He worked on tugboats, freighters, private jobs, or out of the union hall. He also had Coast Guard documents. This past winter he had been on a freighter bringing back ammunition from Operation Desert Storm. They had returned from the Middle East late in the spring. By the time his boat *Nadine S* was out of storage and had been repaired, he had missed the start of the lobster season. It wasn't until the long Fourth of July weekend that he began getting his gear out—fixing pots, lines and buoys, then finally setting out his traps. Hooper had 750 traps this year, many more than he could set or haul in a day. During the coming week he would manage to set out half of them.

5

Late in the afternoon of July 7, two women were leafleting cars parked on Derby Street near Pickering Wharf in Salem. Both women were former practitioners of witchcraft who now embraced Christianity. They were spending that day distributing fliers depicting realm of darkness/realm of light diagrams. The two had taken cups of Dunkin' Donuts coffee onto Derby Wharf for a short break. When they returned, they targeted a red Fiero in the National Park Center lot, across from the old custom house.

As they stuck a diagram under the windshield wiper, a tall, dark-haired man in his forties with a small, cream-colored dog walked up. Obviously, he was the owner of the Fiero. He struck them as handsome, healthy, tanned, well built, and "well preserved." As a conversation ensued, the women further found him "astute, interesting, very gentlemanly." Articulate, sharp, professional, debonair. Commanding in stature, world-wise, alluring. "Sort of a Magnum P.I. type," they remarked, alluding to the television hero.

Thomas Maimoni was wearing khaki shorts, sneakers, and a red shirt with PCYC stitched on the front. Below was an insignia bearing a witch on a broomstick. The insignia is common in Salem, appearing everywhere from police patches to ice cream stores. The witch rides the masthead of the *Salem Evening News* and the garage door at Witch City Auto. A witch on a bicycle, in the familiar *ET* silhouette, graces the front of Salem Cycles on

New Derby Street. It was this insignia that launched the three into a discussion of witchcraft in Salem, the sociopolitical climate of the region, metaphysics, the occult, and life in general.

Maimoni suggested the women needed a really good plan to offset the existing reality of witchcraft in the city. "You can't just use your religious icons," he insisted. The two answered that they did indeed have a plan. They thrust a flyer into his hands. Maimoni read it with interest and told them he was impressed by their depth of knowledge of the occult.

They talked further. Tom Maimoni invited them both for a sail sometime. One of the women, who was single and enjoyed sailing, had a sudden, chilling reminder of the movie *Dead Calm* and was spooked. She regarded him carefully. But the man seemed nice. So trustworthy. Sane. Charming. She pushed aside the stray thought. They all exchanged phone numbers and cards. Maimoni said he was an "engineer from Connecticut" working in this area. He had a condo on Settlers Way in Salem and a sailboat at Palmer's Cove Yacht Club. He loved the ocean and Salem Sound. Come by anytime, he offered.

Commenting on their cause, Maimoni explained how to "shift the focus metaphysically, in a hidden way" to create a plan to change things. "I use my boat that way—it's called *Counterpoint*. You see? Point/counterpoint."

Maimoni related that he had been raised a Catholic but did not practice his faith anymore as a result of bad memories. Because he had described unresolved personal conflicts with the Catholic Church, the women decided to forego the sail.

The women said good-bye and then worked their way down the street toward Pickering Wharf. As they rounded the corner, they passed by one of Salem's street people—an elfish woman with flowing white hair who walked around the city each day. The elder woman stared straight at them. "Death," she intoned. "There is so much death over this city."

6

Shortly before Patti Maimoni left for Kansas, she and Tom and two other couples took their boats on a weekend sail down to Provincetown, at the tip of Cape Cod, south of Boston. One of the sailors was Dr. Raymond Mount, a family psychologist and fellow member of Palmer's Cove Yacht Club. He owned a thirty-one-foot Hunter sailboat. With him was his girlfriend Charlene Colella, who had a passion for diving. Sailing and diving were two things they all shared in common, though their styles differed substantially. On the way down, Tom—a more conservative sailor and diver—hugged the coast and radioed his nervousness to the others about patches of fog along the way. Ray and the others forged eagerly ahead. He and Charlene often felt Tom spent more time polishing *Counterpoint* than raising its sail. Tom also seemed pretty hesitant about diving in less than perfect conditions.

When they all had reached their destination safely, the three couples moored their boats and socialized together. It turned out Tom Maimoni had a streak of homophobia. Provincetown was well known for its large, openly gay community, which Tom seemed to find disturbing. He angrily berated the gay lifestyle to his companions, who were put off by his attitude. "I'm not staying another night here," Tom proclaimed to the group after his dinner excursion into town. The others prevailed upon him to relax a bit. They had paid for two nights on the moorings. They had no desire to leave. Tom finally gave in.

Ray and Charlene also found Tom's attitude toward women hard to take. Tom, generally aloof and unable to connect, seemed overly controlling toward women. Particularly on his boat, Tom needed to be in charge. When Patti described all the meals she had frozen for Tom for her upcoming trip, Charlene stared at the man. "What's wrong, can't you cook?" she felt like asking him. Charlene thought Patti was "a real sweetheart" who sometimes would shoot the breeze about child psychology with Ray—something in which both had a professional interest. What the hell was such a nice woman doing married to a boasting, useless man like Tom, Charlene wondered. Since Charlene was unemployed that summer, Tom suggested that she go sailing and diving with him sometime. Charlene politely declined.

As they chatted that day in Provincetown, Tom took out his chart book that showed maps of the waters off Salem, Beverly, and Marblehead. They had been talking about good dive spots, and Tom asked Ray for recommendations. Ray thought of two. He pointed them out on Tom's chart. The first was the shipwreck of the *New Hampshire*, a wonderful, easy dive off Grave's Island to the north in only thirty feet of water. Designated a National Historic Site, the cove in which she lay was strewn with great oak ribs and copper spikes forged in Paul Revere's foundry. The second was Ray Mount's favorite lobster spot, northeast of Cormorant Rock behind Cat Island, owned by Salem but located just off the coast of Marblehead.

Tom marked both spots on his chart.

7

"This would be perfect for my out-of-town clients," said Maimoni as he surveyed the spacious den belonging to Rosemary Farmer. He had given her the name of Tom Mahoney. Rosemary—who had a delicate frame, light brown hair, and fragile eyes—was an artist and a substitute teacher living in the exclusive Pride's Crossing section of Beverly, Massachusetts. She was going through a divorce and was anxiously trying to sell what had been a home but what was now to be merely a house. Three weeks earlier, the prospective buyer had come to the door and had left his name and number with her niece, who was baby-sitting Rosemary's small kids that afternoon. After Rosemary made contact, he arranged to visit the house on Tuesday morning, July 9. Mahoney explained upon his arrival that he preferred not to go through a realtor and that he had been looking at several properties in the area. He went through the house carefully. He was particularly interested in the den. The space seemed adequate. Mahoney described how his office was packed with computers. He went on for awhile talking about satellites and things on the moon.

Rosemary told the man about an offer that had come in that morning. Since a 6 percent realtor commission would be owed, she suggested that if Mahoney wanted to match the offer she'd split the commission savings with him. Mahoney indicated interest and said he'd think about it. Parking was a concern for him. Could the neighborhood handle the increased traffic of his clientele? If everything checked out, he would ask his lawyer to draw up a purchase and sale agreement. He explained to her that he was on vacation for the week, had recently sold two townhouses in Salem, and was living in Rockport aboard his boat. Rosemary told him she had to respond to her earlier offer by eight that evening. So the two arranged for an afternoon meeting on board between Mahoney and Rosemary's husband Peter at a public dock in Manchester, just up the coast. Rosemary planned to visit the boat around 3 P.M. to check on their progress.

When the teacher arrived at the dock, Mahoney and her husband had finished talking. She waited until Peter had left and then approached the boat. Mahoney invited her aboard and showed her some typewritten pages—some sort of an informal purchase agreement. Rosemary looked it over, and they began discussing the terms.

"How about going for a sail?" Mahoney asked her.

"I don't really have time," she answered. "I have to meet my realtor at 4:30."

"Why don't you call and postpone it? Look, there's a public phone up at the train depot. We'll just be going out to the end of the harbor and back."

Hesitantly, Rosemary agreed. Mahoney walked with her to the Manchester train station, where she placed a call and changed the appointment to 6:30 that evening.

They returned to the boat, cast off, and motored out into the harbor. At the entrance, Mahoney raised the head sail and set off toward Baker's Island, about two miles to the south.

Rosemary said uneasily, "I don't have a lot of time, remember."

But Mahoney reassured her. Having learned she was an artist, he began to chat warmly about all the art courses he had taken at the Rhode Island School of Design. He also told her about his job with NASA, designing biomedical equipment.

They reached Baker's Island. Mahoney headed the boat around the side. By now the conversation had drifted to the recent loss of Mahoney's wife after her tragic battle with cancer. Rosemary was sympathetic. She had lost her own brother to the same disease three years back. Somehow Mahoney had known this. Perhaps Peter had mentioned it.

Mahoney disappeared below and brought up a chilled bottle

of white zinfandel and a pair of glasses. Rosemary allowed him to pour her half a glass, which she then sipped carefully. Along with the wine, Mahoney poured out his pain and sorrow over the death of his wife. "She looked so much like you," he explained to Rosemary. He began to touch her shoulder, her arm, and her leg.

Rosemary became increasingly uncomfortable and unsure how to handle this situation. The guy wasn't some leering Lothario trying to make a quick score. He seemed highly educated, well mannered, and suffering a great deal of pain. Maybe his groping was a genuine need for human contact, for some measure of comfort. Rosemary consoled him until Mahoney began touching inside her shorts and under her blouse. The woman tried blocking his hands and saying less and less gently, "Don't!" But she wanted to keep her demeanor civilized and to keep her own reactions from encouraging a more persistent—even violent—assault. Instinctively, she tried to remain calm in her noncompliance. Rosemary repeatedly attempted to steer the discussion back to real estate.

They had reached the far side of Baker's Island. But instead of sailing back to Manchester, Mahoney headed toward another offshore island—Grave's Island. Upon reaching it, he dropped anchor. By now Rosemary was reminding him about the appointments she was late for and all the people who were waiting for her. She stuck to reasoning, hoping against hope that he would remain reasonable if she did. But Mahoney ignored her pleas. Then out of the blue he asked, "How modest are you?"

Rosemary tried to be truthful. "Well, it depends on the context."

Mahoney didn't wait for an explanation of what constituted an appropriate context. Instead, at that point, he took off all his clothes. The ensuing exchange was surreal.

Mahoney asked, "Would you like to go swimming?"

"I really don't care to go swimming. I need to get back, Tom."

"Mind if I go swimming?" he continued. "You know, if you're worried about swimming naked, I have a suit down below that used to belong to my wife. You are welcome to use it."

"No, thank you. I don't want to swim," she repeated.

Mahoney leaned toward her. "I'm sorry, could you move over for a minute? My dive gear is stored underneath your seat. I'm going to clean the bottom of my boat, if you don't mind."

Rosemary had been riveted to her spot ever since boarding

the boat. She moved aside and watched as this man, so completely oblivious of her pleas, reached into the compartment and removed a wet suit, dive gear, and a scrub brush. When she refused once again to join him, he rustled around for some paperwork to occupy her time, including reprints of research papers he had written for NASA. He then climbed into the wet suit and jumped overboard.

How do you defend yourself against a sexual assailant who shoves a pile of scientific reprints in your face? Something they *never* taught in school. Rosemary looked over his paperwork, her exasperation now bordering on genuine fear. As she tried to read, she heard Mahoney below, scrubbing the bottom of his boat.

A few hundred yards away was another boat. Rosemary noticed that two young boys were aboard, fishing. She considered yelling, but her terror wasn't quite full-blown yet. She still felt that her best strategy was to keep this man calm. Who knows what he would do if she cried out for help? Would that in fact be gaining control of the situation or instead relinquishing what little she had? And who was to say whether the two boys—strangers— would be any safer?

After fifteen or twenty minutes of scratching away at the bottom, Mahoney emerged and climbed up the swim ladder at the back of the boat. He stripped off his wet suit, dried himself, and went below to put on some shorts. Then he invited her down for some homemade brownies. Reluctantly, she climbed down into the cabin and sat down at the tiny table. Mahoney set out the rest of the wine and a plate of brownies that a "neighbor" had made for him. Unfortunately, the brownies contained walnuts. Rosemary didn't like walnuts, so she declined them. He also showed her the swimsuit. It was small, about her size. She had no intention of trying it on.

Mahoney sat down next to her and resumed his groping advances. He told Rosemary again how much he missed his wife and how much Rosemary reminded him of her. He laid his head on her shoulder, then on her lap, and clung to her.

Rosemary kept telling Mahoney that she was *not* his wife, that she felt badly for him, and that in time he would heal. He would meet someone else. Interspersed with her comments were her polite but firm refusals as his hands wandered too far up her shorts.

"You know, your work with NASA really seems interesting,"

Rosemary said, desperately trying to keep the situation normalized. *Get him to talk about his work. How can he be assaulting me if he's talking about biomedical engineering?* Maybe it would reawaken his sensible side, redirect his hormones into a passionate discussion of science. Allow the higher cortical functions to reemerge and the reptilian brain would go back to sleep. Rosemary, like many women, had grown up with such strong nurturing instincts and a distaste for confrontation that crossing certain lines was inherently difficult. Particularly those lines where *acceptable* situations must suddenly be branded *unacceptable.* Could she dare hope to encourage this man to behave more appropriately by pretending he was even when he was not? This man was big. She was not.

And, for a moment, Rosemary's tactic seemed to work. Mahoney stood up abruptly and asked, "Would you like to see my bionic hand?" It was here, right here on the boat, in the sleeping quarters.

Rosemary wanted to believe him, wanted to make it true. So she rose as he stepped toward the berth area. As she stood by the doorway, Mahoney rummaged around in a compartment just inside the door. Then, suddenly, he swung around and grabbed her about the waist with his free hand. Rosemary reached for the doorjamb and held fast.

"Let go of me! You can't do this!" she finally yelled.

"Just...just lay down with me. I just want to hold you. It'll be all right," he pleaded over and over again, tugging at her.

"You have to let go of me. I'm not going in there."

"Just for one minute."

The harder he pulled, the tighter she gripped the doorway and the louder she protested. As she did, his hands locked more tightly. Only by relaxing a bit did she sense his own grip easing. A subtle biofeedback mechanism. But Rosemary felt fear when she looked into his eyes. They had changed from pitiful to something completely different—a violent, far-away look that terrified her.

All of a sudden he released her. Rosemary swung around and headed for the steps. When she had climbed halfway up and was reaching for the hatch, Mahoney once again grabbed her, encircling her waist with his arms. He lifted her off the ladder and swung her around into a tight embrace. Somehow his pants once again dropped to the floor.

Rosemary tried her stern, in-control voice. "Tom, you *have* to let go of me. You know, maybe another time we could get together, but right now isn't the time. You need to let me go. I need to go home."

Mahoney clung to her for several minutes, moving his hands all over her, talking to her softly about his dead wife. And then, once again, he let her go. "I'm sorry," he said quietly.

Rosemary scrambled up the ladder and resumed her former position in the cockpit. Mahoney put his clothes on. Then he followed her up topside.

It started again. He couldn't keep his hands off her. Finally Rosemary crossed the line. She reached for her car keys on the bench, next to her shoes and dark glasses. Scooping them up, Rosemary stood on the bench and stepped onto the edge of the deck. The boat with the two boys was far up the shore now, out of shouting range. The beach at Grave's Island looked close enough to swim to. Yet to be trapped on the island, where Mahoney would surely follow, would probably be worse than her current situation. Manchester was visible, but not attainable. With little hope of survival, the sea seemed more welcome than the fate unfolding aboard this boat.

"If you touch me again, I'm going to jump overboard," she said flatly.

Mahoney stopped. "OK. I'm sorry. I'll take you home."

It was nearly dark. Her 6:30 appointment was long overdue, and the 8:00 deadline was in jeopardy as well. Not only was Tom's bid on the house looking less and less likely, he was also ensuring she would lose the one real offer she had. Worse—after nearly five hours of being pawed, all she wanted to do was throw up.

Rosemary was shivering. After Mahoney had turned the boat back toward Manchester— nearly a half hour away—he went below and brought up a pair of sweatshirts. Rosemary pulled one on, and tucked herself into a fetal position on the bench with the sweatshirt drawn over her knees and her ankles like a cocoon. She remained frozen in that posture until they reached the public dock in Manchester Harbor.

The distraught woman tried to keep conversation centered on the house deal until they finally docked. As she climbed off the boat, the two briefly discussed a possible follow-up meeting so that her abductor could "measure the rooms." Mahoney stayed aboard. The name *Counterpoint* emblazoned the stern below him. Rosemary turned, made her way up the pier, and trembled as she walked to her car.

As soon as she got behind the wheel, Rosemary Farmer collapsed, sobbing for several minutes before she could turn the key. It was just now 8:00. She felt terrified. She felt violated. Involuntary tremors still racked her body. Her shaking foot eventually found the accelerator, and she pulled the car onto the road.

8

Thomas Joseph Maimoni was born in Framingham, Massachusetts, in 1945. He moved with his family to Pawtucket, Rhode Island, when he was still an infant. Tom's grandparents had come from Italy. His Sicilian grandfather spoke little English, to Tom's embarrassment. His father was a laborer who worked in construction and on the docks of Pawtucket. Tom grew up in the shadow of textile mills, once powered by the dirty, dark waters of the Blackstone River, its edges lined with smokestacks. Tom's first job as a teen was in the mills. His father felt it would be a good experience for him. Nothing wrong with good, honest hard work. Mrs. Maimoni packed her son a lunch bag each day before he set out for the mills. Tom unwrapped his sandwiches by the big, grimy windows and stared at the black river as it lumbered down to Narragansett Bay. The river transported him away from the mill town, and out into the ocean, which he knew was in his blood, then away to some far-off land.

Tom was a dreamer throughout his childhood and frequently followed his own path in life. He preferred reading, tinkering, and painting to participating in things like contact sports with his peers. At the Catholic school he attended, the nuns held him back in third grade, describing him as having an active imagination and difficulty with attention. When he was older, the nuns recommended his parents send him to a technical school to better "ground" him. At sixteen he painted a picture of Gainsborough's famous *Blue Boy* from a paint-by-numbers kit. Tom used the box cover as guide, rather than the instructions. Tom marched to the beat of a different drummer. His father built a frame for the painting. His mother hung it in their living room.

Although he often watched his father fix things around the house, Tom was not encouraged to do so himself. "You'll never be able to do it," he was often told. Tom's father only hoped his son would land a good, steady job as a laborer like himself. One could do worse in life.

9

On Friday morning, July 12, 1991, Martha Conant Brailsford laid the last of her hand-painted T-shirts on her roof deck to dry in the sun. From this deck, which she had dubbed the "yard," the slender thirty-seven-year-old artist could look out over Massachusetts Bay and see the islands it embraced. Great Misery lay to the northeast, Cat Island to the south. Martha often dove in the waters surrounding these islands. Cat Island with its rocky backside was a haven for the marine life whose images now emblazoned the soft fabric between her fingers. Wrenched from their underwater obscurity, these brilliantly colored creatures swam again in Martha's artwork in the sunshine on her rooftop.

She climbed back down into her studio, leaving the trapdoor wide open. Despite the extensive renovation Martha and her husband Bill had put into it, their Salem Willows house retained the memory of the seaside cottage it once was. Old houses benefit from the summer breezes of July. The salty smell of the Atlantic followed the artist down the ladder.

The eastern tip of Salem Willows had been a famous resort at the turn of the century, a lovely waterfront community made up of parks and summer cottages strung close together at the end of the mile-long peninsula. People had once come from all over the country to stay in its hotels and rooming houses and to benefit from the ocean breezes and warm sunshine. Over time, families in the Willows renovated and winterized most of the cottages and now lived in them year-round. The hotels and rooming houses were gone. A generation had grown up calling the Willows home.

Martha Conant met Bill Brailsford on a blind date in 1972, when she was a seventeen-year-old student taking art courses at Endicott College in Beverly, the city just north of Salem. She had journeyed from her landlocked home in Ohio to be near the sea. Martha's father was originally from New Jersey and was one of the many descendants of Roger Conant, founder of Salem.

When the two met, the twenty-one-year-old Brailsford was working as a launchman at a yacht club in Marblehead. Martha was his date for the dinner and dance the club gave for its launch operators at the end of each season. From that point on, the two were inseparable. They went together until the fall of 1982, when they were married.

Bill Brailsford was an experienced sailor who had owned a number of boats over the years. The couple spent most of their spare time on the water. During the wintertime, they substituted skiing for sailing, still craving the outdoors. Both worked for awhile at a local ski resort. But once the weather again grew warm, Martha loved to swim and windsurf. She became certified in scuba diving. Despite her petite frame, she was a strong woman.

Meanwhile, Martha finished at Endicott and enrolled at Boston University, where she earned a bachelor's degree in German in 1977. Two years later, her husband began his current job working for a ferry company in Boston. The first year he and Martha spent six months in the Caribbean operating and living aboard a fifty-foot charter sailboat. Bill was the captain and Martha was his only crew. During that time and subsequent years, Martha became an expert in performing every conceivable shipboard task.

After living a number of years in Marblehead, Bill and Martha purchased a gutted house on narrow Cove Avenue in the Willows near a small beach. Over several years, the pair renovated what had been an uninhabitable three-story shell until it took on an eclectic beauty typical of the creative individualism the neighborhood sported. The results of Martha's artistry and sense of design were featured in a 1988 home and garden supplement of the local paper.

Martha looked at her watch. Two hours she'd had to herself to create, to work. Laid off three weeks earlier from her job as a kitchen designer, Martha was experiencing both the exhilaration and the fear of being self-employed. She was suddenly dependent on her own resourcefulness. She was free to grow, to weave, to paint. Free to expand her own clothing business, Uncommon Threads. She was also free to enjoy a lower standard of living. More pressure on Bill, who worked long hours during the summer as captain on the Boston to Provincetown ferry.

In her studio, Martha shifted gears from creating to nurturing. She began by pulling out a pad of note paper and drawing her stool up to the workbench next to her loom. An elderly neighbor down Cove Avenue had entered a nursing home. She composed a note telling how much the neighborhood missed him. When she finished, she gathered samples of her recent artwork, plus copies of brochures and résumés she was trying to put together to market herself. She stuffed them into a brown canvas bag. Downstairs, she set the note on the fireplace. It lacked only a stamp. Martha checked the refrigerator. Bill might get home early that night for a rare chance at dinner together. She wanted to plan something nice. Vegetarian, but still nice. Of course, on a Friday night in July, "early" meant 7:00 if they were lucky—twelve hours after he had kissed her good-bye that morning.

Martha also planned to call her twin sister Muriel that evening to determine whether they had really recovered from their last squabble. That argument was stupid: how to cut a tomato properly. When sisters are as close as these two were, tolerances are very slim indeed. Martha's relationship with her twin was complex. All of the family's emotional baggage formed the bonds as well as the walls. Muriel was pregnant. Martha was ecstatic for her sister and, deep down, a little jealous. Even more important Muriel now learn how to cut a tomato properly.

The third occupant of the Brailsford's home was a mongrel dog named Rudy, the next patient on Martha's list. Rudy was their surrogate child. Martha was renowned for her protective passion for the environment and for her love of animals—rescuing strays, ministering to their wounds. Today her own dog was recovering from an injured paw. Rudy was pining a bit, so she led him onto the sunny porch where he could bask in the attention of the neighborhood. Martha tied his leash to the banister, checked his paw once more, shut the screen door, threw the bag over her shoulder and leaned down to hug the dog's neck. "I'll be back in a little while," she explained to him, as dog owners do. "Be a good boy." Her relationship with Rudy was simple and wonderful.

Dressed in shorts and a colorful top, her sandy blonde hair pulled back into a braid, Martha set out toward Salem Willows Park at the end of her street. Little fishlike earrings dangled from her ears. A decorative bracelet and a Seiko sports watch encircled her wrists, but her left finger felt sadly bare after the theft of her wedding ring over the Fourth of July weekend. Her appointment was to spend some time with a friend in need—Tom Maimoni, a new acquaintance. He was still despondent and lonely from the recent loss of his wife to cancer.

Martha was acutely sensitive to the repercussions of this disease. Her own best friend's husband had succumbed to cancer three years earlier. The two couples had long been friends and had sailed and enjoyed the sea together for countless years. Martha still remembered the pain and the poignant beauty of the group's final sail together. With their families, they took the young man's ashes out to sea. In the final days of his all-too-brief life, he had planned the details with his friends. The boat, the time, the destination, even the caterer. The result had so moved Martha. The serenity, the companionship, the colors of the sky at sunset when they scattered his ashes and wildflowers over the water. "What a touching and beautiful way to remember him," she had commented. "If I ever have to go, this is how I'd like it to be."

Martha had become experienced in consoling people. She visited her best friend daily. Today, however, a different soul would be the recipient of her compassion. The artwork and brochures were designed to distract the widower by eliciting his suggestions. She knew instinctively the feeling of well-being derived from answering another's plea for help. Tom was a dog owner and a sailor like herself. Salem had once attracted the French Canadians, Polish, and Irish to its cotton mills and leather tanneries a century ago. Now Salem was a mecca for dog owners and lovers of the sea. And sailing, like walking dogs, was good for the psyche. Today, they would sail. Today, perhaps, they would help each other.

Passing by the local beach, Martha waved to a couple of women she had met there earlier that morning. "Gotta meet a friend. We're going for a sail," she called out.

It was a little after one when she arrived at the pier. She gave another wave to the owner of the boat livery there, but his head was buried in paperwork as customers crowded into his tiny shop. She didn't see him look up. Martha walked to the public landing ramp and made her way down to the float.

The dock was crowded. Boats were maneuvering in and out. The white sailboat she was heading for was having a hard time docking. Nearly hitting another boat, it finally managed to back into the edge of the float. On the stern was inscribed *Counterpoint*. With one nimble leap, Martha jumped aboard.

Around 6:15 on Friday evening, the Maimonis' friends Ray Mount and Charlene Colella pulled into one of the transient slips at Palmer's Cove Yacht Club. Accompanying them were friends who had spent the afternoon sailing and diving near House Island, just outside Manchester Harbor. Although Ray had been a member of the club for about five years, given the long waiting list, he was still several years short of getting a permanent slip there. Ray used a mooring far out in the harbor and paid three dollars a day whenever he docked in one of PCYC's transient spaces. The club duly recorded each date and billed him monthly.

Charlene looked at her watch. They were scheduled to pick up another couple around six for a cookout. As usual, Ray was late. They jumped off and started up the dock to find their friends. The transient spaces were directly opposite Tom Maimoni's slip, about five or ten feet away. Both Ray and Charlene noticed *Counterpoint* tied up as they passed by. Ray observed a wet suit hanging on a lifeline to dry. He and Charlene looked at each other and joked, "Wow, maybe he actually went in." It was a sunny, calm day. Perhaps Tom Maimoni had chanced a dive.

A couple of brightly colored towels draped on the lines caught Charlene's eye. Sailors and divers were always hanging stuff on their boats. Half the time it blew away. The Maimonis' towels were fastened with little clips. "Nifty!" thought Charlene. "I'll have to ask them where they found those clips."

For a moment they wondered if Tom and Patti were below. Charlene considered calling out, "Hey, you guys down there?" But she caught sight of the padlock through the latch of the companionway—the door down to the cabin. The padlock wasn't closed, but its presence made it unlikely anyone was aboard. Charlene and Ray continued up the dock to meet their friends. Shortly afterward, they all went back out for an evening sail.

A little after 11:15 on Friday night, a local registered nurse picked up the phone and dialed the Salem Police Department. She had just returned from working a private duty job in adjoining Marblehead.

"Salem Police Department, your call is being recorded."

"Yes, I want to report a...well, screaming," said the nurse. "I just got back from Fuller's Lane in Marblehead. I was standing there looking out over the water this evening around eight or so, and I heard the most horrible scream coming from a boat offshore. A woman's scream. I think someone should go out there. It looked like the boat—it was a sail boat—was heading northeast, up toward Cat Island."

"You're in Marblehead, ma'am?"

"No, I live in Salem. I was taking care of a lady down there. I saw the same boat earlier. I could hear two people arguing."

"You'd be better off calling Marblehead police, ma'am. Probably just some sort of domestic dispute."

Marblehead police offered to check out the report but turned up nothing.

10

There are two moments in his life that Officer Frank Baccari will never forget. The first is a surprise birthday party hosted by his young sons in an Atlantic City hotel room. A Hostess twinkie with a lit matchstick crowned his present—a brand new chess set. Chess had always been his greatest love. The two kids had smuggled the whole party inside their suitcases during the long car trip from Massachusetts. Balloons, birthday banner, spray-on string. He couldn't ask much more from life.

The second is the moment a forty-year-old ferry captain from the Salem Willows neighborhood walked into the Salem police station during Baccari's late eleven to seven shift on the night of July 12, 1991. Baccari, whose lined face and skeptical eyes suggested he had lost more than his share of chess matches, was working the house that night, booking prisoners and handling walk-ins. He looked up through the grimy Plexiglas.

"Hi, what do you need, sir?" he asked.

Bill Brailsford had curly, light brown hair, stood medium height, and was lean and tan. In a quiet, controlled voice he told the officer that he had called earlier about his wife's disappearance and had come to fill out a formal report. Baccari dug out a missing person card and took down the sea captain's information.

Martha Brailsford, an attractive, self-employed artist and designer, had walked out of their house in the Willows community of Salem sometime Friday. By all appearances, she had fully intended to return home after a short while. The dog had been tied to the porch. Her pocketbook and car were there, the lights were off, the shades open, the doors unlocked. No note or message. Brailsford had been running the Provincetown boat out of Boston on that long, busy summer day, returning late around 9 P.M. to an empty house. After two hours with no word from his wife, Brailsford had tried going to sleep but had risen sometime between midnight and one. Still no Martha. Totally out of character for her not to contact him. He finally called Salem police headquarters and went down to get help.

"You sure she didn't go over to a girlfriend's house?" Baccari asked him. He explained again, as he had on the phone, that people tend to turn up on their own if you let them. Brailsford's initial call had been at one in the morning. At that time, Baccari had suggested that the bars were all about to close. Perhaps she would roll in shortly.

Brailsford insisted his wife would have let him know about her plans. Anyway, Martha didn't go to bars. He gave Baccari a photograph of Martha. Wearing a smile and no makeup, the woman looked radiant and natural under a branch of fuchsia, oblivious of her own beauty.

The police officer told Brailsford that he would enter Martha's name into the statewide computer system. "Call and let us know if she turns up so I can cancel it out." He asked Brailsford for a phone number where he could be reached. Brailsford warned that he would probably be out looking for his wife most of the time.

When he returned home, Brailsford checked with Salem Hospital. No unidentified female patients five foot three, slender, with sandy blonde hair had been admitted. No amnesia victims, no accident casualties.

Brailsford was unable to sleep. Around 3:00 his mounting fear pushed him out into the early morning, flashlight in hand, to search for his wife on his own. Martha had a set route she took each day through the Willows with their eight-year-old dog. Brailsford followed her course along local beaches, over rocks, and through the adjoining parks. When dawn broke and the light improved, he walked the route again. He then permitted himself to start calling family and friends, who were quick to respond. People began gathering at his home. Someone designed a flyer. A search party was organized.

Brailsford stopped by the police station again. It was the end of Baccari's shift. With Baccari at the desk was Lieutenant Pete

Garrette, who jotted down the man's statement while they talked. Brailsford told the officers that his wife had still not shown up and insisted that her disappearance was totally out of character. To his knowledge, no problems had been heavy on her mind, and there had been no marital difficulties. The two were happy.

Brailsford added that Martha's habits included yelling at people she came across, those who in her estimation were doing wrong. She never hesitated to point out the transgressions of polluters. The same trait that made her a protector of the environment made her a protector of the defenseless and the vulnerable as well. She had a penchant for picking up strays, aiding the wounded, tending to the needs of strangers. Martha gave generously of her time and friendship to neighbors of all ages. Stubborn, argumentative, steadfast, loyal. She had a mouth. She had a heart. Brailsford worried that one or the other might have gotten her in trouble.

Brailsford last saw his wife at 6:30 on Friday morning, when he had said good-bye to her and had left for work. It had now been more than twenty-four hours. He now questioned the police about what they intended to do, what resources they would use, what plan of action they would take. Officer Baccari reacted to Brailsford's questions and self-controlled tone with suspicion. The sea captain's steady, light blue eyes conveyed an unsettling calm to the officer. "I thought it was strange, him asking all those questions," Baccari said later. "But then I felt bad after. Felt real bad."

On Saturday morning, Muriel Conant was consumed with dread as she and her husband drove to Salem from their home in Cambridge. Muriel and her twin sister Martha had only a few days ago reconciled their differences from their recent squabble. She wondered where Martha could have been at that moment. She wondered where her sister could have been the day before. And she thought about her own last few hours leading up to Bill's 6 A.M. call, the very hours when Martha was officially listed as missing.

The previous evening, Muriel and her husband Greg Garvey had gone to see the Friday night production of *King Lear* at the American Repertory Theater on Brattle Street in Cambridge. As they were walking home they passed by the churchyard where Mary Joe Frug, a Harvard Law School professor, had been slain three months earlier on a breezy April night. Muriel had paused and had directed Greg's attention to the fresh flowers, which still adorned the spot. A foreboding had begun to envelop her, like a darkness closing in. And during the night it had developed into sleeplessness, her first spell since the onset of her pregnancy. Now, Saturday, her active unborn baby was strangely still.

One of the spots along Martha's route was a park known as Winter Island, adjoining the Willows by a short causeway. Less than half a mile long, Winter Island contained a number of tiny, secluded, rocky beaches, a public pier, a clam shack, a former Coast Guard hangar, the ramparts of Fort Pickering, and a parking lot that was currently home to a herd of Winnebagos. Bill Brailsford walked the park a second time on Saturday morning. This time he was lucky and ran into one of the caretakers, who knew Martha by sight. Bill explained the situation.

"Martha? Sure, saw her yesterday morning. 'Bout this time," the caretaker replied. "She was with some guy with a little dog. Balding, dark-haired guy, tall."

Bill was heartened by this sighting. It was a start. He also recognized the description. The guy was one of Martha's strays. Martha's "new friend," she had called him—a widower she had met last spring on one of her walks. Bill had seen him once in front of the house. Martha had introduced them. Bill couldn't remember the man's name, though Martha had talked about him frequently and about how sorry she felt for him. Brailsford knew the man lived down on Settlers Way.

A friend rode with him over to the condos. One of the neighbors was out early in the morning working on his car. With his help Bill was eventually able to determine the name and address of Tom Maimoni. The first time Brailsford knocked, there was no answer. Returning a short time later, he found Maimoni home.

When Maimoni greeted him, Brailsford explained why he had come and asked Tom if he had seen Martha the day before.

"Martha who?" was Maimoni's response.

Brailsford reminded Tom that he had walked with Martha several times a week. Both families owned dogs. Neither had a yard. Martha and Tom each made the rounds of the Willows every morning, she with Rudy the mutt, he with Salli the corgi. Another of Martha's habits was to replay for Bill conversations she had shared with the people she met on her daily walks. Maimoni was one of those people. "The girl with the dog," explained Brailsford.

"Oh, the girl with the dog," repeated Maimoni. He indicated that he had seen her in the early morning on her walk, but not afterward. "But say, we should go for a sail sometime. Both of you come. I'll bring a girlfriend along."

Brailsford asked if Maimoni had gone sailing with Martha on Friday. Maimoni insisted he would never have gone sailing with her alone. He denied sailing at all on Friday, though he did say he had taken the boat out to a mooring in the afternoon to wash it.

The ferry captain tried a few more questions but got no useful information. He turned to leave.

From the door, Tom Maimoni said encouragingly, "I'll be sure and say a prayer for her."

Detective Sergeant Conrad Prosniewski was the investigator on call Saturday. When the chief of detectives, Sergeant Dick Urbanowicz, learned of Brailsford's report, he had another reason to instruct the desk officer to contact thirty-seven-year-old Prosniewski. A fourteen-year veteran of the Salem Police Department—five as a detective—Conrad Prosniewski had also spent his youth in the Willows and knew the people down there.

Prosniewski was awakened at 8:30 on Saturday morning. The dark-haired, mustached detective hauled his six-foot frame out of bed. Embroiled in some personal battles of his own, he had been looking forward to spending the day with his eleven-year-old son Michael. It was an opportunity he would soon lose. His two kids were moving to Florida. After Prosniewski hung up, he woke Michael, and the pair went down to the station. The desk officer and the lieutenant on duty filled him in. First was some normal, standard speculation that the husband had been involved. Missing people usually appear within a day or two. When they don't, they very often know their abductors. Spouses are always the first suspects police consider. The detective gathered up his son and headed out to the Willows to talk to Bill Brailsford.

Cove Avenue ended at Salem Willows Park, with its public pier, adjoining beaches, and an arcade of food concessions and attractions. Detective Prosniewski pulled into the park, led his son Michael into the video game hall, purchased five dollars worth of quarters, and told him that he needed to talk to a man down the street for awhile. Michael had no objections.

Prosniewski arrived at the Brailsfords' home around nine on Saturday morning to find Brailsford surrounded by a tight knot of friends and family. Brailsford had called every acquaintance he could think of. A couple of neighbors indicated that Martha had been planning to sail with "a friend" on Friday afternoon. The only "friend" Brailsford could not fully rule out was Thomas Maimoni, a newcomer to the Willows who had told people that he had lost his wife. Brailsford related his earlier conversation with Maimoni and the suspicions he was left with. Brailsford's companions offered information about Martha that they thought might help the detective. Many confirmed that she was a head-strong, independent woman. Never one to try to diffuse a situation or back down in an argument or confrontation.

The group was anxious to widen the search, to get the media involved, to distribute their flyers, and to make a public appeal. Some, including Brailsford himself, owned boats and wanted to scour the local waters.

As he was trained to do, Prosniewski first had to consider the possibility that Brailsford himself might have had a hand in his wife's disappearance. Although the man described walking around all night searching, he didn't look the least bit tired. His voice bore no emotion. However, the people around him—who seemed to know him well—were confirming his statements and supplying the emotion for him. Apparently, this was just the man's style. Bill Brailsford's self-control belied his fear. Prosniewski put himself in Brailsford's shoes for a moment. He could well understand how adrenaline could drive out fatigue in such a situation. In his gut, he quickly eliminated Martha's husband as a suspect.

Prosniewski's next stop was the arcade at the park. His son Michael was happily attached to his favorite game. A quick count of the remaining quarters indicated Prosniewski could afford an-other interview. He climbed back into his gray, unmarked cruiser and rolled down the street to Settlers Way.

The Maimonis' unit was the second from the end. The build-ing was of blue-gray clapboard with a colonial ambiance tacked around the front entrance. When Conrad Prosniewski knocked on the burgundy front door, there was no answer. He placed a quick call to Maimoni's answering machine from his car phone and headed back down toward the park. Within minutes, the station radioed him that Maimoni had called back. Prosniewski turned back toward the condos.

11

Sergeant Prosniewski made himself comfortable in a chair facing the deck and water and set his radio on the end table. This should be simple, he thought. Either the guy knew where Martha was or he didn't. Dressed in shorts as though he were between sails, Maimoni settled back on the living room couch with a relaxed posture and an expansive manner. The forty-six-year-old host's gaze was steady, attentive, and concerned. When Prosniewski explained the purpose of this mid-morning visit, Maimoni showed momentary confusion but then spoke freely of Martha once he appeared to recognize her name.

The two had met the past spring while walking their dogs near the ruins of Fort Lee, tucked in the hills above Salem Willows Park. Their daily schedules had overlapped a couple of times a week, and the pair had become friendly, chatting comfortably as they made the circuit around the Willows and along the road to Winter Island. Martha had told Maimoni about a nude sunbather who parked himself each day on one of the Winter Island beaches. Prosniewski added the sunbather to an ever-growing list of small leads, names, and numbers to track down.

Maimoni said that on Friday, July 12, the day in question, he had seen Martha in the early morning around seven near the parking booth on Winter Island in the company of two women. She had approached Maimoni for a brief conversation, and then had rejoined her friends. That was, Maimoni said, the last he saw of her. She did *not* go sailing with him. In fact, Maimoni had not sailed at all on Friday, he said. He kept his boat at the Palmer's Cove Yacht Club in Salem, he explained with pride.

The detective managed to combine attentiveness, doleful eyes, and an easy smile in winning confidences and putting witnesses at ease. And suspects. Tom Maimoni warmed to him and chattered on. Out of the blue, he turned to the detective and offered that Martha was a "free spirit," overly friendly. Had he so desired, he could have gotten her to go out with him, even sailing alone with him. However, Maimoni said he was married and would never do anything to jeopardize his marriage.

Prosniewski heard little cop bells going off inside his head and scrambled to keep track of them all. First, the man's arrogance and boasting was offending him. Second, by previous accounts, Maimoni was a widower. Maimoni launched into a discussion of how his previous wife had indeed been a victim of cancer and mentioned that her death had been a topic of conversation with Martha. Martha had been extremely sympathetic, having lost someone close to cancer as well. Prosniewski asked whether Martha knew he was presently married.

"Oh, yes, she knew I was married," said his host. "We talked about the possibility of her and Bill going sailing with my wife and me." Maimoni added that he was grateful Patti was out of town and that she did not have to go through this.

Prosniewski had to explore the possibility of an affair between the two but was unsure how to ferret out the information. He asked, "Did Martha ever talk about her relationship with her husband Bill?" Maimoni said although Brailsford was apparently away for long hours at a time, Martha had never given any indication of marital problems.

Yet another brick wall. Prosniewski finally asked point blank: "Look, Tom. I'm investigating a missing person. I need to know— were you two having an affair? This is between you and me. Maybe she's upset over something, and is just getting away to think things through."

Maimoni denied the suggestion vehemently. His relationship with Patti was good, he insisted. His relationship with Martha had been casual. He then added, reassuringly, that he and Patti were deeply religious and would say a prayer for Martha.

Bells sounded in Prosniewski's mind. Out of the corner of his eye he scanned the room and searched his visual memory. No crucifixes in sight. No Stars of David. No buddhas, no pentagrams. He was trained to sniff out incongruities. "That's nice,"

Prosniewski commented. This guy's a bullshitter, he thought to himself. Casually, he checked Maimoni's forearms, face, neck, and exposed skin, looking for fresh scratches.

As Prosniewski was shown the door, he glanced around the hall and dining room. Stenciled ivy and custom switch plates gave the rooms a cozy exuberance. The house didn't fit the avowed piety. The wife didn't fit with Brailsford's story. And then Maimoni offered one more comment which raised the small hairs on the back of the detective's neck.

"You know what always bothered me about Martha?"

"What, Tom?" Prosniewski asked in a steady voice. But the detective was already thinking, Oh my God! Here it comes.

"The fact that she took so easily to strangers," said the man.

Prosniewski digested this obvious suggestion to look elsewhere. Find the nude sunbather. Find the strangers, Maimoni was saying. Direct the search away from Settlers Way. And a chilling conclusion came into Prosniewski head: Martha Brailsford is dead. What we have here is a murder.

Prosniewski sat in his car a few moments. Raindrops covered the windshield. He would call this a "garbage day," the sky reflecting his mood. He wondered what the hell to do next. He started up the Crown Victoria and headed down the street toward the park.

Suddenly, Thomas Maimoni's voice crackled from the car radio. Prosniewski jumped, then swore. "Salem police," the voice was saying in pseudo-police-speak. "Please inform Sergeant Prosniewski that he forgot his radio at my house." Maimoni had commandeered his radio.

Prosniewski grabbed the mike in embarrassment. "I got that," he said in a low growl. He did a quick U-turn and went back to the condo. Clicks spewed out from the speaker as patrolmen all over the city keyed their mikes in derision.

Maimoni was standing out front with the radio in his hand. Prosniewski retrieved it. He looked at Maimoni. Maimoni looked at him. Nothing was said. They mentally circled each other, then each retreated. Tom Maimoni entered his townhouse. Prosniewski headed back to the park to retrieve his kid.

The battle had begun. The paths of the two men were now inexorably entwined.

12

Conrad Prosniewski's father claimed much later that he knew his son was going to be a police officer when, at the age of five, Conrad stood in the intersection of Derby and Turner Streets with a couple of empty popcorn boxes on each hand, directing traffic.

Born on the North Shore in August 1954, Conrad grew up in Salem, where his parents had eventually settled after leaving their native Poland during World War II. His parents had both escaped slave labor camps during the war and had then made their way separately to England. There his father flew for a time in the Royal Air Force. His mother happened to work ground control and was the voice on his father's radio. After they met and married, Conrad's elder sister Barbara was born. The family then moved to the United States, where the senior Prosniewski found employment as a leatherworker in one of the many tanneries for which Salem and its neighbors were renowned.

One of Salem's most illustrious homicide cases occurred when Conrad was in grammar school. On a sunny September day, a woman was found sexually assaulted and brutally murdered in a Lafayette Street apartment downtown. Conrad remembered coming home from school and seeing all the neighbors milling around on the sidewalk. The victim's death was attributed to the infamous Boston Strangler, who was stalking women and terrorizing the area at the time. Ultimately he was caught, tried, and convicted. Although the Boston Strangler later died in prison amid controversy surrounding his confessions, the case planted seeds in Conrad's mind: where evil rears its head, justice will ultimately prevail.

Conrad went to St. John's Parochial School in Salem until high school. The nuns, who all spoke Polish, considered young Conrad a pretty wild kid. Later on, public high school came as an unbelievable shock to Conrad, who felt like a "meek little saint" next to his classmates. Here kids talked in the hallways and threw spitballs at the teachers. "Holy shit!" he said to himself when he ducked his first flying eraser. The nuns would have had fits. Conrad wasn't sure whether he was now at a giant party or in a war zone.

Prosniewski adapted quickly. Once caught smoking in the boy's room, he learned about the true meaning of the "board of education." Not dissuaded from his ongoing acculturation, Conrad graduated from being just a "screw-off" to an emerging radical—growing his hair long, wearing fatigues and bell-bottoms, skipping classes occasionally to attend talks and rallies protesting the Vietnam War. His inspiration was his sister Barbara, then a college student with a strong political conscience. The last thing he ever had in mind was to become a police officer.

At fifteen, Conrad began working after school as a dishwasher and cook at a busy restaurant in neighboring Peabody. There, another significant seed was sown. The establishment was a popular hangout for the Peabody police. A couple of the regulars were really nice guys. They often went back into the kitchen and wrestled with the young dishwashers, trying to dunk their heads in the sink. The kitchen crew loved them.

Many of the kids depended on the head cook for rides home after work. The man had a drinking problem, however. Each night the employees argued over who got to ride in the backseat for the extra margin of safety. As the cook's drinking got worse, some of the cops took pity on the young help and started giving them lifts home after closing. The rookie whom Conrad often rode with was Jack Dullea, the youth's first exposure to "the man behind the badge." Jack became his friend for life.

As things turned out, the head cook was the son of the owner. The two frequently had family tiffs during their shifts. These quarrels developed into heated fights after the cook had had a few. One night it escalated into an all-out war during a banquet for a local bowling league. The meal was running late. The argument became physical. The cook began to tip over stacks of plates and platters of food. Then the meal became airborne, course by course. The father grabbed a pot of boiling string beans from the stove. The son hurled a kitchen knife across the counter. Conrad and the rest of the young dishwashers dove beneath the big steel sink to escape the weapons and hot beans flying through the air. By the time Conrad had climbed into Jack's cruiser for his ride home, he was beginning to wonder which of the two had the more dangerous job.

Nevertheless, Conrad worked as a cook for years, eventually supporting himself while earning an associate's degree at nearby Essex Tech. Conrad found college made much more sense than high school had. He enjoyed his courses, did well, and began to visualize a future for himself. Along the way, he developed a passion for flying. Each week he cashed his paycheck and headed up to Beverly Airport to buy another flying lesson.

Conrad also loved hiking and camping outdoors. As a youth, he had been an Eagle Scout, an important milestone in his life and one which he credits with steering him away from trouble. When he realized how expensive obtaining a commercial pilot's license would be, he instead considered studying to become a game warden or conservation officer. He began working on a second associate's degree to improve his chances, this time in criminal justice. In the late 1970s, his classmates all began studying for civil service exams to become police officers. When the test came up, Conrad figured, why not take it? Everyone else was. And it might prove useful.

Useful indeed. As fate would have it, Conrad Prosniewski passed the exam and was hired by the Salem Police Department in 1978. Somehow, he had become a cop.

In the beginning, his parents were surprised by his sudden career choice, despite the prophetic image of directing traffic with popcorn boxes. They had witnessed their homeland, Poland, being taken over by a police state. There the police were oppressors of good people, to be feared and avoided at all costs. Due to their deep distrust of police, many of Conrad's relatives in the old country were never told about his new job. His parents, however, came to accept it and even to feel pride. Conrad initially felt he was a "fish out of water" at the academy and feared he'd have problems adjusting to this new culture. Ultimately, he reconciled his own value system with that of being a police officer. He went on to join the motorcycle patrol, to serve as assistant harbormaster, and to help form the police dive team.

After ten years on patrol, he joined the Criminal Investigation Division in 1988. Prosniewski was promoted to sergeant in early 1991.

Jack Dullea, who had rescued the teenager from the flying beans, eventually left Peabody to join the Salem Police Department, shortly after Prosniewski had joined the force. Returning briefly to the station from Settlers Way on Saturday morning, Prosniewski ran into Dullea in the hallway.

"How's it going?" Dullea asked him.

Prosniewski stopped and looked his friend in the eye. "I just talked to a murderer," he said.

13

Go back to the neighbors. Now Prosniewski had to piece together every step Martha had taken on Friday. Reconstruct her trail and see where it led. The insignificant details of an ordinary day so casually flow into oblivion when the next one dawns. Each yesterday is eclipsed by tomorrow. Martha had walked through Friday. Her footsteps, fingerprints, and visual image were dissipating with each passing hour. Every person whose seaside path she had crossed now had to pluck the memory from the tide.

After lunch, Conrad Prosniewski swung by the arcade and bought another roll of quarters for his son. "Try the helicopters," he suggested.

Two neighbors placed Martha near the local beach at close to one in the afternoon Friday. She had told them both she was going sailing with a friend. Martha was walking north on Beach Avenue, away from her home, carrying a canvas bag, dressed in shorts and a T-shirt.

OK, she was walking. She wasn't sitting on her front step waiting for a ride. She had left her car at home. There were three docks within walking distance of the Willows. One was on Winter Island, but she would have headed west on Cheval Avenue if that had been her goal. That left Salem Willows Yacht Club and the Willows pier, both in the park. Prosniewski started with the yacht club.

Salem Willows Yacht Club consisted of a small clubhouse

built on a pier jutting out toward Beverly Harbor. As Prosniewski approached the clubhouse gate, he heard music coming through the windows.

At the screen door, Prosniewski gave a perfunctory rap and stepped inside. Some sort of affair going on. The place held not an accidental clumping of members but instead a more homogeneous and dressy crowd in loose affiliation. It shortly dawned on him that this was a wedding reception. The detective held back with momentary discomfort, regretting the intrusion. This young couple, about to start their life together, hardly deserved to have this moment clouded by a stranger's misfortune and marred by the harshness of a police investigation. Yet every passing hour would more certainly seal Martha's fate.

Conrad Prosniewski pushed his holster and radio further under his jacket and slipped in as unobtrusively as possible to locate one of the employees. He conducted his errand quietly. While he waited, his questions were circulated among the staff. Who had been around on Friday? Had anyone seen a woman of Martha's description that day? Any possibility she boarded a boat at the yacht club pier? Who was running the launch?

The music had a good beat, carefree, full of promise and hope. The bride, aglow in satin, moved about the room. A perfect setting for a celebration—surrounded by the sea and accompanied by a chorus of halyards clinking against masts with every pitch and roll. Amid the nautical ambiance, the families would send these children off, setting them adrift together to make their own way as two paths now became one.

For a moment, Prosniewski shared with these strangers their good wishes for the couple. May their marriage be a smooth sail, may the wind be always at their back. May it be smoother than his own had been.

The detective was self-conscious of his own rather inappropriate attire as he waded through the responses from the staff. They had yielded nothing. This route was a dead end. Finally, he cut bait and went back out into the hard rain. "What a lousy day for a wedding," he sighed, and turned toward the park. Michael might be running out of quarters by now, but at least the kid was dry.

Despite lacking a raincoat, Prosniewski's threads were dressy enough for Dan Sweeney's bait shop at the Willows pier. The shop and boat livery had been in Sweeney's family for three generations. Dan's business and livelihood depended on the activity on the pier. And nothing that went on there escaped his eye. Dan and Prosniewski were old friends.

The detective entered the shop and flicked the water out of his eyes. "Dan," he said to the boatman, "would you believe I'm actually here on official business?"

Sweeney was tanned, with impish eyes and a mustache the size of a cowcatcher. He extended both fists toward his friend. "OK! Lock me up!" he shouted.

"We've got a missing person. She may have picked up a boat here yesterday. Martha Brailsford. You know her?" Prosniewski asked him.

Sweeney didn't disappoint him. "Hey, yeah, I know Martha." Not only did he remember seeing the young woman Friday afternoon, he also nailed down the time. Martha and Rudy were regular visitors to the pier. Friday was unusual in that Martha had come without the dog, and Sweeney had been too busy with a boat rental customer to engage in their usual chitchat. Nevertheless, Martha was sufficiently attractive to require a quick glance as she passed. A good enough glance to remember what she had worn, and a strong enough impression for Dan to remember the customer he had been with at the time. Dan retrieved Friday's rental slips, located the pertinent one, and read off the rental time to Prosniewski: 1:20 P.M. Prosniewski had obtained his first hard evidence.

Sweeney could not identify Martha's destination, but he pointed to his dock hand Dan Mahoney, who had also worked the previous day. Mahoney was presently down working on the boats. All of Sweeney's bright orange dories were at the dock today. The rain had shut down business, and the pier was deserted.

Prosniewski repeated his questions to Mahoney. By his side, Dan Sweeney elaborated on Martha's description: light-colored shorts, raspberry shirt, boat shoes, French braid. Apparently Sweeney was good at noticing these things.

Mahoney did not know Martha by name but did remember a woman of that description walking past him and boarding a sailboat on the public side of the dock. He described the boat. And he described the sailor.

Prosniewski's first big break on this gloomy day shone down on his investigation like sunlight from heaven. Young Mahoney's partial description fit that of Tom Maimoni.

"Will you do me a favor?" Prosniewski said to the kid. "Will you take a quick ride with me? I wanna show you some boats."

Mahoney agreed. The detective turned to his friend. "OK if I take him?"

Sweeney smiled. "Just pay for his time."

Prosniewski stopped at the arcade and retrieved his quarterless son. Then the three drove downtown to Palmer's Cove Yacht Club, PCYC, as it is locally known. It was just after three in the afternoon.

On the way to the club, Prosniewski was figuring out how best to handle this identification so that it could be admissible in court. He couldn't just lead the witness over to Thomas Maimoni's boat and say, "Is this the one?" He had to assemble a little collection of similar boats, like a lineup. Or he could present Dan Mahoney with a whole crowd of boats, like asking the witness to pick out a face in a courtroom or like running a photo ID.

Prosniewski decided that the latter approach was by far the simplest and that he could probably get away with turning Dan Mahoney loose in the marina. The detective wasn't sure where Maimoni's slip was located or whether his boat was in.

When they arrived at PCYC, the three walked slowly down each dock. Each boat was wrong. Wrong color, wrong size. The boat Mahoney remembered was white, twenty-eight feet long, possibly with gold trim. The fenders were hung horizontally, rather than in the more typical vertical position. As they strolled down one of the fingers off the main dock, a boat motored up and began to pull into one of the slips. Prosniewski recognized the man at the helm immediately. Tom Maimoni called out, "Hey, Connie!" He had a couple of people with him, and the boat was *Counterpoint.*

Detective Prosniewski's first reaction was, "*Connie?*" So now we're good buddies? His second reaction was more serious. If Mahoney realized this man was a suspect, it would screw up the objectivity of the identification process. Dan Mahoney might be the only person in the world who could place Martha on Maimoni's boat.

The detective gave a quick wave and turned away, avoiding conversation. Mahoney was staring at the boat. They walked on. The sixteen-year-old looked back over his shoulder a couple of times and finally said, "It looked a lot like that one."

There was no gold stripe on *Counterpoint,* but a teak rub-rail ran along the side. Mahoney was not positive about either the man or the boat, but both fit to the best of his memory.

Prosniewski sensed that Maimoni might feel the police were dogging him at this point, bringing witnesses around to see his boat. Michael, now following his father's case with interest, started to ask something. Prosniewski quickly shut him up.

Dan Mahoney reaffirmed the partial identification. It was suggestive, but not strong enough, for probable cause. The detective took him back to the Willows.

On the way back to the station, the detective apologized to his son. "I had a bad feeling about that man, Michael. I'm sorry I yelled at you, but I have to be real careful what I say to him, you understand?"

Michael nodded and looked up at him. "Dad, is she dead?"

"I don't know. But we gotta keep looking till we find her."

The detective was amused by the encounter with Maimoni. The twentieth century Argentinean writer Jorge Luis Borges portrays the universe as a "garden of forking paths," where there is not one straight route through time but infinite paths—divergent, convergent, parallel, and cyclical. Each person's maze-like routes through time and space double back again and again, often as coincidences. One is greeted at every turn by one's own reflections, alternate realities, pasts, futures. The investigation into the disappearance of Martha Brailsford was leading Conrad Prosniewski straight into Borges' garden.

14

Virginia McCarthy met Patti Maimoni in the spring of 1989 when both were teaching at the Carlton School in Salem. The two fast became friends. Virginia, or "Ginny," and her husband Gerald were avid boaters themselves. They kept their own boat, a thirty-two-foot Grand Banks called *Sarah B*, at Pickering Wharf. The McCarthys were an older couple. Ginny's welcoming nature often filled the void left by the death of Patti's mother.

Before Patti departed for Wichita, she extracted a promise from Ginny to look in on Tom from time to time and to have him over for a meal. This was the first separation the happy young couple had endured since their marriage in 1987. On Saturday afternoon, July 13, Ginny fulfilled her promise by phoning Tom at the condo. She found him in.

"Tom, it's Ginny. Keeping yourself busy?" she asked.

"Well, I'm trying to get the washing done," he answered. He told her about all the frozen homemade dinners Patti had prepared for him.

Ginny suggested he come down to their boat Monday night and have supper with them on board. They agreed to meet at the *Sarah B* at around 6:00.

The sole female in the Salem police's Criminal Investigation Division (CID) was Detective Mary Butler. On Saturday afternoon, she came down to help out Sergeant Prosniewski. One of her first tasks was to accompany him as he went to update the Brailsford family and to see what else the CID could learn from them.

As they entered the Brailsfords' house, Mary noticed Martha's dog, waiting with sad eyes on the front porch. Inside she observed a warm and welcoming home with open, light-filled rooms, exposed beams, and polished wood floors immersed in beauty and love. After introductions and Prosniewski's news, she asked Brailsford if she could check through Martha's purse. He located it and handed it over. Mary sat for awhile on a kitchen stool, pulling out a wallet, comb, and assorted items from the pocketbook. But she began to feel self-conscious, aware of Brailsford's gaze. How must it feel to have your wife missing and watch some stranger paw through her purse? she thought. Mary wished instead she could say something to this man to make him feel better, to help him through this. She didn't stop being a person just because she was a detective. But she could think of nothing to say.

Instead, she glanced around the living room. Martha Brailsford was clearly not a person who had left without intending to return. Her very soul was in this house. And the dog. Who's going to explain this to the dog? She looked at the family. Mary Butler had a husband and child of her own. This is more than anyone ever anticipates in life, she thought. How are they going to get through this?

There were business cards, an appointment card, and other items they would need to check out more carefully, but she couldn't bear to do it here. "I'd like to take this back to the station," Mary said to Brailsford. "We'll get it back to you as soon as possible." Brailsford nodded, and the detectives left.

At the office Prosniewski answered a few calls. He followed up with some of the people who had been on the beach. His yellow-lined pad was filling up with chronological notes, names, phone numbers, and lists of things to do. Folks to talk to, like the ubiquitous neighbor who would know everything about everybody. At 4:00 he turned the pad over to Jim Page, one of the detectives on the Saturday night shift. Page agreed to contact the Coast Guard and get a search-and-rescue mission under way. Local harbormasters had all been notified. Page dug into Prosniewski's list:

TO DO

PCYC - WITNESSES, BARTENDER, LAUNCHMAN
WHO SAW WHAT THERE
CALL PARKER BROS: SHOW UP WORK FRI?
WIFE - AT SISTERS? OR IS MAIMONI LYING?
NEIGHBORS - FIND THE NOSY LADY -
BILL WORKED TILL 9? MAKE SURE -
PHOTO OF BOAT

Sergeant Prosniewski went home to shake his head out a bit and to make arrangements for Michael to go back to his mother's for the remainder of the weekend. If Martha somehow had fallen overboard, seven to nine days would pass before her body rose to the water's surface. In the meantime, Brailsford's friends focused their own investigation on Maimoni and appeared annoyed that the police were wasting time barking up other trees. Prosniewski had to work at keeping his own prejudices under control. He was as convinced of Maimoni's involvement as the family was. Yet Prosniewski had to think ahead to the courtroom and be prepared to convince a jury that he had explored all other possibilities, every step of the way. Thomas Maimoni could be a ruthless killer. Sloppy police work could set him free.

15

Detective Jim Page had been a Salem police officer since 1985 and a detective for the past three years. Page, thirty-two, when he wasn't working overtime liked to ski, golf, and run. His tall, lean frame attested to his athletic nature. With dark blonde hair, clean-shaven square jaw, and impassive expression, the youthful-looking Page had found much success in working the department's undercover drug cases. Thorough and methodical, Page was the designated evidence officer. He also had a reputation for tinkering with anything mechanical and was dubbed "Inspector Gadget" by his colleagues. Jim Page now tackled Prosniewski's list with a vengeance, continuing the trail of notes on his yellow pad.

Page first contacted the pier tender at Palmer's Cove Yacht Club, where Tom Maimoni kept his boat. The club had been slow on Friday. At one point in the afternoon, there had been a power failure in the clubhouse. Staff and patrons had gone outside. The pier tender and bartenders knew about three-quarters of the members by sight. The bar was a "regular soap opera," Page wrote in his notes, a close-knit family club in which everybody's business was also everybody else's business. Still, no leads turned up, although several names and numbers awaited call-backs. Someone else was checking the PCYC guest book.

Muriel Conant, Martha's sister, called late Saturday afternoon demanding a search warrant be issued for Maimoni. Page told her what the police had been up to and carefully explained why there was insufficient probable cause to justify a warrant. If Dan Mahoney's identification had been absolutely positive, if enough evidence had surfaced, the warrant would have been written and executed by now, Page assured her. Martha's sister was not satisfied and announced that she would call a judge.

Later in the evening, Bill Brailsford called to suggest that Martha's picture be broadcast on the local news. Page told Brailsford he was free to call the news stations himself.

In Martha's purse a note had been found with the notation "5:15—Towne Lyne House" and a phone number. Towne Lyne was a restaurant on Route 1. Brailsford believed it was for an old appointment. Nevertheless, Page tried the number five times during his shift.

By early evening, Page had contacted the Coast Guard. The weather was still poor. At 7:30 on Saturday night, the Coast Guard authorized a search of Salem Harbor and its perimeter to begin Sunday morning "at first light, weather permitting."

Jim Page added numerous notations regarding mariners' bulletins, local harbormasters, arrangements for the Coast Guard vessel, and the rippling involvement of more and more members of the department. Sergeant Peter Gifford, who came on duty at 4:00 on Saturday afternoon, had dropped by the Willows and had found neighbors and friends flocking around him with questions. Gifford had not known about the incident, and, justifiably annoyed, went to the Criminal Investigation Division to be filled in. Not only was Gifford an assistant harbormaster, he also had grown up in the Willows. He knew the neighborhood, knew the hiding places, and knew the waters better than anyone else on the force. He was also as member of the police dive team and later was pulled into the search efforts.

Family and friends of the victim were both an asset and a liability to an investigation. Bill Brailsford's companions were eager to help. Martha was well loved. The flyers they had created were tacked up throughout Salem and neighboring Marblehead. Late Saturday and well into Sunday morning, Brailsford's supporters climbed aboard lobster boats in the hours before they were to embark, leaving the posters to alert their crews. All along the shore, people were asked to be on the lookout.

A number of Brailsford's friends contacted Maimoni on Saturday, some by phone. In each case, Maimoni's response was,

"Martha who?" After the first time, this answer hardly seemed credible.

Someone in the family contacted the FBI in Washington, D.C. A Boston agent, Tom Cassano, was alerted.

A close inner circle of family and friends reached out to the surviving victim to surround, comfort, protect and insulate their loved one. Increasingly, Prosniewski found himself communicating to Brailsford through Martha's brother-in-law, Muriel's husband Greg Garvey, who appeared to be heading up the family's own investigation.

16

On Sunday morning, July 14, with a few hours of sleep stoking his body, Prosniewski reviewed the efforts of the night shift. He appreciated Jim Page's careful notes. Now Prosniewski picked up the case again. Things were already heating up by 7:30 A.M. A forty-one-foot Coast Guard patrol boat was already searching the harbor. Soon afterward, the Coast Guard issued a missing person's description over marine radio. Although the Coast Guard would not provide helicopters, Corporal Richard Welby of the Massachusetts State Police Air Wing Unit had managed to make one available for an aerial search that afternoon.

The calls continued. People who had seen Martha, people who had not. Both could be significant. Many calls were a waste of time, but all had to be politely, painstakingly followed up. Between calls, Martha's family had to be updated and reassured.

Tom Cassano, the local FBI agent, called Prosniewski on Sunday. He explained to Prosniewski how he had been called into the case. He offered his services but agreed to stay out of the way. In a series of serendipitous coincidences for which this case would later become famous, Cassano mentioned that he just happened to be a member of Palmer's Cove Yacht Club. Prosniewski perked up. This could be useful. Then the agent said his boat slip was adjacent to Tom Maimoni's. Just so happened. Prosniewski smiled. Cassano offered to photograph *Counterpoint* for the Salem detective. Prosniewski loved this man!

Prosniewski contacted the company for which Bill Brailsford

worked. Their records confirmed that Martha's husband had been working all day Friday during the hours he had claimed.

Staff and other members of PCYC began to call in. Out-of-state members of the Brailsford family telephoned for information. A local resident called to say that he had not seen the boat on Friday but that he had been dozing at the time. He recalled seeing Maimoni's wet suit hanging in the cockpit of *Counterpoint* to dry. Upon further questioning, it turned out the local resident had seen the wet suit on Thursday, not Friday.

Bill Brailsford pointed out that Maimoni claimed he had been washing *Counterpoint* on Friday afternoon. Prosniewski made a note to look for people who could confirm or disprove this claim.

Then Tom Maimoni himself called to say that his wife Patricia was expected back from Kansas later in the week. The man wanted to assist in any way he could. What would the police do without Tom's help?

The detective arranged to meet Corporal Welby of the Massachusetts State Police and his chopper at 1:45 in the middle of Bertram Field at the local high school. The football field was a popular landing site for emergency medical flights in the area.

Around lunchtime, Prosniewski picked up the phone to check in with his fiancée Julie, who was also working. Julie Michaud had become concerned about Prosniewski's whereabouts when she couldn't get through to him during yet another long, unscheduled shift. She was resigning herself to the fact that his work always, always came first. Another Sunday morning without him, without the renewal they both badly needed. On Sunday afternoons, Julie tended bar at a Derby Street restaurant called In a Pig's Eye.

The Pig's Eye was located a short block from Salem's famous House of the Seven Gables and a stone's throw from the wharves and the custom house, where Nathaniel Hawthorne had worked while he wrote his American classics. Derby Street had once been lined with taverns servicing the needs of sailors, local and foreign, when the golden era of East India trade had brought wealth and industry to this seaport. When Prohibition ended, a handful of bars reemerged, each catering to a different subculture. Witches Brew, on the corner of Derby and Daniel Streets, hosted visiting seamen seated alongside shopkeepers, city workers, and carpenters—Salem's working class. Directly across the street, the Pig's Eye was a hangout for a more eccentric population—artists, musicians, and the eclectic community of Salem Willows. Several members of the staff pursued fledgling careers as singers or actors on the side. Members of tiny Wharf Rat Productions, a local community theater group specializing in benefit performances, paid their rent by waiting tables and tending bar at the Pig's Eye.

Conrad Prosniewski was an anomaly there. Then again, Conrad Prosniewski crossed freely the countless social and cultural borderlines of Salem. When he called on Sunday afternoon, he was greeted warmly by the waitress who answered the phone. Today she was serving up the daily catch to the missing woman's worried neighbors. Tonight she would be down at Pickering Wharf playing the murderous sister in Wharf Rat's dinner theater production of *Crimes of the Heart*.

This weekend, the Pig's Eye was packed. Rumor mongers, information seekers, and concerned friends seeking company all shoved their way inside. With Julie's updates and a small TV perched in the kitchen, customers at the Pig's Eye heard it first. The week of the search and investigation broke all previous sales records.

In the midst of the day's blitz of activity, Prosniewski also attempted to negotiate the sale of his house in neighboring Danvers. His ex-wife was about to move to Florida, taking their son Michael and young daughter Kristina. Earlier in the year, Prosniewski had battled the proposed removal in the courts. He had made a sad, fruitless last attempt to maintain regular contact with his children. Losing his bid to remain a full-time father, Prosniewski was now relegated to being a vacation getaway for the kids. Probably three-quarters of the police department had gone through a divorce or two. Families were casualties of the job. Losing the kids cut deeply.

His ex-wife was anxious to move but could not do so until the house was sold. Prosniewski was not eager to sell short. He had an interested buyer and had to deal with a realtor, his ex-wife, the numbers, and his conflicted heart through the entire weekend—all the while engaged in his highest profile case.

Finally, an agreement was reached. The president of the real estate office personally delivered the papers to the station for Prosniewski to sign. The realtor had heard about the case and gave assurances that Prosniewski need not worry about the details and distractions of the sale. He would personally look out for Prosniewski's best interests.

On that same Sunday, Tom Maimoni had woken early, unable to sleep. Maimoni called his wife Patti when an appropriate hour had dawned in Wichita and asked her to cut short her trip. Patti phoned the airline, then called back to say she would return Tuesday or Wednesday.

After checking in with Prosniewski and passing on this information, Maimoni calculated that he was now left with a day "in between." Patti should never have gone to Kansas. Her place was by his side. Now he needed her. Now he had to wait to get her back.

In need of company, Maimoni decided to drive to Rhode Island and drop in on friends in Jamestown, twenty miles south of Providence. When he arrived, however, they were not home. He turned his car around and headed back north, picking up Interstate 95 again. Just as he neared Providence, he caught sight of a hitchhiker standing on the shoulder of the highway.

The woman was in her twenties—pretty with long, light brown hair, clad in jeans and a T-shirt. Maimoni slid the silver Taurus into the right lane and pulled over just beyond her. She climbed in. She was making her daily trek to the methadone clinic downtown, she explained, and her car had broken down. The clinic closed at 11:00 on Sunday morning. It was 10:50, and she had no time to find a service station. She either had to find a quick ride, or miss her dose. She said her name was Jennifer. Jennifer Eccleston. Her name was as wholesome as her face. She certainly didn't look like a heroin addict.

"Oh, I've read all about methadone." Maimoni said knowledgeably, "I understand." He flew into town, got her to the clinic on time, then offered to wait outside in the car while she got her dose. "Listen," he said. "I'll wait and give you a lift home. I wouldn't want some weirdo to pick you up."

When Jennifer returned, Maimoni asked if she felt like having lunch. The young woman was feeling a little better. The methadone meant she wouldn't have to score drugs later. The distraction meant she wouldn't be tempted to. Food would be nice. A ride home would be nice. And the guy had this cute little dog in the car, fitted with a collar decorated with tiny sailboats. The dog settled on Jennifer's lap. Its presence reassured her. Jennifer relaxed and accepted the man's offer.

Maimoni drove to Newport. They talked while they ate, had a few beers, then went for a ride along the coast. Maimoni stopped the car along Cliff Walk. The two took the dog for a stroll overlooking the water. The little corgi trotted alongside them at the end of a retractable leash.

They found much in common. Jennifer had lost her mother to cancer the year before. And Maimoni, the "lonely widower," told her about his dead wife. Cancer, too, as it turned out. Skin cancer, stemming from a bad sunburn in Florida, he explained. To Maimoni, in need of someone today, the "in-between" day, here was a pretty woman with problems. A perfect companion.

Jennifer lived in the country on a farm with one of her older brothers and their father, both fishermen. The well-established Yankee family had owned land in the county for generations. Bright parents, attractive children. Despite her farm-fresh appearance, Jennifer Eccelston had also acquired a measure of street sense and distrust she hadn't learned on the farm.

Methadone made Jennifer sweat, one of its unpleasant after-effects. Outside Bristol, Maimoni pulled over by a channel and watched as she ducked in to cool off. When she returned, they continued on their drive. He talked about his boat and his plans for a cruise soon. He suggested she join up with him as his first mate. "You could sail with me to Florida," he said. Jennifer actually considered this offer. He was middle-aged and unattractive, she reflected. Today they were pretty much using each other. She was feeling lonely and isolated and couldn't bear to be with people she knew. But Florida? Hey, for months she had been spending her afternoons on her bed planning her own funeral, how to do herself in and still look good for an open casket. Would news of her death reach her friends and family out on their fishing boats and move them to ask their captains to return to shore for her burial? This haunted her. Would she go into the ground alone because everyone she loved was at sea? Maybe Florida with this guy was a better alternative. Maybe it was a way out of here, she mused.

Maimoni wanted to go to a beach. Jennifer directed him to Narragansett, where they sat on the sand and looked out over the bay. A couple of divers crossed the beach toward the surf, carrying weight belts in their hands. While they watched, Maimoni's mood changed abruptly, and he "spaced out" for several minutes. The young woman asked what was wrong. "Oh, I guess I'm getting old. Those guys, they still carry their belts back and forth. At my age, I tend to keep mine on my boat. Too heavy to lug back and forth."

Jennifer decided she was about done with this guy. His new

mood made her uncomfortable. "I can get home from here," she said. Her home town was only ten miles away. She could thumb a new ride.

"No, no," Maimoni insisted on keeping his promise. He drove her to her father's farm. On the way, he made a few half-hearted moves.

The young woman turned him down. "Thanks a lot, but you're a little old for me." She knew lots of ways to say this, but after all, the guy had bought her lunch.

Maimoni asked if maybe he could just touch her a little, "in certain places," as if those places were unnamably dirty to him. This guy has a problem, she thought. She shook her head. They pulled into the driveway leading to her house. Jennifer got out. Maimoni reached over and handed her his business card.

"Don't forget, we're still going sailing," he hollered out to her.

Jennifer Eccleston held up the card and waved. "Yeah. I'll call you." Florida no longer seemed the best alternative.

17

hen the helicopter arrived Sunday afternoon at the high
school, Detective Sergeant Conrad Prosniewski climbed
into the right seat and the air search got underway. For
Prosniewski, a licensed pilot on his first chopper ride, the two-
hour flight Sunday afternoon was both beautiful and thrilling.
They scanned every island in the waters near Salem and Beverly
from a height of about fifty feet. At times they hovered still lower,
and the skids almost touched the water. The propeller wash bit
the water's surface, shattering the peace above and below. They
studied every rocky crevice for pieces of clothing, canvas sail
bags, or shoes.

Sunday was a gorgeous day. Sunbathers were getting annoyed. The aircraft flew so close to the ground that the vegeta-
tion flattened in the wind. Calls flooded the local police stations
complaining about the disturbance. To each caller the dispatchers
patiently explained about the search.

Inside the cockpit, the two occupants were protected from
the din. Prosniewski talked frequently on the radio to pinpoint
articles they spotted that warranted checking out by boat.
Through the calm, shallow water he could see probably ten feet
down. Lobster pots partially submerged in sand on the bottom
masqueraded as bags and shorts. They scrutinized the coast as far
south as the city of Lynn and as far north as Gloucester Harbor
before turning back. They found no sign of Martha.

Before Prosniewski returned to the station, the desk received a call from a woman named Ruth Buck, a summertime resident of nearby Baker's Island. Mrs. Buck had heard all the hullabaloo and thought she might have some information.

Prosniewski arranged to visit her in the evening. Salem Harbormaster Andrew Syska agreed to find transportation. The Salem harbormaster's own boat was a dog, a twenty-seven-foot Nausett called *Bowditch*, converted from some prior commercial use. Power enough, but incredibly slow. Syska rounded up Beverly's patrol boat instead. Beverly Assistant Harbormaster Bill McGrath agreed to take Prosniewski and Syska to Baker's Island at 6:00.

At 5:30, the detective swung by Cove Avenue to update the family. Bill Brailsford listened in silence, holding back his emotion. His face reddened, and he swallowed hard as the detective's lack of good news sunk in. The bottled-up reaction pained Prosniewski, who felt the anguish that lay beneath. He wanted to shake the man and say, "Hey, man, let go!"

Martha's sister Muriel was there with Bill's father, Paul Brailsford. The senior Brailsford told Prosniewski that years ago he had been a bobby in London. He shared a policeman's perspective on the case. He was polite, not wishing to nose into Prosniewski's case, but had a few thoughts. The detective listened patiently. Most of the suggestions had already been taken. But this was not a time to cut short anyone's ideas. Martha was still missing. No one had any answers. And no one at this point was above seeking help.

Prosniewski contacted headquarters and asked that all local hospitals be called and checked for possible amnesia victims. He also fielded a few calls from the news media.

At 6:00, Syska, McGrath, and Prosniewski kept their appointment for the visit to Baker's Island. Baker's is the only inhabited island of fifteen that belong to Salem. Four and a half miles out to sea, its mournful foghorn can be heard from the mainland year-round. Several dozen summer cottages and a lighthouse pepper the sixty-acre terrain occupied by sumac, wild roses, granite, and woods. Fires have always been the island's plague and constant fear as bolts of lightning seek it out. Homes, though they lack electricity, are all fitted with lightning rods.

Ruth Buck was waiting for her visitors aboard her seventeen-foot Boston Whaler, tied to the island's pier. When they pulled up, she told Prosniewski her story. On Friday afternoon, Ruth had been at the Willows pier, preparing to ferry a young Salem couple to the island. Richard Lis, an engineer for the city, and his wife Jennifer were boarding the whaler at 1:15 P.M. when they noticed a large white sailboat backing into the float on the public side of the pier. The boat had caught Ruth's attention because smoke was billowing from the exhaust pipe and dirty water was being pumped into the ocean. Ruth was something of an environmentalist and had bristled at the sight.

Prosniewski asked her to describe the boat she had seen. Ruth Buck had come to Baker's Island every summer for over fifty-five years. Considered the local historian and Grande Dame of the island, she knew boats well. She told the detective this one was very similar to a "Nicholson with a Marconi rig." She estimated the length at thirty-eight or forty feet. The boat was fiberglass, single-masted. The sails were down, and the name on the transom began with a C, the letters scrolled and worn. Something like *Concession*, she said, or perhaps *Concussion*. She did remember the home port Boston in block letters below the name.

Ruth Buck had also caught sight of the sailor. She described a man about fifty with salt-and-pepper hair, mustache, baseball cap, about 6 feet tall. Handsome, she said, and of medium build.

She then described his passenger, a slim young woman about five feet four with sandy blonde hair, light shorts and top, standing on the float with a beach bag. Ruth was leaving the dock about that time. She last saw the white sailboat as it motored past Hospital Point, further up the coast toward Beverly.

Prosniewski took down information about Ruth's passengers and arranged to pick her up the next morning to show her some boats. Then the three headed back to Salem.

Back in the detectives' office, an intriguing call came in from a resident of the Willows who claimed to know Tom Maimoni. The guy told Prosniewski that Patti was Maimoni's third wife. The previous two had divorced him. He knew one of them well, a Mary Ellen, who did indeed have cancer. The man also told Prosniewski that Maimoni may have had a couple of kids.

Tom Maimoni had been less than honest with more than a few people around him. In fact, Patti Maimoni was Tom's fourth wife, and all were currently alive. Tom did have two kids. It just so happened they were named Michael and Christina, just like the kids of his new friend, Conrad Prosniewski.

On Sunday evening at 8:45, Prosniewski called Brailsford and again brought him up to date. Brailsford thanked him quietly. The detective's heart went out to this man. Martha's husband continued to trudge through the whole episode with poignant dignity and grace. He never lost patience, never interfered, and never questioned the integrity of Prosniewski's investigation.

Martha's family was still clinging to hope. With each passing hour, Prosniewski's own hope diminished. For now, however, he wanted to leave this family with theirs.

One member of the family was stuck on the West Coast, wanting to return sooner than her airline reservation allowed. Jim Page faxed a letter to Delta Airlines explaining there was a police/family emergency so that she could get home as soon as possible.

The calls continued into the night. Sandy Doyle, another Willows neighbor, reported that a couple of weeks earlier she and two friends had been walking dogs along Beach Avenue. Martha had joined up with them, and together they had continued down to the park. Near the public men's room, known as the Men's Cottage, they had caught sight of a man with a small dog. Martha had left the group at that point to talk to him. Later in the day she had apologized to Sandy and had explained that the man was her recently widowed friend. Martha had said she felt sympathy for the man, who had lost his wife to cancer. Maimoni had told Prosniewski of that encounter but instead had placed the incident at Winter Island on Friday morning, July 12. Sandy Doyle reconfirmed that she had not seen Maimoni for over two weeks and that her only encounter with him had been in the park. Prosniewski checked with her friends. Both repeated Sandy's story. Another minor Maimoni mystery. Why was he trying to throw the time and location off?

The drone of the state police helicopter engines could be heard over Salem off and on, well into the night. For the local residents below, it was a chilling and eerie reminder of how close to home tragedy could strike. The neighbors who knew Martha's bouncy, casual, sharing nature lay awake Sunday night listening to the deafening roar as the search for the young woman came into their own backyards.

Sometime after the midnight shift had ended, Prosniewski packed it in. He prayed that the next day he might stumble on some better news to carry to Martha's husband. But in his soul he knew it was increasingly unlikely.

18

Monday, July 15, began early for Prosniewski. He came in shortly after 6 A.M. to look over his notes and gather his thoughts before the phones started jangling. The detectives on the day shift would be coming in at 8:00, and the regular business was enough to keep them scrambling. Thankfully, the commander of the division, Detective Sergeant Dick Urbanowicz, was at his absolute best when the pressure was on. During the course of this investigation, he would shine in his role as something between a head cook and an orchestra conductor. One of his most important jobs was to ensure that Prosniewski got the time and privacy he needed to conduct the investigation with few distractions. He was also skilled at triaging the barrage of issues that came in—designating the ones that couldn't wait, setting aside the ones that could. Most importantly, the chief of detectives managed to set a galvanizing tone throughout the department.

Nearly every member cooperated fully, giving Prosniewski unquestioned support wherever and whenever he needed it, sharing the footwork, never fighting for the spotlight. The division worked in extraordinarily rare harmony. Under normal circumstances, Dick Urbanowicz was known to cultivate an abrasive and sometimes terrifying facade. His reputation was described in all manner of terms during periods of relative quiet. But in the heat of the battle, Urbanowicz was a good cop and an effective leader.

Prosniewski met his future supervisor Dick Urbanowicz under less than friendly circumstances, back when Conrad was a college student hanging out at the Willows boardwalk with his friends. On warm summer nights, they brought beer down and sat on the benches shooting the breeze. On one such night Urbanowicz, a Salem police rookie at the time, approached the kids. Drinking was illegal in the park.

"Hey, you're making me look bad. Put the bottles away!" Urbanowicz warned them. Then he drifted off into the crowd.

Conrad and his friends used their imagination to switch the contents of the bottles to paper cups, obeying the letter of the request. To a twenty-year-old, this gesture seemed more than sufficiently cooperative.

Urbanowicz didn't see it that way. When he came back and found them still drinking, he flipped out. As he yelled at the group, he grabbed his radio and summoned every cruiser on the force for backup. One by one they rolled into the park, picked up the bad boys, and took the whole bunch down to the station. There the boys were "PC'd," thrown into a cell under protective custody for a few hours.

Conrad Prosniewski spent his first encounter with the Salem Police Department "sweating death" in a jail cell. All he could think of was what his parents would say when they found out. Their certain disappointment, especially knowing how they felt about police, killed him worse than the cell. He silently vowed never to stand on this side of the bars again.

One of the first calls on Monday came from Elaine Fernald down at the Willows. She told Prosniewski that her two sons and a friend had been fishing off the Willows pier Friday afternoon and that they may have noticed something of importance. Prosniewski talked to both of her sons. He learned to his chagrin that Greg Garvey, Martha's brother-in-law, had already spoken to the boys. The family's investigation was pretty efficient. It could also do a lot of damage.

The boys remembered seeing the same boat that Ruth Buck apparently had seen. Eleven-year-old Brandon remembered that the boat had tinted windows and thought that it had a clear patch on the sail. The woman he caught sight of wore sunglasses, a pink top, and baggy shorts. His older brother Brent suggested that the back of the boat was shaped like a half-moon and that the steering wheel was in the middle, not off to one side as many are. Later in the morning, Prosniewski also interviewed their thirteen-year-old friend, Timothy Vassil. Tim said that the woman had a French braid.

"How do you know what a French braid looks·like?" asked Prosniewski.

"My sister wears one," answered the boy. The woman had been sitting on the edge of the deck, he added, and he had watched the sailboat go out toward the islands.

Later on Monday morning, Patti Maimoni's friend Ginny McCarthy heard a knock at the back door of her house in Beverly. It was Tom, dressed up in a navy blue suit and pink shirt. He had come to ask what the McCarthys had heard in the way of local gossip. Ginny had grown up in Salem Willows. Tom knew she had close friends there.

As it turned out, Ginny's husband Gerry had picked up some news at the Willows the previous day from Buddy Hobbs, owner of the popcorn stand. Hobbs told him that a girl from the neighborhood was missing and that she had last been seen on Tom's boat. Ginny asked Tom whether any of it was true.

"You know better than that, Ginny," he responded. "I have a nice slip at PCYC. Why would I take my boat over to a public place like the Willows pier?"

"Well, it's what they're saying. They're trying to tie you to this somehow."

Tom proclaimed, "As God is my judge, I had nothing to do with her disappearance. You know I would never do anything like that. You know how happy I am with Patti. And how much I miss her."

Tom looked shaken. Ginny felt badly and offered him some more coffee.

"Where'd you say Gerry heard that?" Tom asked.

At 9:30 on Monday morning, Conrad Prosniewski picked up Ruth Buck at the Willows pier and took her to Palmer's Cove Yacht Club to try to identify the boat. The woman walked slowly by every slip, scrutinizing each boat. She eventually stopped at *Counterpoint*, as had Dan Mahoney. Ruth was more certain, however, after reconciling every discrepancy in her own mind. "It had the same rigging. The exhaust pipe's in the same place.

Boston is in the same place." Ruth said that she had the length wrong but that her mistake could have came from viewing the boat from behind on Friday. She also didn't remember blue sail covers the first time. Or the canvas dodger, which shaded the cockpit. No other boats in the marina came close, she told Prosniewski. "I'm almost certain that was the boat."

Palmer's Cove Yacht Club continued to be a major hub of activity all morning. Shortly after Prosniewski's departure, daytime bar manager Bette Putnam finished putting away her liquor delivery and went outside to the dumpster to get rid of the empty boxes. On her way out the front door, she kicked down the doorstop so that she wouldn't need her key to get back in. Only members and guests were allowed in the club. The members had keys. All visitors had to ring the buzzer and identify themselves through the bartender's speaker.

As she approached the parking lot, Bette noticed that Tom Maimoni's silver Taurus had pulled alongside the container. Maimoni was a member and a regular at the club. This summer he had been down nearly every day. Usually he'd blow through on his way to or from his boat. He rarely stopped to socialize. He never came to club meetings, never worked weekends when members pitched in to repair the floats. One of the "window walkers," the regulars called him. He walked by the window of the lounge without so much as a wave.

Maimoni often had his small corgi tucked under one arm or trotting behind on a leash. Bette had asked him countless times not to bring dogs to the club. Maimoni ignored her requests. Not that the dog was ill-behaved, though now and then other members had yelled at Maimoni to clean up after the animal when she pooped on the docks.

As Bette neared her destination, she saw Maimoni standing by his car. Suddenly a dark mass sailed from his hands and landed squarely inside the nearly full dumpster. It was unusual for members to discard trash there unless they were returning from their boats. Bringing garbage from home was frowned upon, unless you were one of the really old-timers. They pretty much did what they wanted with their garbage.

Maimoni then returned to his car to slam the trunk door shut. Bette had been hearing Maimoni's name all morning in connection with the missing woman from the Willows. His sudden appearance gave her the creeps. She tossed her cartons in quickly and went back inside, kicking up the doorstop on her way. The glass door swung shut behind her. Let him use his key, she thought.

A few moments later, Maimoni came into the club with a loop of wire in one hand. He took a seat at the bar. Bette Putnam set aside the delivery slips she had busied herself with and came over to him. Maimoni had set the wire on the counter and was fiddling with a clip on one end. He looked up. "Hi, Bunsie," he said. All her patrons called her Bunsie.

"What'll it be, Tom?"

His usual fare, when he bothered to stop by, was a hastily consumed Miller Draft and a Maple Leaf hot dog, the club's specialty, steamed in one part water, two parts beer. Tom Maimoni wasn't a drinker. He never had more than one, he never drank in the morning, and he rarely sat at the bar.

"You know, the 'real' beer," he said, indicating Miller Draft.

Bette suppressed her astonishment. It was only 10 A.M. She poured a glass, set it in front of him, and glanced at his face. Maimoni's countenance surprised her even more. It was as if he had put on a mask. Normally his expression was pleasant but self-absorbed. Today he wore the weight of the whole world on his face. The loop of wire clanked against the counter. Maimoni seemed to sense her stare.

"A lifeline," he explained. "You can't have enough safety equipment on a boat." He continued to fix whatever he was fixing. Lifelines normally stretch around the perimeter of a boat on short posts, affording those on deck something to grasp if they start to fall. Given the rumors this morning, the broken lifeline seemed ominous.

Bette went about her business. Maimoni sat for awhile nursing his beer and fiddling. One of the regulars sitting nearby, a former commodore, struck up a little conversation. "These damn lifelines, sometimes they just don't work," Maimoni explained to him.

Palmer's Cove Yacht Club was proudly described by its members as a "poor man's yacht club," a "working man's club." It was perched on the site of a former dump at the southern end of the sprawling Shetland Properties on the Salem Harbor waterfront, where the Pequot Cotton Mills had employed thousands of French Canadians at the turn of the century. The neighborhood that grew up across the street from the mills to house its workers became known as the Point District. Now predominantly Hispanic, the Point had been French until the late 1970s and early 1980s.

During the Great Depression a guy named Dumas operated a neighborhood club out of an old wooden shack, on the water near the dump. Since it was sited in the protective lee of Palmer's Cove, a handful of local Frenchmen got together in 1934 and bought out Dumas in order to form a yacht club, initially just a glorified hideaway for the boys. Palmer's Cove Yacht Club was born. The same year another venerable Salem industry, Parker Brothers, was developing the *Monopoly* board game.

Over time, PCYC saw improvements. The Army Corps of Engineers dredged the cove so that the boats tied up at the club's floating docks were in water all the time instead of resting on tidal flats twice a day. Boaters could then get out to the harbor channel at any hour. The green wooden shack built on stilts grew into a solid building with cinder blocks and aluminum siding on the exterior with lounge, bar, kitchen, offices, and function room inside. The marina expanded over time to include multiple finger-like floats with street names like "Main Street," "Party Lane," "Wall Street," "Lookout Lane," and "Expansion Lane." More and more of the dump was reclaimed so that an asphalt parking lot and a dry storage area could be added.

Over time the list of chartered members grew to 350. Since each member also became a shareholder and part owner of the club, the charter limited membership to this number. The fees were low, a hundred-something, plus sixteen hours of required work a year. The slip fees were a mere seven dollars a foot per season, a fraction of the fees charged elsewhere. It was no surprise that membership was coveted, today a four- or five-year wait. Boaters on the waiting list checked the obituaries in the *Salem Evening News* each day. Once a member, one had another five or ten-year wait for a slip. Those who waited had to content themselves with a mooring out in the channel and had to rely on the club's launch service for access to their boats.

Tom Maimoni endured the waiting list to become a member of PCYC back in 1981. He then waited another seven years to finally procure his slip on the farthest finger, "Expansion Lane," across from the general tie-up for visitors. Tom Maimoni had "arrived."

The former commodore of the club who sat at the bar Monday morning was a little amused to see Maimoni rubbing elbows after ten years at the club. Most of the chartered members at PCYC tended to be powerboat owners, in keeping with their working-class roots. "Work hard, play hard," they said with pride. And playing hard meant spending time at the bar, bonding with their fellow members while they gave as much business to the club as they could.

To powermen, sailors were a whole different breed. After a day's sail, they tended to stay out in their slips and open bottles of wine for their own private parties. They "put on airs." They passed by the big glass windows absorbed in that strange world sailors inhabit, oblivious to the patrons inside. They didn't mix with powermen, whose boats they considered stinkpots. A couple of years back, one of the powermen tried taping large paper hands all over the inside of the windows to see whether the sailors would notice. On each hand in big letters was scrawled, Hi! The window walkers never looked up.

Tom Maimoni was a sailor. He was also considered part of the "oddball" minority in the club that didn't mix well, that didn't particularly support the bar. One who marched to a different drummer. The regulars at the bar on Monday morning July 14 wondered why he had come in, this man whom people were somehow tying to the disappearance of the woman from the Willows.

At this point Bob Montague, a good friend of Maimoni's and a sailor himself, walked into the lounge. Although Montague lived in New Hampshire, he kept his boat at PCYC. Noticing Tom at the bar, he stopped for a quick chat. The two had planned to rendezvous for a sail on Friday, July 12, but Tom never showed up. Montague was used to being stood up by Tom, however, and he let it slide. Instead, he described some problems he was having with his onboard refrigeration unit.

"Why don't I take a look at it," offered Tom.

"Sure. I'm heading down now to work on it."

"I'll join you in about fifteen minutes," said Tom.

Montague nodded, gave a wave to Bunsie, and headed to the marina.

When Maimoni had finally drained his beer, he paid Bette and went down to the boats. The bar manager watched him go out the rear door leading to the marina. What was he doing in here? What was he looking for from us? Rumors? On every pole outside was posted a picture of the missing woman, her sweet face visible from where Bette stood. As Maimoni disappeared from view, she gave a shudder, reached for the telephone, and dialed the Salem police. The bar manager left a message with one of the detectives, who promised she'd be contacted later. Bette briefly dictated her concerns: "lifeline," morning beer, creepy facial expression.

And the dumpster. As soon as she hung up, Bette considered whether she should go out to find the bag she had seen Maimoni toss. Laidlaw, the dumpster company, came on Monday mornings to empty the container. Members tended to know every trivial detail of how the club worked, what went on, how their dimes were being spent. Like all other members, Tom Maimoni probably had known this morning was trash pickup day. This bag might be important.

She hesitated leaving her post at the bar. But as she stood there, the front door speaker crackled faintly as the familiar beeps and hydraulic noises of the Laidlaw dump truck put an end to her plans.

"Shit," she sighed.

Maimoni never showed up to check Montague's refrigeration unit. It was typical of Tom to make plans and not keep them. Just another day with Tom Maimoni, Montague thought to himself.

Conrad Prosniewski followed up with Ruth Buck's two passengers, questioning them in separate interviews Monday afternoon. Jennifer and Richard Lis each corroborated pieces of the emerging scenario. Mr. Lis worked for the city and was acquainted with Prosniewski, since Lis called the police station whenever his crew was scheduled to dig up a street. He remembered in particular that the helmsman of the boat in question had trouble docking, nearly hitting another boat. The white sailboat had finally backed up to the dock, and a blonde girl with a shoulder bag had hopped aboard. Lis was also taken to the yacht club on Monday. He, too, selected Maimoni's boat out of the numerous possibilities in the marina, way out on "Expansion Lane." He recalled a red stripe on the boat, the word Boston, the position of the steering wheel, and the black tinted windows.

Prosniewski had accumulated a sufficient number of witnesses whose memories held enough certainty to punch severe holes in Maimoni's claim that he had never sailed with Martha on Friday. Accompanied by Dick Urbanowicz and Detective Mary Butler, he went to visit the Brailsfords late Monday afternoon.

After updating the family, the police were provided with yet more names of witnesses who could place Maimoni at various spots around the area during the day. Bill Brailsford and his friends were sure Maimoni was involved. They were very anxious for the police to take action. The hope they still held was pinned on this one suspect. In the meantime, the group's own search efforts seemed to keep pessimism at bay.

Prosniewski was now ready to confront the man. Get him in, read him his rights, tell him he's lying. He placed a call to the Settlers Way address shortly before 6 P.M. and asked Maimoni to come in for questioning.

Tom Maimoni was also expected that evening at Pickering Wharf for dinner with Patti's friends, the McCarthys. Ginny McCarthy was making preparations Monday night in the galley of *Sarah B,* tied up in its slip. On the dock her husband Gerry was chatting with a friend, the principal of Ginny's school in Salem. Tom strolled up shortly after 6 P.M. Greetings were exchanged, then Tom explained he needed to drop by the police station before dinner. He was helping them out with something important. With that, he left.

Maimoni got to the station a little before seven on Monday evening. With Dick Urbanowicz as a witness, he was given his *Miranda* warning. Conrad Prosniewski read each line slowly, looking up at Maimoni after each statement. "You have the right to remain silent," said Prosniewski. Maimoni showed no surprise, and nodded silently. "Anything you say can and will be used against you in court...." When Prosniewski was done, he asked Maimoni to sign the back of the small blue card. Then he breathed a sigh of relief.

The detective explained that the police had talked to numerous witnesses who had observed Martha boarding his sailboat at the Willows pier on Friday afternoon. He looked carefully at Maimoni and said, "Look, you can tell me that Martha never got on your boat Friday and walk out that door. Or you can stay and tell me what happened."

Tom Maimoni was at a critical branch in his own garden of forking paths. He considered one route, then said softly, "Maybe

I should talk to my lawyer." The statement struck Prosniewski as rhetorical, and he waited in silence. After a few quiet seconds, Maimoni looked up.

"She was supposed to bring her husband."

The two detectives were motionless.

Maimoni continued. "Martha showed up without her husband. Around 1 P.M. There was no room at the dock there, at the Willows pier, so she just jumped on. I thought she was going to come with Bill."

And so began the second story.

19

"It was her idea to meet at the pier," Maimoni explained. "I didn't have time for a sail. The intent was not to go sailing but to review her artwork. She had some consignment work to do. We just motored over to Winter Island. I dropped her off at the float there and put on a wet suit to check the bottom of my boat. I went to a mooring I have at Derby Wharf, Paul's mooring—Paul from Palmer's Cove Yacht Club. Martha took everything with her when she left. She had brought a bag filled with résumés, I think."

"Why did you go to Winter Island?" asked the detectives.

"The Willows pier was full and tough to land at," replied Maimoni.

"What color shorts was she wearing?" asked Prosniewski.

"Pink. If the papers said pink, I'll go along with that. I think her shoes were white. Not sneakers or boat shoes."

"Did anybody see you when you let her off?"

"There were no boats at the dock. Some people were there at the pier. Maybe they saw her."

Prosniewski did not mention to Maimoni that witnesses had spotted him near Hospital Point, in the opposite direction of Winter Island. Instead, he asked Maimoni why he had withheld this vital information from the police.

"I didn't want my wife to know I was with her," said Maimoni.

"Why did Martha tell all her friends you were single?" asked Prosniewski.

"She knew I was married."

"And Bill? Did you tell Bill you were married?" the detective inquired.

"I never had a conversation with Bill about being married or single." Maimoni then said, "Let me tell you about my walks in the mornings with Martha." He went on to describe both routes. The young woman's path had taken her through the Willows, over the causeway to Winter Island, behind the old Coast Guard hangar, along the shoreline over isolated beaches and rocks. "She could have fallen. She could have run into some nut. I would never let my wife do that. It's treacherous there." Maimoni was careful to ascribe blame where he felt it was appropriate. Apparently, he surmised, if anything had happened to Martha, Bill was at fault for allowing his wife's reckless behavior.

Maimoni mentioned the nude sunbather on Winter Island again, a man in his fifties, potbellied, with a mustache and receding hair. The man's name was Bob, he told the police. Perhaps he would be a useful witness, or even more usefully, a suspect.

Maimoni went on to say that he had cleaned his boat from about two-thirty in the afternoon until about seven on Friday night. Getting the "salad" off the bottom, as he described the slimy growth. The water was clearer out on the mooring than in the slip. Afterward, he had gone home, had walked his dog Salli, and had stayed home the rest of the evening. His only companion and witness was the corgi. Alone all afternoon. Alone all night. Four and a half hours cleaning his boat.

On Saturday, Maimoni explained, he had gotten an early morning call from some friends who wanted to arrange a meeting later in the afternoon. He then took the dog for a walk and was informed by neighbors along the way about Martha's disappearance. He cut the walk short. When Bill came by about 8 A.M. and asked whether Maimoni had made arrangements to go sailing, he answered no. Strictly speaking, he explained to Prosniewski, it was Martha who had made the arrangements. But mostly Tom had decided not to get involved. He now apologized for lying to the police and said he would do anything to help. The interview concluded. Thomas Maimoni had invited the CID to explore a new path.

20

Fate dealt Tom Maimoni an unkind blow after he departed the police station on Monday night, July 15. Conrad Prosniewski bumped into Bob Callahan in the hallway. Lieutenant Callahan was four things: the four to midnight shift lieutenant that evening, the commander of the police dive team, the close friend of Prosniewski, and the consummate visitor to Winter Island.

The two chatted about getting the dive team ready to do a search. They talked about the mooring where Tom claimed he had washed his boat, how to locate it, and what he may have thrown overboard. Callahan had to make sure the diving equipment was ready and to arrange shift coverage for the members of the team.

Now Callahan spent a great deal of his time off either docked at Winter Island or reading a newspaper and sipping coffee on shore. It just so happened to be his thing. Prosniewski mentioned that Maimoni had just told the police he had dropped Martha off at the pier there Friday afternoon.

"That's bullshit," was Callahan's analysis. "I was there Friday afternoon. I woulda seen them."

"Bobby, what time were you there?" asked Prosniewski.

"All afternoon. I was trying to unload at the pier, but it was too crowded. There were two boats docked there for hours. Since there's a twenty-minute tie-up period over there, I finally got so pissed I called Andy Syska."

This was beautiful. A witness to refute Tom's story happened to be a police officer. And if Harbormaster Syska had cited the boats, there would be records with dates, times, and names of more witnesses.

Actually, being a police officer didn't always help in court. Prosniewski recalled one time he had appeared to testify on behalf of a fellow member of the department. The patrolman's lawyer rose and informed the judge that Officer Prosniewski was there to corroborate the defendant's story. The judge responded, "I'm quite sure *Officer* Prosniewski will say whatever your client wants him to say." Prosniewski wasn't sure he had heard the judge correctly, so he leaned over and quietly asked the attorney, "What did he say?"

The fuming lawyer leaned back and said in a loud whisper for the benefit of the entire courtroom, "He called you a fucking liar."

"That's what I thought he said."

From the station, Tom returned to Pickering Wharf on Monday night and rejoined the McCarthys. Their friend the principal was getting ready to leave. But he loitered long enough to hear Tom retell his sad story. Tom claimed he had been unfairly accused of involvement in this disappearance, just because he knew Martha and had seen her that morning.

When the school principal departed, steaks were thrown on the grill. Tom went below to talk to Ginny. "Have Gerry come in here," he said to her. "There's something I want to say."

Ginny called her husband in. The three sat down. Tom was calm. "What I told you before is not quite true," Tom began. "Actually, Martha was on my boat. She came to work on some résumés. We were out maybe ten or fifteen minutes. It didn't look good. I mean, I'm a married man. I was uncomfortable with the situation, so I sailed over to the Coast Guard station at Winter Island and let her off. Then I went back to PCYC."

Ginny and Gerry were speechless. They stared at the man they had considered a close friend, one of the nicest guys they knew. A man who had waited to confide in them only after he had unburdened himself to the police? What were friends for?

Tom was on a roll. He explained how he met Martha, about the dogs and walks, about her route, about the nude sunbather who may have had something to do with this. The guy had a fat belly, Tom added. "Not like mine," he said with pride, and to restore his credibility he stood and flexed his stomach muscles for them.

The steaks were served, but Ginny was still too shocked to eat. Tom consumed his with voracity and animation. As supper wore on, the McCarthys' comfort and trust sank with the setting sun. Tom looked out at the harbor, noticing lights and activity in the distance. From where he sat he could see the mouth of the PCYC marina, now host to a team of divers, a scanning searchlight, and the harbormaster's boat.

"Look out there," he said to them with a hint of bemusement. "All those lights. That's the police. They're checking out my mooring, my boat. They think they're going to find something. They think her body is tied up down there." He chewed his last piece of meat. "But they're not going to find anything."

He turned and gazed at Ginny's steak, now congealing on her dinner plate, cold as her heart. She still looked as if she had swallowed a sneaker. "Anyone eating that," he asked, gesturing with his fork.

She pushed it toward him.

After rehashing the investigation with Dick Urbanowicz late Monday night, Conrad Prosniewski went home to bed. Julie was asleep. He pulled the blanket up to his chin and appealed to his God, as he had done the previous two nights. "Please let me find her. Please let me find her."

He rolled over. Then feeling greedy, he added a postscript: "And then maybe just one small shred of evidence so I can nail the bastard."

He would recite this prayer for two more nights.

21

Early on Tuesday morning, July 16, Conrad Prosniewski
called Andy Syska, the Salem harbormaster. Syska remembered the day of July 12 well.

After Lieutenant Callahan's complaint, the harbormaster said
he had shown up at 1:15 that afternoon and had made a note of
the boats tied up at the pier. About an hour later, he had returned
from circling the harbor to find the two still there. One of them
was a boat he recognized. Syska recalled having issued a citation
to the same boat on July 4 for speeding in the harbor and
creating a wake. He now located a copy of the citation and gave
Prosniewski the name and address of the violator, a Dr. Ronald
Plotka of Marblehead.

Detective Mary Butler, like the other members of the Criminal
Investigation Division, had a penchant for names. Hearing about
Plotka, she recalled that among the items in Martha's purse there
had been an appointment card with, she thought, the names of
Doctors Plotka and Smith. They located the card. As fate would
have it, it was the same name.

The police contacted Dr. Plotka. Sergeant Urbanowicz asked
him about the pier. Plotka recalled having arrived before noon
and then having tied up at the public dock for well over two
hours while he cleaned the vessel and lunched on fried clams.
With him had been two women from his office.

Urbanowicz described Martha Brailsford and asked Plotka if

there was any way a woman matching her description could have disembarked while he had been tied up at the pier.

Plotka said no way. "I oughta know. I'm her dentist."

Martha, a patient of many years' standing, was characterized by her dentist as friendly, outgoing, a great flosser, and possessing perfect teeth. Dr. Plotka would have one more appointment with Martha. Sadly, the teeth would no longer be perfect.

Conrad Prosniewski reflected briefly on what he was sure would turn out to be his first lead role in a homicide investigation. He was certain this was a murder but was flabbergasted at how the case was progressing. "Is this how it's supposed to be?" he kept asking himself.

One got the impression that for a city of nearly 40,000 inhabitants, Salem behaved like an incredibly small town, as if it were a down-and-out repertory theater group with members of the cast doubling up roles. The dentist was the violator, the complainant was the police diver. FBI agents passed as local yacht club members. The entire ensemble wandered back and forth around the Willows. And of the 40,000 people who lived in Salem, it seemed as though Conrad Prosniewski knew 39,000 of them.

22

The local news media had camped out in front of police headquarters for a couple of days now. Satellite trucks from the major Boston TV stations were starting to clog the adjoining street and municipal parking lot. The customers at Red's Sandwich Shop next door to the station were greeted by TV crews popping in to capture the "man on the street" reactions to each new turn of events. The story was now being picked up in the Boston papers as well. The detectives had gotten used to being followed whenever they left the building and were starting to invite reporters along when they stepped out for coffee.

Early Tuesday morning, the fourth day of the investigation, Detective Sergeant Urbanowicz ventured out to throw them a crumb. The police had identified a sailboat that apparently had picked up Martha Brailsford Friday afternoon. The name of the boat and owner were not going to be disclosed at this time.

Shortly afterward, Detectives Jim Page, Dick Urbanowicz, and Conrad Prosniewski set out on the route Martha followed each day. It was close to 7 A.M. They hoped to run into the people Martha was likely to encounter at that hour. They were also on the lookout for any evidence along her path.

Albin Zegorowski, a retiree living on nearby Columbus Square, was the first to approach the detectives on their walk. The gentleman told them he indeed had seen Martha and her dog Rudy near the old barracks on the island. With her had been a tall man wearing a baseball cap and walking a small dog. He sensed, as people often do, that the cap was meant to cover baldness.

They continued along the shoreline. They came across William Nunn, who lived at the Plummer Home for Boys next to the Winter Island park. When the group explained they were searching for Martha Brailsford, Nunn suddenly realized who they were talking about. Shock filled his eyes. "Oh, my God! Martha. Martha's the missing girl! I didn't know her last name, and the poster doesn't look like her." He, too, had seen her with the tall man wearing the hat. Prosniewski made notes in his leather portfolio stuffed with business and *Miranda* cards.

Near the rocks between Waikiki Beach and the boatyard to the north, Detective Jim Page spotted—or rather, uncovered—Bob, the nude sunbather. Bob turned out to be a professional clown from Beverly, available for children's parties. He was not particularly dangerous looking. Literally from nowhere he produced a business card. It depicted his professional visage, not his off-duty one.

Bob knew Martha by sight. She frequently had stopped to talk to him, most recently about losing her job with the design company. He had also met Bill. He remembered the tall man accompanying her late last week, on Thursday or Friday. It had not been Bill.

Like the Little Prince, who journeyed from planet to planet meeting all manner of curious adults, the group of Salem detectives continued on, this time they met "Rocky" in a parking lot. "Rocky" was John "Rocky" Lord, a Marblehead fireman in his thirties, a good friend of Brailsford's. Prosniewski recognized Rocky. It just so happened the two had grown up together in Salem. Rocky told the detective that early Saturday morning he had driven over to Palmer's Cove Yacht Club to talk to Maimoni after Brailsford had exhausted other leads. He had located the slip number for *Counterpoint* on a bulletin board at the club. When he found the boat, he had noticed diving gear and a wet suit set out to dry in the cockpit.

Maimoni was on the dock. Rocky confronted him and asked about Martha. Maimoni said, "Martha who?" as he had to the others. Rocky knew Brailsford had gone to Maimoni's condo earlier that morning. So like Brailsford's other friends, Rocky didn't buy Maimoni's professed ignorance. Martha from the Willows, Rocky explained.

"Oh, Rudy's Martha. No, I didn't see her. And I didn't go

sailing." As if to explain the wet suit, Maimoni added, "I was cleaning the bottom of my boat." Rocky told the detectives that Maimoni had looked shaken and that he never once had questioned who Rocky was.

The police team split up. Jim Page joined Mary Butler on Columbus Avenue to get statements from others who often had seen Martha on her daily rounds or who had seen her with Maimoni. The statements were all the same.

On Tuesday, Tom Maimoni drove up to Ginny and Gerry McCarthy's place in Beverly three or four times "to check the local gossip." He repeated the story he had told them on the boat. On one of his visits, he told them that he wanted to call his mother. The McCarthys let him use their phone.

When he hung up, Tom had tears in his eyes. He went over to Ginny and said, without explanation, "I am *so* sorry!" Tom put his head on her shoulder and said he was sorry, again. Then he went back to the table and sat down. Resting on his elbows, he announced: "If this ever ends, I am going to have a bronze plaque set up on the Willows pier in memory of Martha Brailsford."

Back from their walk on Tuesday morning, Prosniewski checked in with the coordinator of the Tenth Special Force's dive team from Fort Devens. The Salem police divers trained with them a few times a year and welcomed their expertise.

The rest of the day passed much as Monday had with the kind of painstaking police work that rarely led to success, to appreciation, or to glory in the media. Yet what little success was ultimately attained could not have been reached by any other means.

Calls came into the police department from people who thought they had seen Martha or white sailboats up and down the coast. White sailboats, unfortunately, were not uncommon. Prosniewski stuck pushpins into a large-scale nautical chart mounted on his wall, one pushpin for each sighting. And each got checked out. A caller claimed to have seen the young woman boarding a bus at Logan Airport in Boston. Someone else had seen her sailing in the Cape Cod Canal.

Then there were the psychics. As in any disappearance case, psychics called Prosniewski with inspired and graphic imagery. Martha, they said, had been beaten by a gang. She was stuffed in a blue sleeping bag, face down in shallow water, surrounded by red flowers on a sheet. There were bees. There was gray spaghetti. There was a stick in the water nearby. She was behind the bathhouse at Winter Island. "I see Martha in a dream." "Thistle comes to mind." Prosniewski thanked each of them for their help.

For a pet lover, there was no greater joy than taking a housebound dog to a place like Winter Island, ten acres of pure dog heaven: hills, paths, mud, sticks, trash, critters, and smells. Whatever concern one brought over the causeway was momentarily driven away by watching one's dog charge around unencumbered. There might or might not be hope in this world, but there surely was pleasure.

Walking his dog was a rich part of Mark Steele's life. He had been to Winter Island during the past week with his four-year-old dog Katy. Mark was an on-line editor for WGBH-TV who lived in Salem with his wife. On that walk, his path had crossed that of a woman who also carried an unattached leash. She, too, had a dog somewhere, in one of the bushes overlooking Cat Cove and the power plant on the opposite shore.

Dog walkers are frequently like ships passing in the night. They had stopped for a few minutes of conversation in the sun. They had talked about their pets and in conspiratorial tones about the schedule kept by the city's dog officer. The young woman knew the officer's pattern, and precisely when it was safe to run free with a dog off its leash. They had talked about Salem, and other dog walking topics. But it didn't take many minutes or weighty topics to uncover a kindred spirit. The woman had seemed happy, decent, and very centered. She had a free quality that Mark had often found in "old hippies" he knew. Her congeniality was contagious, and Mark had felt sufficiently buoyed by the chance encounter to mention this to his wife when he returned home.

Tuesday's *Salem Evening News* ran a picture of the woman reported missing in the previous edition. Mark hadn't known her name, of course, but he knew her picture when it hit him in the face. Such a brief encounter, such a happy impression, and now such sudden sadness.

Dot Chainey's son Ian cried out, "Hey, that's Martha!" *Our* Martha. The same woman who had designed the Chaineys' kitchen the previous year. Martha had helped them from start to finish, through good and bad, as the Chaineys endured that special hell people go through when remodeling their kitchens. The same woman whose picture was now on the evening news. Like Martha, Dot had studied art and had shared with her a mistrust of microwave ovens. Martha had planned a special bread-making counter for Dot's kitchen. Ever mindful of the needs of animals, Martha had also designed a custom-made food tray for the Chaineys' cats. She had been mindful of five-year-old Ian's needs as well, handing him crayons and scrap paper when he visited Kitchen Place in neighboring Middleton with his mother to discuss the remodeling project.

On Tuesday evening around six, Tom Maimoni called Prosniewski at the police station to ask if there was any news about the missing woman and to again offer any help he possibly might lend in the investigation. He told the detective he was in Rhode Island at the home of his wife's father and stepmother, Mr. and Mrs. Charles Stochl. He felt the need to be with relatives at this time and thought he might spend the night.

Prosniewski asked him for more details about the mooring to which he claimed to have tied up on Friday afternoon. The harbormaster had not come up with anything based on Maimoni's description. Maimoni gave vague directions to the location of the mooring and said he thought the owner was Polish, the name sounding like "Louassa." Prosniewski thanked him and hung up.

Assistant District Attorney Kevin Mitchell had gone into his boss's office an hour earlier to request a vacation day. There, he and his colleagues chatted about the missing person case with Trooper Mark Lynch, a state police detective with the local Crime Prevention and Control (CPAC) unit assigned to Essex County. Most police departments outside the city of Boston got some degree of assistance from the state police in homicide investigations or whenever their resources were needed. In small towns, the state took over the case. Salem was large enough to have its own detectives, so responsibility was often more or less shared.

Mark Lynch was concerned that he had not yet been called in on Prosniewski's investigation, even though they had no evidence of a crime at this point. He remarked to the group that he and Corporal Jack Garvin were about to go over to the police station to get filled in. There was some discussion about whether the troopers needed company.

"Urbanowicz over there?" someone asked.

Lynch answered in the affirmative.

"Forget it," they chorused.

Mitchell, whose wife and kids were away at the Cape, had nothing better to do that evening. He also considered himself pretty tough skinned. What the hell. No pain, no gain. So he volunteered to tag along.

Conrad Prosniewski had just brought them up to date when the call from Maimoni came in. Assistant District Attorney Kevin Mitchell was amused. "That was him? That was the guy?"

Prosniewski explained. "He calls a lot. We can't get rid of him."

"Shoot, let's talk to him. Where is he now?" asked Mitchell.

"Rhode Island."

They agreed it was indeed time to get Tom Maimoni in again. No one had seen Martha being dropped off Friday. With the number of people in the neighborhood who saw her go by each day, it was inconceivable that she could walk anywhere on Winter Island or in the Willows and not be noticed. No one, *no one*, had seen or had heard from Martha the rest of that day.

Bertini's was an Italian restaurant near the bottom of Canal Street in Salem, a favorite haunt of the CID for grabbing a pizza and beer after a late-night drug raid. On Tuesday evening, Chief St. Pierre and Dick Urbanowicz slipped into one of the back function rooms for some dinner and a strategy meeting on the Maimoni case. So far, no one could fault the quality of the investigation. But concerned citizens, friends of the family, elected officials, even the mayor were calling out of concern for the missing woman. Everyone wanted to know whether the police were doing everything they could. Part of the chief's job was to be the point man when problems with the media arose or when the pressure got heavy. Urbanowicz was the acting chief of detectives. St. Pierre wanted to be sure that as the case developed, it would continue to be managed as well as possible and that the police—not the media or political concerns—controlled its direction.

Chief St. Pierre had every right to be cautious. Boston police had recently stumbled badly in a high-profile case involving the murder of a pregnant woman named Carol Stuart in the Roxbury section of Boston. Her husband Charles, who was wounded in the shooting, had been driving his wife home from childbirth class in October 1989, when he claimed they were robbed and attacked by a black man who shot and killed Carol. Charles called for help from his car phone, then later picked out William Bennett—a convicted felon—from a police lineup. Tips from area residents had implicated Bennett, however, the residents later claimed police had coerced them into falsifying their testimony.

The following January, Stuart's brother Matthew fingered Charles in the murder of his own wife. Apparently, he had planned Carol's death and had managed to wound himself to make it look credible. Stuart then allegedly tossed the gun and Carol's purse into his brother's waiting car before summoning the police. The day after Matthew Stuart came forward, Charles leapt off Boston's Tobin Bridge to his death. William Bennett was dropped as a suspect.

For three months, the black community of Boston had endured intense police harassment that had ultimately led to the wrongful arrest of one of their members. Media and political pressure had driven the investigation, and, many claimed, had corrupted it. Ultimately, a federal grand jury investigation found serious misconduct but no criminal violations. The police department was subsequently pressured into ordering an internal affairs investigation. The *Boston Globe* later filed suit to gain access to police notes and files. There were outcries that the police not only had botched the case but they had also managed to cover up the extent of their wrongdoing. William Bennett, meanwhile, filed a civil suit against four Boston police officers for violating his civil rights. Years later, the Boston Police Department was still reeling from the fallout of this case. Even after the national attention and inflamed racial tensions in the city had died down, the deep wound remained.

"Let's not let this be another Stuart case," the chief said to Urbanowicz at Bertini's. No one else was going to drive this case.

No one was going to push the police into violating rights or scaring away their only suspect. Conrad had a great rapport with this guy. Tom Maimoni was still talking to them. He was talking a lot. The chief wanted to keep it that way.

23

At 7:00 on Tuesday night, Conrad Prosniewski called Maimoni at the Rhode Island number. He gave him two choices: you come up here, or we go down there. Maimoni asked if he could bring his father-in-law along. "Sure," said Prosniewski. "Bring the Pope if you want," he almost added.

While the group waited, some friendly discussion ensued over why the state had not been called in earlier. They might not officially have a homicide yet, but a woman in a high-profile case had been missing four days. Chances were she was not alive. The last person to have seen her seemed incapable of telling the truth. Protocol should have won out over semantics.

Tom Maimoni and Charles Stochl arrived at the office around 9:00. Without a greeting, Maimoni bounded up to Prosniewski and announced exultantly that a Mr. and Mrs. Tony Bova had seen him at the mooring on Friday. They would back him up, he said.

Maimoni was asked to take a seat. The police inquired whether they could search *Counterpoint*. Maimoni said "absolutely" and signed a consent form. He gave them the combination for the cabin lock: 1-9-5-6.

Then Prosniewski read the *Miranda* rights to Maimoni a second time and asked him to tell Trooper Lynch about Winter Island. Jack Garvin, Dick Urbanowicz, and Kevin Mitchell busied themselves by piecing together the lengthy affidavit for a search warrant. They lined up the state chemist, photographer, and the rest of the forensic team. Other detectives were called in. The clerk of courts, who had to sign the warrant, was located.

With Patti's father seated next to him, Tom Maimoni related to Mark Lynch the Winter Island tale—all the way to Tony and Connie Bova, owners of *Nefertite*, who would back him up.

At this point, Prosniewski suggested that Stochl step out of the room for a moment. Maimoni assured them that Charlie and he had a close relationship and that he had nothing to hide from his father-in-law.

Prosniewski replied that the information was pretty sensitive. There were inconsistencies in the interviews, and Maimoni might not want his father-in-law to hear what was about to be discussed. Maimoni glanced at Stochl, who stepped out into the hall.

When they were alone, Mark Lynch minced no words. Maimoni's story was baloney. The police had witnesses to prove it.

Maimoni looked at him, then turned to Prosniewski. "You don't believe me either, Connie?" he asked.

"No, Tom," answered the detective.

Maimoni lowered his head. There was a very heavy pause. Then he looked back up. "There was an accident," he said. Martha Brailsford was dead.

At approximately 10 P.M. on Tuesday, Thomas Maimoni gave the police his third story. His signed statement read as follows:

> There was an accident. The wind had freshened up. We were sailing around, Martha and I. We were really supposed to look at her art work. My wife was out of town, Parker Brothers closing—I lost two job opportunities. I felt like I needed a day out on the ocean, I needed to get away. We sailed out. Sailed all over the place—out as far as Gloucester. Heading to Stellwagen Bank. We didn't make it out that far. The sun was going down. She wasn't wearing the right shoes—any shoes. I de-powered—got the mainsail down—she insisted on helping and ran over—she wasn't a good sailor.
>
> There were good size boats off in the distance. I jibed around to make a 180 degree turn. The head sail got hung up on the stay—no big deal—she tried to help. A rogue wave hit—maybe two. Her face hit the mast twice. The boat pitched. She grabbed for the head sail and went over. The winds were 10-15 knots out of the southwest. She went right in and down. I was trying to control the

boat and look for her. She disappeared behind the dodger. I saw the depth at 102' (feet)—This happened half an hour after sunset. She was wearing one of her designer tops and shorts. I could probably put you right over the spot. My hands were on the radio. I wanted to call the Coast Guard, but I froze. There was no alcohol involved. Neither of us had a drink. I may have had a beer. Her bag fell over at the same time—shoes were in her bag—the bag was heavy. I assumed it went to the bottom. However, the bag may have gone in...I don't remember what caused the bag to be lost.

Signed: THOMAS J. MAIMONI, July 16, 1991
Witnessed by: CONRAD J. PROSNIEWSKI and MARK LYNCH.

At Prosniewski's suggestion, Maimoni stepped into the hall and told his father-in-law to go to the condo. The detective arranged for a cruiser to take him to Settlers Way. Maimoni explained to Stochl that there had been a tragic accident and that he would be staying a while longer to heroically help the police in their search efforts. When Stochl was gone, the police sent someone to procure navigational charts from the harbormaster's office.

While they waited for the charts, Maimoni chitchatted with relief. His corgi Salli was about to have her first birthday party. Maimoni had intended to invite Martha, Bill, and Rudy. He also talked about his experiences in Vietnam as a C-130 pilot. Lynch asked him whether it was true such aircraft were called "trash haulers." Maimoni didn't know.

A search of *Counterpoint* was underway. The boat was moved to the Hawthorne Boatyard on White Street on Tuesday night, where the public could more easily be kept at bay. Robert Pino, the state police chemist, shined a Polylite over the various surfaces of the boat. Its special filters would illuminate traces of human bodily fluids, even those invisible to the naked eye. Pino played the light on every surface and angle, using the wavelength and filters appropriate for blood. Deck, sides, top, lines, the galley sink, head, seats, floors, mast, channel on mast, boom, sail. Visible blood was found on the mainsail, in six distinct groups of drops. No other blood was found.

Pino removed the sail and took it into custody. Within two

days, he would determine the blood to be human. He also took a Dirt Devil vacuum cleaner from the cabin to test whether someone had cleaned up—and, if so, what? The team noted a collection of teddy bears and other stuffed animals down below. Patti's, or Tom's?

Meanwhile, on the floor of the detective's office, Maimoni had the Cape Ann navigational chart spread out. He had requested rulers, pencils, and a compass. He was on his hands and knees doing elaborate calculations and talking about current deviations, wind corrections, deltas, and vectors. He drew circles, lines, and a triangle on the chart, which Prosniewski asked him to initial and date. The depth at that spot was 102 feet. Not feasible for diving. Bottom time for divers was too short at that depth, and the risk of going through gradual decompression or getting injured was too great. The body certainly would have drifted by now and should soon surface on its own. Nevertheless, they agreed to go out with Maimoni to the spot sometime on Wednesday.

Lynch and Prosniewski drove Maimoni home sometime after 1 A.M. On the way, Maimoni remarked how glad he was to finally get this tragic accident off his shoulders. His relief seemed genuine. His remorse was somehow absent.

After the detectives dropped Maimoni off at Settlers Way, they joined the rest of the team at the boatyard. Assistant District Attorney Kevin Mitchell had come down to watch. Some small part of him had always wanted to be an investigator. The night was too beautiful to waste on sleep—still nearly eighty degrees after a blistering day. The sky was full of stars, brilliant and taunting. They combed the boat until four in the morning.

Conrad Prosniewski climbed aboard. Remembering the call from the PCYC bartender, he wanted to check the lifeline on deck. He found the usual bending and wearing but nothing that told him anything.

The state police photographer snapped his roll of film, exterior and interior shots, including the chart book lying open in the cabin. Bob Pino packed up his Polylite and glanced up at the stars, then out at the glassy, black harbor. They all shared the same fantasy: Why don't we just take the boat out? But the crime scene stayed at the dock.

24

Early Wednesday morning, July 17, Ginny and Gerry McCarthy were awakened by the urgent sound of their doorbell. Maimoni was standing at their front door with his father-in-law Charles Stochl. The sun was barely up. The McCarthys let the pair inside, and Tom poured out the story of the tragic accident. Gerry urged Tom to seek legal guidance. Tom borrowed their telephone. He woke Patti in Wichita and begged her to come home on the next flight to Boston. Then he called a lawyer.

When Tom hung up, he asked Ginny and Gerry if they would meet him at the airport just before Patti arrived, so that they could stand next to him in apparent solidarity when she got off the plane. After that, they could essentially get lost. "I want you and Gerry to come as support for only two minutes because I want you to be there for Patti to see you as support. Then I will whisk her out to the car." Tom's plan was to then go with Patti immediately to Cumberland, Rhode Island, to see Patti's father. The McCarthys agreed.

Tom's face clouded for a moment. "Patti should never have gone. She knew better than to leave me alone." Ginny was shocked and angered at these words. How dare he blame this all on Patti.

Later that morning, Maimoni called the Criminal Investigation Division and said that he wanted his attorney to accompany him on the boat ride with the police. However, the attorney was unable to make it that day, Maimoni said. The trip was rescheduled for Thursday afternoon at 4:30.

The next recipient of Maimoni's early morning networking was Jim Brown, who lived next door on Settlers Way. Brown was a freelance photographer. In fact, a few years earlier he had photographed a Cal 28 for an article about its designer, C. Raymond Hunt Associates, which appeared in a 1987 issue of *Nautical Quarterly*. Jim Brown was also a sailor. His own boat, a thirty-foot O'Day 302, was another C. Raymond Hunt creation built in the same plant as the Cal 28.

"Jim, this is Tom, your neighbor. I just want you to be aware that the place is going to be crawling with the media."

Brown had just returned from out of town and had no Salem news. "Oh, why?" he asked.

"Didn't you hear? I had a little accident on my boat over the weekend, and I would like you to be a character reference." Maimoni proceeded to tell his story of the accident aboard *Counterpoint*, referring to Martha only as "the girl."

"The girl" had suggested they go for a sail, Maimoni explained. This was to be his nautical version of the event. He described their sail past Gloucester toward Stellwagen Bank, a favorite spot for whale watching. As darkness descended the wind was blowing about fifteen knots and the water was choppy. Maimoni had decided to return and jibed the boat around. The girl had known nothing about sailing.

Brown thought that since Maimoni had been sailing alone, jibing— turning the boat away from the wind—was a rather stupid thing to do. Coming about—turning into the wind—would have been less dangerous under those circumstances, Brown felt.

Maimoni continued. At that point the Genoa jib, the smaller sail in front, hung up on the weather shroud, one of the wires that held up the mast, on the windward side of the boat. The girl had gone forward to free the sail, despite Maimoni's urgent warnings not to. Then a rogue wave—a wave out of nowhere, not part of a normal set or pattern—hit the boat. Simultaneously, the sail let loose, caught the girl, and threw her from the high side (the weather side) to the low side (the leeward side). In the process, the woman had hit her head and was tossed overboard through the shrouds. Maimoni told Brown he had lost her in the waves and had stayed out most of the night searching for her.

After he had returned to shore, Maimoni explained, he denied the event to himself for a number of days. At last, he had come to grips with it and had gone to the police. Now he wanted the truth to come out, he said to his neighbor.

Jim Brown later granted an interview to a reporter from the *Boston Globe*, but insisted they first sit down and review the facts carefully. Brown felt sorry for Maimoni and wanted to be sure his story was accurately rendered. He felt he was doing his neighbor a favor at the time.

Early Thursday morning, July 18, the article appeared in the *Boston Globe*. Tom Maimoni immediately got on the phone.

"Jim, this is Tom. I understand you have been talking to the media in explicit nautical terms."

"Yes, Tom. You said you wanted the truth to come out."

"That was not what I wanted you to do," replied Maimoni.

Brown then said he thought he had been complying with Tom's wishes. As far as Brown was concerned, he wanted nothing more to do with this case.

One of Prosniewski's first tasks early Wednesday morning was to let Bill Brailsford know about Maimoni's statement. The detective took him the news and watched again Brailsford's darkened face and his swallowed despair. Around him, his friends and family refused to give up. Until Martha was found, no one wanted to let go of hope. Tom Maimoni had lied to police so many times before. What if this, too, were a lie? God knows what his motivation might be, but how could they believe anything Maimoni said at this point? Maybe Martha was being held somewhere, and ultimately a ransom request would be made. Maybe something had happened on the boat, and Martha had swam to safety. With no body, they could only substitute theories to keep from giving up. Prosniewski knew that soon he would have to start helping them prepare for the worst. Martha might never be found.

The detective, accustomed to backtracking on dead-end paths, was now focusing on proving or disproving Maimoni's latest tale. There was always the slim possibility he was telling the truth this time. They had to go on that assumption and make contingency plans for air, sea, or underwater searches as warranted. Salem Harbormaster Andy Syska, with help from the Coast Guard, spent five hours Wednesday searching the waters Maimoni had outlined on the chart. They turned up nothing, to no one's surprise, after days of tidal changes and currents.

The local media had managed to discover the name of the sailboat and its owner the preceding day. The morning papers splashed Maimoni and *Counterpoint* across their front pages. Even the Boston papers, the *Globe* and the *Herald*, were starting to give this case front-page treatment. Boston readers had short memories and waning interest in the occasional drive-by shootings and the all-too-frequent domestic homicides that normally filled the papers. But people lost at sea command attention in New England, a region whose lifeblood is the ocean. A missing woman from a world rarely touched by violence, loved by an involved family unafraid to ask for the public's help, the mysterious appeal of Salem and its sailboats in the summer—all these ingredients fueled the media's attention. The calls began to stream into Salem police headquarters.

Roxcy Platte had not paid much attention to the news stories about a missing woman last seen on Friday, July 12, with a man aboard a twenty-eight-foot Cal sailboat. Tom Maimoni had called her early that morning to say he had to go away on business. She hadn't heard from him since. Nevertheless, Roxcy's eldest son became afraid for her and hassled her to check with the police. Roxcy dismissed the suggestion as a joke. How could it possibly be the same guy? The waters were filled with white Cals this time of year. And Tom's was thirty feet, longer than the boats listed in the news article. Finally, on Wednesday, she was convinced it might be time to call. When the Salem police answered, Roxcy asked about the name of the boat. "Don't you read the papers?" the officer at the front desk snapped. "It's in this morning's *Salem Evening News*."

"I don't live in Salem. I don't read the *Salem Evening News*. Please tell me the name of the boat," Roxcy insisted.

"*Counterpoint*," came the response. Tom had added two feet to his boat.

Roxcy Platte pushed away the phone, turned, and lowered her head between her knees. Nausea swept over her. She took a deep breath and spoke again into the receiver. "I need to talk to someone about this." Somebody *else* had been the Friday girl.

While Conrad Prosniewski was on the phone with Roxcy setting up an appointment, the other incoming line rang. Dick Urbanowicz picked it up. A very distraught Rosemary Farmer of Beverly, Massachusetts, believed she, too, had been aboard the Cal 28. Urbanowicz arranged an appointment with her for later that morning.

Another caller—a woman who, with a friend, had met Maimoni ten days earlier—was asked to write a statement and send it in. Maimoni seemed to have made the acquaintance of half the female population of the North Shore.

A bartender at PCYC, Gail Rader from Marblehead, phoned and told Prosniewski that she had worked the bar Friday night from five to one. Sometime around midnight, she had spotted Tom Maimoni leaving the back gate and heading toward the parking lot. Gail had been serving Maimoni for the past two years and knew him well. No barfly, Tom came in for an occasional beer, wearing his Greek sailor's hat. In that time, she rarely if ever had seen him on his boat at night. This occurrence had struck her as strange. Even stranger, Maimoni had been carrying a dark canvas bag, which he took to the dumpster and tossed in. This was the second confirmed sighting of Maimoni getting rid of mysterious parcels at PCYC.

Prosniewski had already checked out the dumpster after bar manager Bette Putnam's call. Unfortunately, it had been emptied Monday. But Maimoni's garbage was taking on new significance after last night's disclosure. Prosniewski placed a call to the dumpster company, Laidlaw, and tried to put a trace on that particular load. The manager at Laidlaw explained it was next to impossible. Their trucks went back and forth all day to different areas and landfills in western Massachusetts and Rhode Island. In this case, dumpster-diving for Martha's bag would be no easier than searching for it at the bottom of the Atlantic Ocean.

Rosemary Farmer lived in Pride's Crossing, along the coastal route in the city of Beverly. Urbanowicz and Prosniewski drove up to talk to her late Wednesday morning. She was still very shaken. She told the detectives about her encounter with Maimoni the previous week.

When she left the parking lot on the night of her terrifying boat trip with Maimoni, Rosemary went to the nearby house of an acquaintance. Her friend was having a dinner party at the time. Rosemary arrived, still in shock. She sat down at the dinner table and blurted out her experience to a room full of strangers. The friend and her guests helped calm Rosemary down. Around ten she felt up to driving home. She knew by then her kids would be safely in bed and wouldn't see her in this miserable state. Finally home, she got into the shower and stood there for over an hour.

Despite pleas from her friends to contact the police, Rosemary felt that by putting it out of her mind she'd more quickly get over it. Furthermore, in her own mind, the incident had not actually been a rape. But on this Wednesday morning, her lawyer called her up after the local papers hit the stands.

"What did you say was the name of that boat you were on?"

"*Counterpoint*," Rosemary answered.

"Did you see the paper this morning?" asked the lawyer.

Rosemary hadn't. When she learned that the disappearance of Martha Brailsford was tied to the owner of a boat named *Counterpoint*, Rosemary ran to her next-door neighbor's and broke down. All her fears had been justified. On top of that was the obvious, lingering question. Could Martha's fate have been averted if Rosemary had gone immediately to the police? In her heart, she felt not. Who would have believed her word against his? And since "nothing" actually happened, it was unlikely Maimoni would have been locked up.

The detectives listened carefully. Rosemary was reassured that they believed her. She wished that she had kept the papers Maimoni had drawn up for her to look over to prove it had happened as she had said. Later on, Rosemary fished through her trash looking for the note "Mahoney" had left with her niece, the one with his number and alias. She managed to find it, crumpled up in a ball. Rosemary smoothed it out and clung to it until she gave it to the police. This at least was tangible evidence that what she had gone through may have been a nightmare, but it was no dream.

Prosniewski had handled many of the sexual assault cases for the department during his tenure as a detective and had gone through the necessary training along the way. He knew from experience that Rosemary's chatting with Tom about the house after he dropped her off at the pier was classic behavior for victims of assault. Casual, normal conversation was an instinctive survival tactic of a victim faced with an assailant who could overpower her, even later follow her. It maximized her chances for a clean, safe getaway. In fact, Rosemary Farmer had never returned Maimoni's subsequent calls regarding the purchase of the house. In fact, more importantly, Rosemary Farmer had survived.

Late Wednesday afternoon, Patti Maimoni arrived at Logan Airport in Boston and was greeted by Tom and the McCarthys. "What's going to happen to me?" she asked. Tom whisked her bags into the car. Ginny and Gerry were dismissed, said goodbye, and headed home. The Maimonis proceeded down to Rhode Island, where Tom called a "family meeting" at his father-in-law's house. Tom wanted to explain his situation to his in-laws over dinner. If Patti had been with him on the boat, he declared, this wouldn't have happened. "She would have known what to do," he claimed.

Patti was in shock but decided to stand by Tom, to support him through this crisis, come what may. In her heart, she believed that she and Tom had a good marriage. Patti had seen occasional cracks in the armor like Tom's problems with jobs, his problems with their mounting debts, his habit of sailing with women when Patti was not aboard. And she had grown suspicious that not everything Tom told her was true. Despite all this, Patti loved her husband very much.

As Tom did his explaining, he thought back with bitterness to the moment in the airport when Patti had stepped off the plane. "What's going to happen to *us*?" should have been her question. If only he had known five days ago that Patti's first concern was for herself. If only he had known what this relationship was really all about, things would have been very, very different.

25

On the sixth day of the investigation, God said, Let there be light, and there was light. Detective Sergeant Conrad Pros- niewski's prayers were about to be answered.

Thursday morning at 9:40, Captain Paul Murphy, after some hesitation, called Laurie Cabot, a friend of his who lived not far from the Pig's Eye. In times like these, it never hurt to know a witch.

Captain Murphy met Laurie a few years back, when she had a problem at Crow Haven Corner, her Salem shop. Besides serv- icing the needs of both local and visiting witches, Crow Haven Corner was one of the most popular tourist attractions in town. Occasionally, a religious fanatic or two came in and caused trouble. Store employees sometimes called the police to get them out. In the past, many times the police didn't respond. Laurie Cabot called the station after one such incident to complain. Captain Murphy took the call. It happened that Captain Murphy took very seriously his oath to protect everyone in the city equally. This included witches. He apologized and told her to call him directly if ever she had a problem again. Since then, he has never disappointed her.

Police departments all over the country regularly call Laurie Cabot to ask for her help on tough cases. She claims a high success rate. This was the first time she'd heard from Salem police, however. Trying to find missing persons was a task she did not relish. The feelings she had to experience in the course of working the case were almost unbearably painful. And if she failed, the disappointment was even worse. For these reasons, she never contacted a victim's family or initiated a call. She helped only when asked.

The police captain described the missing woman to Laurie and explained that they were about to conduct another air search over Gloucester Harbor for Martha's body. He asked Laurie if she could help. She agreed to try. Murphy asked whether she needed a personal article that belonged to the victim. She did not. Laurie preferred to work without tools. "All I've ever seen in a crystal ball is my own thumb," she liked to joke.

When Laurie told him the victim was near an island off Marblehead, she added, "You won't find her, though. She's on the bottom of the ocean. She's weighted down. Something's around her waist."

The witch looked further. And then, with agonizing horror, she watched the murder of Martha Brailsford pass before her eyes. She described it to the captain.

"The man knows the area well. He's a good navigator. They're having words. He made advances to her. She was very surprised. She threatened to tell on him. She threatened him with something she knew about him. He waited till her back was turned, then hit her on the head after a struggle. She's screaming for help. He has some weapon—a wrench? He's raped her. He's tied something around her waist. Something weighted. There are bruises on her neck."

Laurie searched painfully for more. "She has a head injury, to the right rear of her head, behind her ear. It's not fatal. She was strangled or left to drown, after being sexually attacked. This man—he's an angry guy."

When she had finished, Laurie erased her mindscreen with her hands, brought them palms downward before her face and body, then pushed them outwards. "I am healing myself and giving myself total health clearance," she said softly. Then she counted herself back up into a fully conscious state.

26

An hour after Captain Murphy had spoken with Laurie Cabot, lobsterman Hooper Goodwin found himself on the far side of Cat Island, hauling back his six-trap trawl. Cat Island belonged to the city of Salem, Marblehead's neighbor to the north.

Hooper was moving his boat along the trawl line from northwest to southeast. Standard practice among fishermen in the area was always to set in that direction to avoid crossing each other's lines. Hooper had five lines behind Cat Island this week. The first was in tight, starting off the tip of Cormorant Rock. These particular trawl lines had been out more than a week. Normally he liked to go back after a few days to gather them. Catching up and trying to get all his gear out for the beginning of his season, this was his first chance to haul back.

On that particular day, the water's surface was glassy. Hooper had calm water, so he hauled from the inside out—coming up close to Cat Island first, the northwest end, and hauling down toward the southeast. The first five traps came up without any problem. The sixth trap—the end trap—was another story.

Twisted and entwined in his ganget was a nylon anchor line, caught in loops. The end points of the anchor were jammed in the trap. And then he saw the rest. "My God!" he murmured. "Oh my God."

In the middle of the jumble protruded a human foot.

Through the clear, still water, Hooper Goodwin saw the entire body, nearly a skeleton, though only one leg broke through the surface of the ocean. He saw long hair, the head, and a multicolored diving belt around the spine. The other end of the anchor line was wound around the ankle, tied in a mishmash of quick half hitches and non-standard knots. There were no clothes, and very little tissue, except on the hands and feet and upper face.

Goodwin knew what he had found, remembering the posters he had seen on the waterfront all week. Now he was terrified of losing her. He lowered the trap below the water where he could still see it and tied it off on a cleat. After letting down the body to minimize damage and to protect her from the prying eyes of nearby boaters, Hooper noted the loran coordinates on his Navstar, then radioed the Marblehead harbormaster on channel 16.

"Marblehead harbormaster, *Nadine S.* Marblehead harbormaster." When his call was answered, the lobsterman continued. "Why don't we switch to a secure channel? I think I found what you guys are looking for." They both then switched down to channel 14 to avoid being overheard, and the harbormaster instructed him not to move. Hooper grabbed his gaff and scooped under the weight belt around Martha's waist. He held on tight. She was so fragile, so brittle looking. His one wish now was to deliver her in one piece. While he waited, he looked for her wedding ring, for he knew the missing woman was married. Though the hands were still intact, there was none. "The bastard stole her ring," Hooper thought to himself.

Within five minutes, the harbormaster pulled alongside *Nadine S* with the Salem police not far behind. One by one, each authority's vessel rafted together to form a long row. When Conrad Prosniewski finally climbed over the *Nadine S* to reach the Marblehead launch, Goodwin's discovery had already been placed in a body bag. As quick introductions were passed around, Prosniewski leaned over and pulled down the heavy black zipper. There was only one person he really wanted to see.

And there she was, wearing an anchor and dive belt as her testimony. "We got him—he's gone!" the detective exclaimed. "Let's go get him. I wanna see the lying son of a bitch's face!"

Goodwin believed that for anyone who earned his living on the ocean, a discovery like this was a curse. Conrad Prosniewski saw it as a blessing.

27

Assistant District Attorney Kevin Mitchell looked at his watch. Then he looked out the window of the Lynn District Courthouse to make certain the weather on Thursday was still good. He was finishing up a case with one of the detectives from Marblehead. But his mind was on the weather. Mitchell had plans this afternoon. He had a friend, lawyer and "master sailor" D. Dunbar Livingston, who happened to have a very nice sailboat. He and Dunbar had a date to go sailing as soon as this case was wrapped up that morning. The Marblehead detective was saying something. Redheaded, mustached Kevin Mitchell was still gazing out the window.

Of course the sail would be "official business." As the prosecutor in the Maimoni case, Mitchell had an obligation to "familiarize himself with the area."

They finished, finally. It was just 11:30. Mitchell quickly started to pack up his briefcase. The detective gave him a quizzical look. "You late for something?"

Mitchell nodded, gravely. "Gotta go look for a body."

The detective's radio began to crackle. Marblehead police were reporting a corpse had been recovered in Marblehead waters by a fisherman. The Marblehead harbormaster and the Salem police had responded. Mitchell paused to listen.

"Christ! There goes my sail!" He snapped shut his briefcase. "Let's go!"

Bette Putnam was working behind the bar at PCYC on Thursday morning. The ship-to-shore radio on the wall was monitoring channel 71, as usual. Sometimes a patron staggered from the club after a couple of beers and set out to sea, leaving a passenger behind. All manner of emergencies and non-emergencies were conveyed over the airwaves on channel 71. Shortly after eleven a friend of Bette's who worked at the *Salem Evening News* called her with the exciting news.

"They found the body! Switch the radio to 16!"

Bette twisted the radio knob just in time to hear, "*Stay right where you are!*" Shortly after that, the channel went dead.

Captain Paul Murphy got the news over his police radio while circling the waters off Marblehead in a small chartered plane. He immediately instructed the pilot to head back to Beverly Airport. The search was over. When he learned the location of the discovery, he silently chastised himself: "Why didn't I call Laurie sooner?"

The Pig's Eye was overflowing Thursday. Prosniewski called Julie from his car phone. "They found the body. Honey, gotta go," and hung up before Julie could congratulate him. She relayed the news to the room, put the phone down, and started to cry.

The owner of the Pig's Eye brought out the small black-and-white TV from the kitchen and propped it on the bar. The cook joined them. Everyone huddled around the tube. People lingered after their lunches were over and their beers were drained, as if the tiny, crowded establishment was an observation deck overlooking the city. They strained their ears and buzzed, "Where's Maimoni, did he say? I saw her last week. What does Conrad think? Was she having an affair? Did they get him, Julie? Did they get him, or what?" This week they were all little detectives, digesting each bit of news along with their clam chowder, passing their deductions and theories around the room like bottles of ketchup.

Word had spread like wildfire along the waterfront from just that brief radio transmission and from scanners monitoring police frequencies. The launch carrying the remains headed to the Hawthorne Cove Marina in Salem, where it would be fairly easy to keep the press out. Only one narrow street led to the boatyard and a gate that investigators could shut. Boaters were swarming around the harbor at a barely respectable distance. News helicopters roared overhead. By the time the launch docked, uniformed officers had cordoned off the boatyard. The chief had come down to greet them. The medical examiner's van was on its way.

Meanwhile, Detective Mary Butler was notified and was hard at work by noon Thursday typing up the warrants in the office. Conrad Prosniewski's nine-page report of the investigation so far was attached as an affidavit to the application for an arrest warrant. Detective William Jennings took one of the unmarked CID cruisers and headed to Settlers Way to sit on the house until the warrants were signed. Divers were quickly assembled to thoroughly search the location designated by Hooper's loran coordinates.

Kevin Mitchell arrived back in Salem and called Dr. Ronald Plotka at his office in Swampscott. When Plotka came on the line, Mitchell asked him if he had located Martha's dental charts and X rays. The police had talked to the dentist about them the day before.

"Yes, I have them here."

"Would you do us a favor, Dr. Plotka? We've found a body. We think it's Martha. Could you come and ID her for us?" Mitchell explained why only a dentist could do the job.

Plotka was shocked. "I'm no expert."

"That's OK. We'll have an expert later. But we're in a hurry right now," said Mitchell. They were in a hurry because the news was already being broadcast all over New England that Martha Brailsford had been found. They were also in a hurry because, technically, they couldn't arrest Maimoni until they confirmed the body was indeed Martha's. If it wasn't, they couldn't touch Maimoni.

"Well, sure. Of course, I'll help. Tell me where to go. I'll be through here around 4:30."

"You don't understand, Dr. Plotka. There's a police cruiser on its way to your office. We need you—now!"

Dr. Plotka rubbed his forehead. "I've got a gentleman in the chair. And another one in the waiting room."

The assistant district attorney told the dentist to go ahead and finish up with the guy in the chair. Whoever else was waiting—tough luck.

An hour later, a state trooper drove Dr. Plotka and the X rays to Tewksbury State Hospital, where the body had been taken for an autopsy. When Dr. Plotka saw the skeleton, he didn't bother to open the X rays. "I'd know those teeth anywhere. Martha had the most incredible teeth," he said sadly.

The dentist's former patient now had one fractured molar and a chip in one front tooth.

28

Detective William Jennings was the man to call if you needed a door kicked in. At 1:45 on Thursday afternoon, July 18, he very effectively kicked in the burgundy door of 2 Settlers Way after his knock went unanswered. On the other side, standing in the ivy-decorated front hall of the Conant model home, were a very surprised and justifiably shaken Mr. and Mrs. Stochl, Maimoni's in-laws. The police officers had drawn their guns on them.

Prosniewski and state troopers Lynch and Garvin were waiting at the back of the condos to ensure Tom Maimoni didn't slip away, a remote possibility considering the legions of reporters and cameramen who ringed the townhouse. Maimoni was far too polite to mow down a reporter during a getaway attempt.

After explaining their rude entrance and flashing the warrant, the detectives asked the Stochls where Maimoni was. Their guns were all back in their holsters. Tom was at the McCarthys' home in Beverly. Mr. Stochl was put in a cruiser to lead the way, and the entourage headed across the bridge.

On Neptune Street in Beverly moments later, Prosniewski's knock was answered by Ginny McCarthy. Prosniewski recognized Ginny. She was the wife of his insurance man, it turned out. "We're looking for Tom," he said bluntly. Standing a few feet behind her was Patti Maimoni, who asked, "What's going on?"

Prosniewski stepped inside with the troopers and explained hastily. "A body has surfaced. We think it's Martha. It had an anchor and a weight around it. We have a warrant for murder, and we're looking for Tom. Where is Tom?" Time was of the essence. They wanted this guy locked up before he did anything else foolish. Apparently, they were too late.

Patti sat down in the nearest chair, unable to speak. Her face drew a complete blank. Prosniewski tried to talk to her. Nothing was registering. Her eyes were glazed. Patti suddenly seemed very, very frail.

Behind him Ginny spoke up. "Tom was here. He just left a few minutes ago. He said he was on his way to meet his lawyer. He said he had to go to Marblehead right away. 'They needed him,' he said. We heard the news on TV. No one said anything about an anchor."

Until the police arrived, Patti had felt relieved that Martha's body had been found. She had hoped they could now put the accident behind them. She loved Tom and was prepared to stand by him. The afternoon sail had been innocent. Tom had explained all that. As he was leaving the house, Patti had begged to go with him, but he had refused. "Whatever happens, Patti, stay with Gerry and Ginny, Tom had said. "They will take care of you."

Detective Sergeant Conrad Prosniewski had just blown away her future. Crumpled up her life. Conrad Prosniewski had just told her that her husband was a murderer. Where did that put Patti? As the full impact hit her, her head flopped down.

Prosniewski knelt beside her. "Ginny, get me a cold, wet cloth. I have to talk to this girl."

Troopers Lynch and Garvin stepped into the other room and started making phone calls. The first was to headquarters to enter a BOLO (Be On the Look-Out) report into the local and national computer systems. The logistical setup for a manhunt was initiated.

Prosniewski seriously doubted that Maimoni intended to see any lawyers at this point. Nevertheless, he gently questioned the man's wife. "Patti, listen to me. I know this is a big shock. I feel bad you have to hear it this way. But it's important I talk to you. We have to find Tom. Can you tell me who his lawyer is? Or where he might have gone?"

Ginny gave him the Lynn attorney's name. Patti was "blotto," totally unaware of what was going on around her. The police got what information they could from the McCarthys and left. Prosniewski was thankful, at least, that Patti Maimoni had Ginny McCarthy with her.

Hooper Goodwin spent several hours that afternoon showing divers the exact spot. When the media finally got their crack at the lobsterman later in the day as he docked, one reporter thrust a microphone in his face. The reporter asked, "Sir, in your mind, was this an accident?"

Hooper was astounded at the question and at his sudden elevation to "expert." "In *my* mind?" he asked incredulously. In case the weighted skeleton didn't convey the same message to the reporter as it did to Hooper, he answered emphatically, "No way. I do not see any possible way it was an accident."

Meanwhile, the news media were already muscling their way into Red's Sandwich Shop next to the police station, eager to hear the reaction of the "man on the street."

By the time Prosniewski got in touch with Bill Brailsford, the family had already learned of the discovery on the news. From that point on, they retreated from the public eye. A note taped to the front door stated: "The family requests that the press respect our right to privacy. We wish to make no comments in regard to recent developments and would prefer that the media make no attempt to contact or speak with family or friends unless otherwise notified."

Brailsford asked to talk personally with Hooper Goodwin by phone later that evening. The lobsterman tried to answer any questions he had and reached out to him with his deepest sympathy. Brailsford listened quietly, then thanked the lobsterman.

"At this point I hadn't even met the guy. He is a real captain's captain. I have such respect for him," Hooper said, describing Brailsford's handling of the conversation.

Prosniewski called Julie at the Pig's Eye later in the afternoon to tell her the news: "Maimoni screwed. He's gone!" Julie relayed this to the dining room. The news was not taken well. Still standing with the receiver to her ear, she was made to feel as if they had just run out of Key lime pie. The little detectives at the bar certainly would have arrested him five days ago. Or had him under surveillance. Outrage was tossed back to her. She whispered into the phone. "They wanna know how he got away. What do I tell them, Conrad? Honey, what do I tell them?"

Prosniewski didn't have time for a press conference, nor did he particularly care what the patrons wanted to know. To make matters worse for Julie, the man she considered her protector announced he probably wouldn't be home that night. In fact, Julie was unlikely to see him until Maimoni was apprehended. This unbearable week with the house issues, Prosniewski grasping for his kids, the missing person, and now a nationwide manhunt. "*I'm losing him to everything,*" she grieved.

By the time her shift ended Thursday, Julie was consumed with terror. She reached Prosniewski at the station after numerous tries from their apartment upstairs in her parents' house. He still hadn't time to talk, and this compelled her to keep Prosniewski on the line as long as possible. "He's out there," she warned him, "and he could have a gun. And he probably knows where you live. He's smart enough to find out!"

Prosniewski could hardly hear her over the din in the CID office. "What are you talking about?"

"He's killed one woman. Look at all the others he's tried to be with. You're the one he talked to every day. He might think no one would look for him at your place. He might try to come after *me*, Conrad."

Prosniewski couldn't help himself: "Oh, right. Now that he's been found out, he's thinking, 'Wow, what should I do next? Of course! Go kill that detective's girlfriend!'"

To Julie, it was of course the next logical move. When she hung up, she grabbed a pillow and scooped up her dog and her quilt, which trailed down the stairs behind her as she took refuge in her parents' apartment. Julie camped out on the living room couch, determined to stay there until Maimoni was captured.

Prosniewski's fiancée was not the only one who was terrified. Rosemary Farmer spent the night in her van, parked in a friend's driveway. Ginny and Gerry McCarthy drove Patti Maimoni to the nearby Beverly Hospital Trauma Center on Thursday evening, where she was treated for shock and was kept for a time under observation. After she returned to Settlers Way, Salem detectives stayed with her through the night. The McCarthys checked into King's Grant Inn in Danvers for the next three days. They were far too close to a man they suddenly didn't know.

Conrad Prosniewski remembers the night he fell in love with Julie Michaud. He had known her for years, since she was a kid and he was newly married with kids of his own. They met at Lydia's Subs on Essex Street, where Julie worked the counter and Prosniewski stopped for lunches.

After Lydia's, Julie worked as a teller at the bank where Prosniewski had his account. A couple of years later, when Prosniewski began night shifts, Julie had a job downtown at Video Paradise. She, too, worked evenings, closing up at midnight and stopping by the bank's night deposit box with the daily receipts on her way home. Prosniewski took to worrying about her. After a time he had gotten in the habit of dropping by while she closed up, following her to the bank in his cruiser. Julie, in return, saved newly released videos for him.

Shortly after his divorce, Prosniewski worked Saturday night details at a restaurant called Jonathan's for awhile, usually at the door. One of those nights he was stationed upstairs in the bar. The dance floor was crowded. Several off-duty police officers had come in for the last call and were lined up at the bar, civilian jackets covering their uniforms. Prosniewski stood with them and talked the usual shop for awhile. The air was filled with smoke and gossip. Then all at once Julie came up the stairs with a friend. Julie wore a red dress with no back that stunned Prosniewski into speechlessness. His colleagues noticed he had dropped out of their conversation. When the first song ended, and the next one began, Julie came up to him. No longer a child, she announced rather than asked: "I think we should dance."

Prosniewski was still immobilized by that dress. But the answer was simple. When he was working, he didn't dance. The cop next to him, however, was suddenly struck by a keen sense of duty, somehow seeing the bigger picture. He offered to take over Prosniewski's detail for fifteen minutes. They accomplished this by trading jackets. Prosniewski unbuckled his gun belt, handed it over, took off his police jacket, and put on his friend's denim one. Then he took Julie onto the, dance floor. They danced to some Marvin Gaye song and fell in love.

PART II

For whatever reason
That warm summer season
She was stolen from where she belonged.

Brought back from the sea
By God and by me,
I pray for her family and soul.

> *My Ballad to Martha*
> W. H. Goodwin III

29

Salem police were bombarded by the media on Thursday because Thomas Maimoni had not been immediately arrested. Joseph Casey, an attorney from Lynn whom Tom had retained, confirmed later that day that his client had not shown up. The Rhode Island authorities were contacted to stake out the house of Tom's parents. People on the run, people in a panic, go back home. Home to hide.

The McCarthys' place was put under surveillance, as was 2 Settlers Way. Police in Groveland, Massachusetts, watched the house of Tom's sister. Kansas City authorities staked out the home of Patti's sister. Chief St. Pierre vowed to news reporters that Maimoni would be apprehended. Responding to criticism that Maimoni should have been watched all along, St. Pierre reminded them that until this morning they had found no body. No body, no evidence of a crime. Surveillance could have possibly violated Maimoni's civil rights, although that point was arguable. One expert, James Fox, a professor of criminal justice at Northeastern University, told the *Salem Evening News* that it was OK to keep track of suspects "as long as you don't interfere with them." He concluded, "It seems the Salem police were a little too laid back about this."

The truth of the matter was that Maimoni was a suspect they couldn't get rid of. Not only did he respond quickly to every message Conrad Prosniewski left him and come immediately whenever beckoned, the police were tripping over him during their investigation around town. When they weren't calling Maimoni, he was calling them. Popping by to help. Telephoning to let them know where he could be reached, just like in the Woody Allen movie *Play it Again Sam*. He was the last person on earth the Criminal Investigation Division thought they'd have to go looking for.

There was a more calculated reason why they had left Maimoni alone. The condos at Collins Cove afforded no cover for hidden surveillance. As each day passed, Tom Maimoni was telling more and more of the truth. Each day brought more information. The police knew that without a body, which they had been exceptionally lucky to find, there would be no case. Their only hope was that out of Tom's stories eventually a confession would evolve. Until Thursday, Tom had still been talking. Had they parked a cop outside his door, he likely would have clammed up.

The detectives got names of friends and other relatives from the Stochls. They suggested Patti cancel all her credit cards as soon as possible. Maimoni's picture was shown on every local news station. Citizens were urged to watch out for a 1987 silver Ford Taurus with Massachusetts license plates T6J.

Maimoni's name was run through all the usual computers: national, local, board of probation, registry of motor vehicles. Other than a few tickets, he came up clean.

Meanwhile, search warrants were procured on the afternoon of July 18 for the Maimonis' condo and for a second examination of the boat. This time investigators removed rope from *Counterpoint* that closely matched the segment found on Martha's body. At the residence the police located Patti Maimoni's diving gear set, complete except for a weight belt that was missing. They also found numerous fake business cards, plus copies of résumés listing schools and degrees—a doctorate from Boston University, among others. In the basement lay a grim reminder of Maimoni's last employer—the popular Parker Brothers game, *How to Host a Murder*.

Evidence "of a sexual nature" was taken from the condo during the search. Police seized a photograph of Tom on a sailboat, close up and nude from the waist down. Tom had a partial manuscript entitled "Illustrated Woman," which they took. They also removed a T-shirt with Just Another Sexy Bald Guy written on the front. Found in the home of anyone else, these items might be considered evidence of questionable taste at worst. In an investigation like this, taste, too, could be on trial.

Detective Bill Jennings dropped a couple of beers on the desk as he and Prosniewski turned on the eleven o'clock news Thursday night at the police station. Jennings plopped down, put his feet up, flipped the tab on his can, and muttered loudly, "Where in Christ can he be?" He had been called off vacation this week and was working overtime every day, helping with legwork, paperwork, and "running interference with the press." Drug informants had been calling him the past few days. Jennings had to pass. No one in the Criminal Investigation Division was handling any non-emergency matters unless it pertained to this case.

All week long, Prosniewski and Jennings had been hanging around the office until the nightly broadcasts updated New England viewers on the latest turn of events in the Brailsford case. Each night they'd get a couple of calls right after the segments aired. "Here they come!" Prosniewski exclaimed when Tom Maimoni's picture flashed across the screen. The number of the Salem Police Department was given at the bottom. Jennings flipped around the other stations. All carried the same lead story. No longer a missing woman's story—a missing fugitive's instead. The phones began to ring.

A woman phoned. "I was on his boat ten years ago. He tried to rape me." She refused to leave her name and hung up. A man reported T6J had gassed up at his service station in Quincy. Another one called and said, "He's in New Zealand." And so it went.

On Friday, July 19, an advance team from the TV show *America's Most Wanted* checked into the historic Hawthorne Hotel in downtown Salem. They had arranged to do a piece on Thomas Maimoni for their next weekly segment. The police and the district attorney's office had agreed to cooperate. On Saturday morning they contacted Steve O'Connell, press agent for the DA's office, and gave him a list of what they needed for the show. It included requests for interviews with the lobsterman and harbormasters, copies of the Maimoni interviews, a chronology of events, a copy of the arrest warrant, a description of the boat, plus photos and descriptions of the victim and defendant for the reenactment. The reenactment would be a challenge in this case. It was anyone's guess what had happened on *Counterpoint* that day. However, they could always pick one from Maimoni's own collection of scripts.

O'Connell passed along the request to the district attorney with an optimistic postscript: "Hopefully we won't even need this segment, planned for this coming Friday night, because he'll be in custody by then. In the event he's not in custody, I should tell you that this show results in the capture of 67 percent of those fugitives it features."

Meanwhile, Captain Murphy decided around noon to talk again with Laurie Cabot, the witch. She had divined the whereabouts of the victim. Perhaps she could also divine the whereabouts of the killer.

A child who grew up Roman Catholic in California in the 1930s, Laurie Cabot was aware she had psychic powers that other children lacked or, rather, had lost. In her late teens, she lived in the Boston area and befriended three women who were witches. They helped satisfy her insatiable curiosity and questioning, giving a name to the powers and beliefs inside her. In high school, Laurie came to realize that she, too, was a witch. She joined her first coven.

In the 1960s Laurie, then a divorced mother with two daughters, decided to buy a house with a friend. As they began their search she announced, "Any place but Salem." Laurie believed that a real witch should never move to a town that bills itself as the Witch City, one historically associated with intolerance toward witches. However, a house that they couldn't pass up turned up in the historic district downtown. So Laurie moved to Salem after all.

After a few years, she opened up Crow Haven Corner and came out of the broom closet, as some like to put it. As time went on, the witch population in Salem grew from a handful to number in the thousands. Although there were a number of witchcraft traditions—not all witches agreed with Laurie Cabot's brand—much of this growth and exposure was indeed due to her life-long commitment to educate and promote the tenets of the craft. She founded the Temple of Isis, became an elder in her religion, and started her own coven, the Black Doves of Isis. To combat stereotypes promulgated by the media and entrenched in popular tradition, she became an active member of the Witches' League for Public Awareness. Her most pervasive decision, however, was to live every aspect of her life as a witch. She resolved to wear only the garb of her religion, despite criticism from some witches that doing so perpetuates flamboyant aspects of their image that eclipse the more fundamental ones. Both of her daughters were raised in the craft. She came to observe witch holidays and ceremonies surrounding all of life's milestones.

Except for small pockets of fundamentalist Christians and other religious fanatics, most long-time residents of Salem came to recognize and tolerate Laurie. Some saw her as merely a colorful character; others revered her. Some viewed her as a "well-oiled machine" since she did so well in the commercial side of her craft. Laurie Cabot managed to wear more than one hat. She served on the board of the local Chamber of Commerce. During one election year, she ran for mayor of the city. She also gained an international reputation, appearing on countless TV programs and interviewed by *Newsweek*, *National Geographic*, the BBC, and hundreds of publications. Laurie was typically booked months in advance for interviews, readings, and counseling. A year, for slots during Halloween.

The official witch of Salem was finishing up a bagel and was trying to focus on a book she was writing. Gazing out at the trees in her backyard seemed at the moment much more satisfying. When the phone rang, she pushed aside one of her cats to reach it. Murphy explained why he had called. Laurie was not up on the details of the case. She never read newspapers because of all the negative aspects and the violence. If a newscast appeared on TV or radio, she'd flip the channel. All she wanted was the weather reports.

"You made a few believers down here last time," Murphy told her. "Can you tell us anything more? Any idea where this guy might be headed?"

It didn't take her long. "He's going to Canada, Captain Murphy. He's shaved his mustache. He's buying a wig." She dug deeper into the character of the fugitive. "He thinks he can con anyone. He thinks of himself as a police officer. He has a lot of rage against women and no respect for females at all. There are problems between him and his wife. I think he's behind on condo payments."

More of the details of the murder were appearing on Laurie's mindscreen. "I saw Martha on deck with some papers. It was such a nice day, so pleasant, until suddenly this happened. She was friendly, and he mistook it as an invitation. But she didn't want romance, or sex, just companionship. She had a very clear boundary. He was surprised at how strong she was. He was planning on coming back later, to move her out to deeper waters. Captain Murphy, she wasn't dead when she went into the water."

Murphy jotted down her words as she spoke. As he had on Thursday, he noted the date and time in the margin.

"Don't worry, he's not going to commit suicide," she reassured him. "His ego is too big. He's thinking about turning himself in. I'll tell you what—I'll put a binding on him to encourage him along those lines or so he does something that gets him caught."

After she hung up, Laurie closed her eyes and pictured Tom Maimoni in a white cocoon, bound up in a thread of light. Around his body. Around his hands. "Correctly, and for the good of all," she concluded.

Help poured in Friday from other sources as well. A federal customs agent assigned to one of the local sections called Conrad Prosniewski and offered his computer imaging skills. The newspaper photo of Maimoni was of a bald, happy man with a mustache. In this day and age, they had the technology to produce images of any possible transformation a fugitive might undergo. Why not make use of it?

Why not indeed? Prosniewski faxed him a clean, crisp copy of the photo.

With the help of Hollywood, a witch, modern technology, and the little detectives at the Pig's Eye, Thomas Maimoni didn't have a snowball's chance in hell.

From a pay phone in front of the station, Julie Michaud called the CID. Prosniewski was already talking with another caller. "He's busy, Julie," Bill Jennings told her.

"Tell him I've got ice cream for him," she pleaded. The ploy didn't work.

Sandy Clark, a victim/witness advocate from the Essex County DA's office, was surprised to discover that she had been assigned to the Maimoni case. Two others in her department would have been more likely candidates, but for one reason or another, they were unavailable. Sandy, who normally worked in Lynn, the city immediately south of Salem, scrambled to catch up on the background of this case. She called Salem police to get copies of whatever reports were produced so far in the investigation. She would need to be available not only for the Brailsford family but also for the women who might testify about their experiences with Maimoni, plus any other potential witnesses who might need moral support or guidance through the system.

Sandy came by to talk to Prosniewski and Mark Lynch and to pick up copies of their reports. Although the focus was on the manhunt at the moment, it was already clear this would be a humongous investigation with a lot of people needing her services. For every little piece of information they gleaned from witnesses, she would have to evaluate the likelihood that each would need to testify. Who would need letters to employers? Who would need referrals to other agencies? Who just needed hand-holding? In Sandy's experience, each individual brought a different level of internal resources to a situation. The degree of help Sandy had to render was rarely related to the seriousness of the crime.

When she sat down, Lynch and Prosniewski told her, "We want you to consider Patti Maimoni as much a victim as anyone else in this case."

Sandy's caseload increased again when the police department received a call from the Rhode Island State Police. One of the troopers had just taken a statement from a young woman who claimed she had met Tom Maimoni two days after the incident. The woman was a drug addict but appeared to be a straight talker, a no-nonsense type. Tom had picked her up south of Providence while she was hitchhiking. They had spent the afternoon together. She had forgotten about him completely until his face was plastered all over the TV news: "Suspect Evades Police." Try looking in Rhode Island, she suggested.

The trooper faxed his report to Salem.

Bill Brailsford was surrounded by friends and neighbors who were effective at keeping the press away from him and who wanted to help him in any way possible. When Bill had to return to work, casseroles would show up in his refrigerator with reheating instructions. Others took over the twice daily task of walking Rudy. People gathered nightly at one house or another to rehash scraps of news and to vent emotions, still running high. The location varied. The address was posted on Fort Avenue on a community bulletin board near the park entrance each afternoon. Bill's grief and fear belonged to the entire Willows neighborhood.

Later that afternoon, Prosniewski's computer imaging friend stopped by with his results. There were four new Xerox copies of the photo. The detective looked through them and smiled.

The first was untouched: *Maimoni with no imagination*. Or no money. The second had the unmistakable gray smudge of white-out correction fluid above Tom's upper lip: *Maimoni with shaved face*. The third had crosshatches drawn all over the lower half of his face: *Maimoni grows a beard*. They looked like pencil lines. The fourth Xerox copy had a shapeless hat perched atop his head: *Maimoni buys a hat*. It had been drawn with a blue ballpoint pen.

Computer technology was a wonderful thing. Prosniewski was touched by the outpouring of help from so many agencies and sources. But maybe they'd stick with the witch.

30

One Salem tradition, perhaps more steeped in history than any other, is the annual Black Picnic held the third Saturday of July at Salem Willows Park. "The picnic that survived slavery," as some attendees refer to it, began in 1741 when a group of twenty-six slaves from nearby Lynn elected to spend their one day off each year at the water's edge. Over the years the picnic evolved and grew. It became one of the biggest and most eagerly anticipated events in the North Shore African-American community. Starting in the 1920s, several area churches took over active sponsorship of the picnic. They chartered trolley cars to transport their black congregations up to Salem for a day of sun, water, fun and good food. Family reunions brought together hundreds of families, traversing both blood lines and color lines. All were welcome at the Black Picnic.

Even during the war years when turnout was low, or years when participants were drenched by torrential rains, the picnic endured and kept its place in North Shore lore. For the African-American community, it has remained a tie that binds. For Salem, the uniqueness of this peaceful and joyous event has only added to its riches.

On Saturday, July 20, 1991, some 3,000 to 5,000 people streamed into the park to enjoy the Willows breeze on yet another hot, hazy, humid day. Some old-timers came as early as six in the morning to stake out the same trees or tables their families had been staking out for half a century or more.

Meanwhile, other Salem residents had elected instead to leave town, escaping the heat by heading north to cabins or lakes in Maine. Chief St. Pierre of the Salem Police Department was spending the day with his family on Sebago Lake, although it bore little resemblance to a day off. The chief's ear was glued to the phone most of the day, checking in with members of the CID and monitoring the progress of the search effort. He was a little nervous about going out on a limb by having promised the press that Tom Maimoni would be apprehended quickly. Not a relaxing day at all. Even on a lake in Maine, it was scorching hot.

Detective Mary Butler was en route with her family to a friend's place in southern Maine, this most popular of states that day. Mary needed the rest, due more to her sleepless nights as mother of a nocturnal two-year-old than to the countless hours of overtime she had been putting in on the Maimoni case. Tom Maimoni was still a fugitive. It was anyone's guess where he might have headed. He could conceivably have headed north through Maine to Canada, a popular route for people on the run. She turned to look at the driver currently passing their car. "Better keep a head's up!" she half-joked to herself.

They had just crossed the small piece of New Hampshire that separates the northern border of Massachusetts from Maine. Welcome to Maine, the sign read, when Mary Butler's beeper suddenly went off.

The Butlers found a phone at the next rest stop. Mary dialed her office. It turned out a couple of the guys in the CID were having a problem with the computer. Mary talked them through it. Some days it struck her that the pay scale for the rank of "mother" wasn't nearly high enough.

Washington County, Maine, was called "Sunrise County," since it was the first spot in the United States to see the light of dawn. The county was big, nearly the size of New Hampshire. It was also remote. And quiet. Four law officers serviced its needs.

On Saturday afternoon, July 20, one of those four—Deputy Sheriff Robert Gross, was covering the scene of a car accident in Topsfield, the town in which he resided. Gross's wife Alice ran the Log Cabin Restaurant in Topsfield. The previous night, chatting with his partner on the telephone, Gross had heard an interesting story. Deputy Sheriff Sydney Hughes had just returned from a week-long drug prevention conference in Nashua, New

Hampshire. There he had met and befriended a detective from Massachusetts, a guy named Jim Page, who on the first day was deep in the middle of a missing person's case. Each day of the conference Page had chatted about its progress.

Later in the week, the case had turned into a murder investigation. And by Friday it had become a nationwide manhunt. Deputy Hughes returned to Maine and shared information about the case along with his impressions of the conference. Nothing like that had ever happened in Washington County. All they got there were those sunrises.

Deputy Gross was mulling over the story and finishing up with the accident scene when he got a call from his dispatcher at 3:30. A burglary in progress had been reported ten miles away in the small logging town of Waite.

His destination was a summer cabin located on the shoulder of Route 1, the highway that leads from Florida to the Canadian border, some fifteen miles east of Waite. When he arrived, the caretaker who had put in the call was standing on the edge of the road in the blistering heat with three other people. Gross knew them all. Washington County, for all its vastness, was also exceedingly small.

He pulled his cruiser over and was told by the bystanders that the subject was still inside the cabin. The caretaker remarked that the strange car parked on the property attracted his attention, as did the humming air conditioners and the damaged back door. "The molding's busted," he told the officer. "There's no one supposed to be here. I was gonna go back home for my shotgun, but I figured let the police handle it."

Gross drew his gun and circled to the back. In a loud voice he identified himself as a member of the Washington County Sheriff's Department and ordered the occupant to come out. Five seconds later, a tall man in white shorts appeared at the back door with a dazed expression. Gross commanded: "Put your hands on top of your head, interlock your fingers, and walk out the door!" When the suspect had stepped outside, Gross gave the next order: "Get down on the ground with your hands behind your back!"

The intruder dropped to his knees, then stretched out on the grass. Deputy Gross leaned down and snapped handcuffs around the man's wrists. Gross lifted the man back up and placed him in the cruiser. Backups from the Maine State Police and local departments began to arrive. Gross asked one of the officers to watch the individual while he searched the cabin.

Inside, Deputy Gross verified that no one else was hiding. An empty soup can was found in the trash, plus a half-gallon ice cream container. A pair of socks were drying in the bathroom. Pieces of splintered wood from the jimmied back door were stacked neatly in the trash can. The burglar had tidied up after himself. Two separate beds had been slept in. Like Goldilocks, the intruder had been looking for the most comfortable place to sleep.

Deputy Gross returned to his cruiser and updated the troopers on the incident. The prisoner interrupted them, complaining the handcuffs were hurting him. Gross let him out to switch the cuffs to the front. As he was doing so, one of the troopers, Timothy McCadden, asked whether the suspect perhaps had been given permission to use the cabin. McCadden knew the owners were from Massachusetts. The stranger's car had Massachusetts license plates. He was a bit concerned that Gross had ordered the guy out of the cabin and had promptly arrested him without first asking questions. Maybe the poor man had gotten his cabins confused, had found his key didn't work, and had forced the door open.

The stranger confessed that he did not have permission and that he did not know the owners. He was only trying to get out of the heat and get some rest.

"Where are you from?" asked McCadden.

"I'm from Salem. Salem, Massachusetts."

"Is that right? I know Salem. I grew up in Beverly. Graduated from Beverly High School. I know Salem real well."

McCadden's mother still lived in Beverly. His brother was a fireman there. McCadden had been down to visit the previous Monday, but he had left before seeing newspaper accounts of Martha Brailsford's disappearance.

"Well, Massachusetts wants me more than you do."

"What are you talking about?" asked McCadden. The suspect was polite, well spoken, a professional type, hardly a guy to be in trouble. McCadden had really believed the arrest could have been a mistake, that in fact the guy might somehow have had the right to be there. He looked like a guy with the right to be wherever he was.

"A woman fell off my boat. And drowned."

Standing beside them, Deputy Gross's jaw dropped. Light

Martha Brailsford, boating in Massachusetts Bay aboard her husband's boat, approximately one year before her death.
Photo courtesy B. Brailsford

Martha Brailsford, several years earlier, on Dane St. Beach in Beverly, MA, after a day of windsurfing.
Warren Patriquin, Beverly Times

Salem Willows Pier, where Martha was last seen on July 12, 1991. *Joan Noble Pinkham*

Thomas Maimoni's Cal 28 sailboat *Counterpoint* after police brought it to Hawthorne Cove Marina to be searched on July 16, 1991. Bloodied sail was removed by the State Crime Lab. *Mike Adaskaveg, Boston Herald*

World-renowned, the Official Witch of Salem Laurie Cabot walks the streets downtown in the robe that is her hallmark. *Kirk R. Williamson*

Lobsterman Hooper Goodwin reenacts for Salem Police how he hauled in his trap and discovered the ensnared anchor, visible at top of trap. Reenactment helped rule out the probability that bruises on the body occurred from his hauling operation. *Salem Police Department photo*

Lobsterman Hooper Goodwin of Marblehead aboard his boat, *Nadine S*, on July 18, 1991, after finding the body of Martha Brailsford entangled in a trawl line. *Nancy Lane, Boston Herald*

Police and Marblehead harbormaster's boats gather around Goodwin's lobster boat to take the recovered body aboard. In the background are Cat Island and Cormorant Rock. *Lynnette Therrier, Salem Evening News*

A manacled Thomas Maimoni is led from an aircraft on July 22, 1991, by Salem Police detective James Page, far left, and Massachusetts State Police, after being flown to Beverly Airport from Maine, where he was apprehended. *Kirk Williamson, Salem Evening News*

Salem Police detectives Sgt. Richard Urbanowicz, left, and Sgt. Conrad Prosniewski, right, at a press conference on July 20, 1991, announcing the capture of Thomas Maimoni in Maine. Det. William Jennings, wearing a cap, is behind them. *Jonathon M. Whitmore, Salem Evening News*

Thomas J. Maimoni as he was booked by Salem Police on July 22, 1991. While on the run he had shaved his mustache and was growing a beard. *Salem Police Department photo*

Friends and neighbors of Martha Brailsford gather around a seaside garden created in her memory in July 1991, at Salem Willows. *Kirk Williamson, Salem Evening News*

Assistant DA Kevin M. Mitchell listens to testimony during the February 1993 trial of Thomas J. Maimoni. *Salem Evening News*

Thomas Maimoni listens with his lawyer Jeffrey A. Denner, left, as witnesses on the opening day of his trial describe Maimoni's sexual advances aboard *Counterpoint. Salem Evening News*

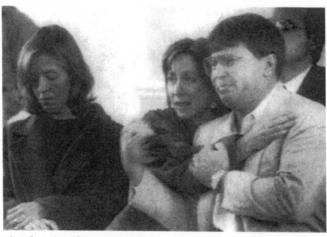

The family of Martha Brailsford reacts to the jury verdict on February 12, 1993. Left to right, Joyce Roy, friend, Muriel Garvey, Martha's twin sister, David Conant, Martha's brother. *Jonathon M. Whitmore, Salem Evening News*

Thomas Maimoni breaks down on the stand February 10, 1993, as he describes his version of the death of Martha Brailsford aboard his boat. *Suzanne Kreiter, The Boston Globe*

bulbs went off in his head. It couldn't be. He pulled McCadden aside and told him the story his partner had related to him the night before. They sent another trooper into the cabin to call the barracks for verification.

Moments later, the trooper returned and told McCadden there was indeed a Salem, Massachusetts, warrant out for this man. A warrant for murder. The deputy sheriff and troopers agreed to wait for the detective division to arrive, and to do no further questioning of their prisoner until that time. McCadden was the senior trooper. He told the rest to hold off reading any rights.

The arrest process in Washington County accommodated the rural needs of its vast acreage. Prisoners typically were not advised of their right to make a phone call to an attorney because usually they were nowhere near a phone. So how could one have that right? As McCadden sometimes explained, the troopers in most situations would "PR bail"—bail the individual out on personal recognizance right from the cruiser. "It's not something that in six years as a trooper I've ever had to advise anybody, 'You have the right to make a phone call,' because most of my prisoners don't go to jail. And at the time that he's taken into the Washington County Sheriff's Department and given due process, he's given the right to a phone call, a cigarette, pat-down search, everything. That's the process we have."

And those were one's rights in Washington County. Another right was not to endure the *Miranda* process until absolutely needed, until the moment of directed questioning. For the next two to three hours, waiting for the detective Saturday afternoon, the ensemble switched Maimoni to another cruiser. They gave him a soda, rotated watch, and took turns enjoying the air-conditioned interior with him. They did not read him any rights. They made a stalwart effort to keep him from talking about his trouble in Massachusetts. Maimoni informed them that he had lied to the Salem police but that he would not lie to these fine men.

The suspect also mentioned to the troopers, somewhat apologetically, that he had borrowed the phone in the cabin to make a couple of calls. One to his lawyer, Mr. Casey, and one to a close friend, a Mr. Montague. Maimoni had left a message on Bob Montague's machine: "Bob, this is Tom. My life is over. But I don't want to talk about that. I want to talk about Patti. I want you to help her in any way you can, and I want you to help her with the boat. Her new name is Patricia Stochl." Thomas Maimoni had renamed his wife.

They talked about home for awhile, McCadden and Maimoni. Beverly, Salem, the Willows, home to both of them. Maimoni was asked why he had come to this particular area in Maine. He told McCadden about a friend of his who owned ten acres near Houlton, up north. Maimoni had been there once before. God's Country, he called it. He wanted to see it again—one last time. He had stopped in Houlton for gas before driving to Waite, but the attendant confiscated his credit card. Maimoni drove off without paying. He decided not to take the time to look up his friend. He explained that he had taken Route 1 all the way up the coast, the scenic route to God's Country.

McCadden then switched with Trooper Jeffrey Parola, who baby-sat until the detective arrived. Two hours of chitchat ensued.

"Mr. Maimoni, we're not going to ask you any questions about any investigation that may be going on in Massachusetts. Do you understand?" Parola asked Tom.

Maimoni buried his face in his cuffed hands. "I was actually going to turn myself in when I saw the state police barracks down in Houlton. I was thinking about turning myself in."

Parola tried hard to talk about something else. "What about those Red Sox?"

They succeeded in talking about baseball for awhile. Maimoni liked the minor leagues better, it turned out. So they discussed the minors.

The trooper was on a roll with "conversation of a sports nature." "So, what about the Celtics? What do you think of the Celtics?"

"I was looking for a Catholic church, you know, before I turned myself in. But I couldn't find one."

Parola paused, then asked, "So, Tom, where do you work?" Usually a safe topic.

"Parker Brothers," responded the suspect. "But I got laid off. I lost my job and then my life went to hell."

"How do you like this hot weather we're having? Been a drought for nearly two weeks now."

"You're taking notes. Are you writing down everything I say?"

"I have to," answered the trooper. "It's my job."

"I was visiting this friend, you know, the one who owns the woodlands outside Houlton. It was two years ago, in the fall. There was this moose. The country up here is very pretty. God's

Country. I wanted to come back one more time to see God's Country before they put me away."

Trooper Parola noticed a tattoo on the suspect's left arm. He asked Tom if he had been in the military. Tom responded that he had done two tours in Vietnam and one tour in Korea. He had been an aerospace engineer for Parker Brothers and had worked on inventing Nerf toys.

Maimoni was quiet for a moment. Trooper Parola found the silence uncomfortable. There were no radio stations this far north that he could pull in to entertain them. He tried another tack.

"So...do you have a nice house?"

"Yes. I have a nice house, a condo. I have a dog, a nice dog. I have a nice wife. Nice neighbors."

The prisoner buried his face again and began to cry. "My wife had gone away for awhile. I took my neighbor's wife out, and I had...an accident. I killed my neighbor's wife! I killed my neighbor's wife!"

They sat in silence for a few moments. Then Maimoni told the trooper that he had left a note for his wife in his car. Inside was his wedding ring. "I completely freaked," he explained. "I left everything to my wife." He asked if he could get his ring back.

Parola had thought of another topic during the wait. He explained to his prisoner how Maine was undergoing financial problems at the moment. Many of them were having to take furlough days.

Maimoni perked up and asked Parola about his job, what his patrol duties were. He took an interest in this for awhile, then became somber again. "The attendant...who took my card...." Maimoni was not thinking anymore about Parola's furlough days. Maimoni was thinking about a furloughed life. "It must have been that Patti canceled them all. I'm glad she did, actually." He asked the trooper about the extradition process and about the laws on burglary in Maine. "Is there any chance I could visit a church? A Catholic church? I think I need to visit a church."

Parola had not tried hobbies or pastimes. He did now. "Tom, do you have any hobbies or pastimes? Do you like to fish and hunt? I like to fish and hunt."

Tom answered, "I like to fish."

"Where do you like to fish, Tom?"

"I like to fish on my boat."

"Oh, what kind of boat do you have?"

"A sailboat," Tom replied wistfully.

"Oh. my parents used to have a sailboat. I used to like to sail in a sailboat."

Thankfully, they were interrupted by the arrival at 5:20 of Detective Joseph Doucette. Maimoni was read the *Miranda* rights, questioned briefly about the break-in, then transported to the Washington County Jail. The silver Taurus followed on a car carrier. It was searched and inventoried at the jail. In addition to an atlas, a compass, and a knapsack, Maimoni's wedding ring was found wrapped in a note: "This car belongs to Patti Maimoni, 2 Settlers Way, Salem, Mass, 01970." Two phone numbers followed. "In Christ's name, amen," the note closed.

When Tom Maimoni arrived, he was booked, given an orange prisoner's outfit, and put on suicide watch. It was 8 P.M. The sun also sets first in Washington County.

"I Killed Her," headlined the next edition of the *Boston Herald.*

Technically speaking, the chief was already on the phone in his cabin when the "call came through." It was as if he had never gotten off. The detectives relayed the news from Maine. A smile broke out on St. Pierre's face. "Whew!" he exclaimed when he hung up.

A little to the south, the Butler family had finished their visit and were heading back home to Massachusetts. They were almost out of Maine, traveling in the southbound lane near the place where Mary had been beeped early that morning. And now, off went the beeper again! She sighed and rolled her eyes to the heavens. They probably forgot how to do a backup. The Butlers pulled over into a very familiar looking rest stop. Mary dialed the office. It was about Tom. He'd been captured.

Detective Mary Butler was elated. She climbed back into the car and they continued down the road. You Are Now Leaving the State of Maine—Come Back Soon! read the sign.

Jubilation in the detectives' office was still running rampant. Bill Jennings went down and told the reporters camping on the sidewalk that there would be an announcement in fifteen minutes. When he returned to the office, he called the home of the manager of WESX, the local radio station serving the North Shore and gave him the scoop. WESX was going on the air live with the news from the manager's house. Jennings, Prosniewski, and Dick Urbanowicz went downstairs for their news conference.

The Brailsford family was relieved and thankful for the news. Bill expressed concern that they might not be able to get Maimoni back to Massachusetts. Prosniewski assured him they would.

Lunch was over. But it was Saturday, and Julie's bar was full. The phone rang. "Honey, we got him!"

Julie put the phone down and screamed the news across the room. The entire Pig's Eye started clapping and cheering. She held the receiver out so Conrad could hear. He could indeed. He broke into a grin.

Later on Saturday afternoon, *America's Most Wanted* checked out of the Hawthorne and headed back to the West Coast.

31

Sunday evening, July 21. Friends, family, and neighbors—some 250 in number—gathered by the sea-wall on the small Willows beach to celebrate the life of Martha Brailsford. They came to say good-bye and dedicate a small garden in her memory. A mahogany plaque was set in cement in the garden of shells, flowers, beach plants, and rocks. The sandy shore was graced with baskets of wildflowers. Flags throughout the close neighborhood flew at half mast.

Hooper Goodwin the lobster man, was included and embraced by the grateful family. The press and camera crews, encamped in the neighborhood for a full week, were asked to grant them privacy. Then, one by one, mourners rose and spoke of Martha's generosity, her beauty, her spirit, her commitment.

The Willows children whom she had befriended shared a tribute of their own, reminiscing about the many special moments they had shared with the young artist. They remembered her sand castles, her first aid, her joy in her dog Rudy, her ready ear, and the hour she spent on her porch trying to fix a neighbor child's watch. One couple recalled that on the day before Martha disappeared she had convinced a child to return a jellyfish to the ocean so that it could live. A man thanked Bill and Martha for joining their neighborhood and for the beauty and love they had brought. Martha, also known for her horticultural skills, had created a garden far beyond the borders of their tiny Cove Avenue lot. Martha's garden walls were defined by the borders of her heart.

Hooper Goodwin, who had come simply to pay his respect, would leave knowing Martha was more than just a woman's face on a poster. Not by the lofty sentiments of poets and sermons, but by pure and straightforward images of those closest to her. They recalled vats of dye and silk dresses on her kitchen floor, her weaver's loom, her vegetarian lasagna. Oreo cookies. Jellyfish. Watches.

The gathering lasted a brief hour. The evening breeze and the sound of the waves on the shore served as a backdrop for numerous elegies. Interwoven with the music of Gluck, Händel, and Bach were a Navajo chant, prayers by a local pastor, excerpts from the writings of Helen Keller, and adaptations of Anne Morrow Lindbergh's *Gift from the Sea*, which asked: *"How can one learn to live through the ebb-tides of one's existence?"* And which observed that *"each cycle of the tide is valid; each cycle of a relationship is valid;"* whatever recedes will eternally return.

A week or so later, Martha's ashes were taken out to sea by those who had been closest to her. The voyage was a sad reprise of an earlier sail when Martha accompanied these same friends to scatter a beloved man's ashes. "This is how I'd like it to be," she had commented at the time. And so on the occasion of this all too familiar rite everything was the same—the boat, the flowers, the spot, the grief, even the rosy cast of sunset. The sailboat used on both trips was the one on which Bill and Martha had first met. Those aboard this time had witnessed the wheel come full circle. They would help one another face the ebb tide, which sooner or later all must accept.

32

Charged with burglary and wanted as a fugitive, Tom Maimoni was held in jail throughout the rest of the weekend. On Monday morning, July 22, he was taken to the Washington County District Courthouse in Machias, Maine, for a four-minute arraignment. The burglary charges were dropped. Looking haggard and nervous, Maimoni agreed to waive his right to fight rendition (as extradition between states is called) and to be returned to Massachusetts.

Detective Sergeant Conrad Prosniewski and State Police Sergeant Jack Garvin flew up from Beverly, Massachusetts, in a chartered plane to bring Maimoni home. They also collected a clear plastic garbage bag filled with evidence from Tom's car. Among the items located in the trunk was a vinyl-covered lead weight that matched those on the diving belt.

On Monday afternoon, Salem Detectives Dick Urbanowicz and Jim Page slipped out the back door, and into a gray, unmarked cruiser. Since it was widely known that Maimoni was due back from Maine today, one half of the media battalion was already stationed at the airport. The other half waited at police headquarters to welcome Tom home.

As the cruiser approached Kernwood Bridge into Beverly, the detectives heard the hated siren go off, signaling the bridge was about to be raised. Numerous times each day, recreational boats on either side waited impatiently for access up and down the Danvers River. But their impatience was no match for the frustration experienced by the motorists on Kernwood Avenue. Working folks fumed for ten minutes at a time while a handful of leisure craft motored in stately fashion into the harbor to play. Beers chilled in the galleys. Music gushed from the cockpits.

The hostile drivers generally took their frustration out on the bridge tender as they passed by. The hapless man who had blocked their way, who brought the summer's heat. He was the source of all the world's problems. He once described his job to a local newspaper reporter: "You know, it's not all fame and glory."

The cruiser stared down the red signal at the base of the bridge, which was just beginning to creak open. Urbanowicz growled, then joked. "Doesn't he know how important we are?" Page was driving. They had rolled to a stop. "Screw this!" Urbanowicz declared. He ordered Page to floor the pedal. They squealed past the bridge tender.

"Hey!" yelled the man. "Hey!"

Urbanowicz responded by giving the cruiser's siren a quick pop. "Doesn't he know we're gonna go get *Maimoni?*"

When they arrived at Beverly Airport, they waited with the camera crews for an hour before the plane bearing their prisoner arrived. The single-engined Beechcraft Bonanza touched down a little after four. As the shackled prisoner was maneuvered awkwardly out of the tiny aircraft and rushed to the waiting police car, an optimistic reporter managed to ask if he wished to make a statement. "No," replied Maimoni.

After she had booked and fingerprinted him, Detective Mary Butler took the first shift watching their new prisoner. Tom was lodged in women's cell number one at the Salem police station overnight. It was easier to have someone on a suicide watch in the women's cells. The men's quarters were cramped and noisy. Hardly enough room to throw a chair. And a female officer would have to endure commentary from the neighboring cells all night long.

Shortly after the prisoner had settled in, Captain Murphy fetched him a chicken salad sandwich from Red's, next door to the station. Word on the bail came back, and Mary Butler was informed that it had been set at two million dollars until his arraignment the following morning. "Your bail has been set for two million dollars," she conveyed to her ward.

"Two million dollars?" Tom asked. "Do you think they'll take a check?" He leaned back on his cement bunk. He clearly was impressed. "Two million dollars. No wonder there's so much media attention on this." This observation puzzled Mary, who had thought the media attention had something to do with the death of a well-loved and loving woman. After a time, Tom announced, "I've made my peace with God." Then he asked to make a couple of phone calls, possibly to make peace with some of the rest: his mother, a friend, his lawyer. His lawyer, Tom later told Mary, wanted a retainer of $75,000. "Seventy-five thousand dollars! My last name's not Kennedy!"

Later on Monday evening, Patti Maimoni came down to the station with clean clothes for Tom's arraignment. The detectives arranged to give them a few moments to talk in private up in the guard room. Husband and wife sat across from each other at a small table. Patti wore a pretty flowered sundress. Tom wore the same pullover red shirt and Bermuda shorts he had worn upon his capture two days earlier. He had shaved off his mustache on the run, as Laurie Cabot had predicted. Now his three-day stubble gave him a whole new look.

Mary Butler and Prosniewski hovered near the door to give the pair some privacy. Tom and Patti talked for about ten minutes—Tom in a businesslike tone, Patti visibly upset. After a while, Patti reached down, removed her wedding ring, and placed it in the middle of the table. Shortly thereafter, she rose and came to the door. "I'm done," she said, concluding her last conversation with the husband she had considered a superstar.

At Salem District Court on Tuesday morning, the restless audience that packed Judge Bonnie MacLeod-Griffin's courtroom was treated to a normal stream of minor offenders, continuances, and arraignments for more than two hours after news cameras heralded the backdoor entrance of Thomas Maimoni. More than 200 pairs of vigilant eyes monitored the doors for his emergence. If ever there was a time *not* to appear in court for a motor vehicle violation, July 23, 1991, was it.

As the judge went through the morning list, the defendant met downstairs with his court-appointed lawyer Hugh Samson and submitted to a routine psychiatric evaluation. Maimoni had been declared indigent, having no job, heavy debts, and little savings. What few assets he owned he was arranging to transfer to his wife.

All eight Salem police detectives had come to court wearing suits and ties for Maimoni's arraignment and had assembled in the front row behind prosecutor Kevin Mitchell. After Maimoni had been led into the courtroom, Mitchell stood and read the murder charge in a loud voice and heavy Boston accent. He then described for the judge what the Commonwealth would establish regarding the events leading to and following the death of Martha Brailsford. Mitchell implored the judge to allow no bail in view of the defendant's flight from justice. "This is not an individual for whom any amount of bail should be set."

Dr. David Swenson, court psychiatrist, testified that during this morning's examination Thomas Maimoni had been oriented to time, person, and place. His ability to recall and think abstractly were intact. He appeared to understand the functions of a judge and jury and to have sufficient trust in his defense attorney. He denied having any overt suicidal feelings. Dr. Swenson felt that he was capable of consulting with his attorney and of assisting in his own defense. Thomas Maimoni, unshaven and wearing a pink striped shirt and dark pants, was declared competent to stand trial.

Hugh Samson entered a plea of not guilty on behalf of his client. Standing slightly hunched in the Plexiglas prisoner's dock, the defendant listened intently, biting his lip occasionally. He showed little emotion during the proceedings. Judge MacLeod-Griffin ordered the defendant held without bail.

Outside the courtroom the attorneys were interviewed. Samson described his first meeting with Maimoni during the hour before the arraignment. "He has a great deal of faith in the Catholic Church and in nature," Samson related. Tom had quoted excerpts from Thoreau during their meeting. Samson also stated that his client was extremely nervous, that he was concerned about his wife's welfare, and that an insanity defense was not being considered at this time.

Kevin Mitchell would next seek a grand jury indictment the following week, thereby moving the case to the jurisdiction of Salem Superior Court. In the meantime, the investigation could now move into the next phase. Could the state put together a strong enough case to convict this man?

Bill Brailsford also filed a wrongful death suit against the suspect, claiming loss of consortium, companionship, and affection. The lawsuit alleged that Maimoni had "intentionally, negligently, carelessly, and unlawfully" caused the death of Brailsford's wife. Later on Tuesday afternoon, a judge in Salem Superior Court issued a million-dollar attachment on all assets (including real estate belonging to Thomas Maimoni) when Brailsford's attorney learned that Tom was transferring everything to Patti and was declaring indigency.

33

The new-man unit at the Essex County Correctional Facility in Middleton was full on the evening of July 23. Middleton was taking in anywhere from twenty to fifty new commitments each day. Prisoners trickled in well into the night. Twenty to fifty guys to book, dress, and find a place to sleep. Tom Maimoni was led through the intake process, was issued an orange uniform designating him as a pre-trial inmate, and was taken to the segregation unit where the overflow newcomers temporarily slept. He was given a sheet, a towel, and a few toiletries.

Middleton is a county facility. Most inmates there are serving sentences of two and a half years or less, or they are awaiting trial. Some are moved to Middleton for their own protection, or due to overcrowding elsewhere, or to await reclassification. Others are there to wrap up the last eighteen months of a stiffer sentence. Serving county time doesn't have the status that serving state time has. County facilities are frequently assumed to house a safer population. But in fact the opposite is true. Even career criminals and mass murderers have to await their trials somewhere. They wait in Middleton. Inside, the county jail is known as a proving ground for inmates. As they like to put it, when guys ultimately go to the state system, "they go wearing a dress or wearing pants."

If they're dangerous, suicidal, child molesters, or ex-cops, inmates are housed in the sixty-bed "seg" unit, along with those segregated for purposes of punishment. In segregation men normally wear red or maroon uniforms and remain alone in their cells twenty-three hours a day. The doors are of solid steel, with a narrow glass window and a small slot for food. Each cell has an exterior window with bars. The glass pane can be opened as long as an inmate doesn't lose this privilege through misbehavior. On hot summer days, the door slots are parked open to tease an occasional breeze through the eight-by-ten foot space. Every man gets one hour a day in the common area by himself, under the watchful eye of a guard in black uniform.

There is no communication among inmates in segregation. No news, no TV. Yet during Maimoni's first night at Middleton, a careful plan somehow managed to orchestrate itself out of thin air. At precisely 7:00 on the morning of July 24th, as mystified guards looked on, fifty-nine food slots opened up. A chorus of baritone voices began to serenade Thomas Maimoni with a husky, if slightly off-key, rendition of "Anchors Away."

The late morning sun was already oppressive when Kitty Babakian slipped into the water behind the townhouses at Collins Cove. The ocean here was shallow but cold. She waded out up to her neck. The lowest curls of her short black hair brushed the surface. When the initial shock had passed, when her body and the sea's temperature had reached a happy reconciliation, Kitty turned around to study the condos as she treaded water. The sunlight reflected off the sliding glass doors at the back of 2 Settlers Way. The interior was impenetrable to prying eyes.

"Here I am in this water," she mused, "and he's somewhere in a jail cell." She felt strange. Not exactly lucky, just strange. She didn't know him well enough to feel more. Her own encounters at the condos with Tom Maimoni, including her refusal to sail, had been brief and uneventful. But the week's events had pulled her to the fringes of notoriety. "Fun-loving Tom," Kitty's father still referred to him. Except for her slight celebrity status among her close friends and family, the farthest side of the fringe was where she wanted to stay. Big event. Small, small part. Just enough to feel a chill, and to shake her head and wonder at the strange paths life can take.

The week after she had last spotted Tom—as he was walking with the angelic blonde woman—Kitty spent a few days on Plum Island, up the coast of Massachusetts. On her return, she found posters of a missing blonde woman all along her waterside route through Salem. She hadn't made the connection when she first saw the posters. But she did make the connection when told of the man responsible for the woman's death. With the rest of the North Shore, Kitty followed with shock as the manhunt progressed, ending finally in the capture and arraignment of the suspect. Fun-loving Tom? She would later write:

I bathed and sunned at the little beach below his condo that summer, and the summer after, and I couldn't help feeling gleeful that the handsome prepossessing condo owner was in jail, and myself, the squatter, was enjoying the sea.

When the local papers asked women who had been approached by Tom Maimoni to contact Salem police, Kitty didn't feel she had anything to contribute. So she never phoned. Besides, people were calling Tom a sociopath. She felt just a little bad for him, suspecting that maybe she had a few sociopathic tendencies herself.

34

Attorney Kevin Mitchell was born in Boston of immigrant Irish parents "right off the boat." When he was fresh out of law school, he began working as a prosecutor, preferring to represent the Commonwealth rather than undergo the particular emotional commitment called for in a defense. Mitchell loved trial work and was lucky enough to move into superior court in his second year of practicing law. Now in his fourteenth year and twenty-five murder cases later, Kevin Mitchell won an indictment for first-degree murder against Thomas J. Maimoni on July 31 from a twenty-three-member Essex County grand jury.

That same day, in the probate court next door, a joint petition for divorce was filed on behalf of Thomas and Patricia Maimoni citing irretrievable breakdown of the three-year marriage. Listed assets included their condo at the Willows, a car, and *Counterpoint*. Liabilities amounted to over $200,000.

Meanwhile, the police were continuing the investigation to assist in putting together the case against Tom Maimoni. *Counterpoint* was videotaped inside and out and was returned to Patti Maimoni in late July. On the hull, detectives noted that the layer of growth normally found on boats had been disturbed recently by a few hasty brush strokes. Had Maimoni tried to clean off something in particular? It was not his usual, meticulous job.

Tom's laptop computer was studied, and then returned. Nothing incriminating in the files. The detectives also uncovered the names of his three previous wives, all alive. And a couple of kids, too. On each new marriage certificate, Maimoni had listed only one prior marriage and had declared that he was widowed. Two divorce records listed "cruel and abusive treatment" as the official cause.

Authorities also discovered on closer examination that Tom Maimoni's whole life had begun to unravel along with the dead wife story. The certified scuba diver patch Tom had displayed in his bedroom had no actual certification to back it up. Degrees held, education completed, prior job experience, even his war stories, had turned out to be largely fictitious. Boston University had never heard of Tom. Nor the Rhode Island School of Design. A couple of evening courses had turned up. But basically all he had obtained was a high school diploma. The brilliant aerospace engineer his wife thought he had been, he was not.

By constructing a world defense experts would later describe as "a Walter Mitty existence," Tom Maimoni protected himself with deceit and self-delusion. He would later list two modes of existence: "business" mode and "emergency" mode. But there was also his "magical" mode. In the labyrinth of Tom's mind, the path of reality led in many directions.

One of the inmates at the Middleton House of Correction stuck his head into cell 733. Inside, a slightly built, dark-haired young man called B. C. lay on his bunk nursing a cup of ice to ward off the heat.

"You got the anchor man," the inmate announced.

B. C. glanced up at him. He looked a little ambivalent at this news. "Now, don't get me wrong, but I don't want to get locked up with any nut."

"He's harmless," the inmate reassured him.

Tom was no nut. In fact, the two soon got along well when Tom was reassigned to cell 733. B. C., who was no stranger to the system, learned this was Tom's first time behind bars. Tom was understandably scared, so B. C., feeling sorry for the guy, expounded a bit on jailhouse survival techniques. "Do your time, don't let your time do you," he explained.

"What are you in here for?" Tom asked his new roommate.

"I was only out like a month, and they framed me for armed robbery. What about you?"

"They're trying to frame me for first-degree murder," said Tom. "I had an accident on my boat." He described how his beautiful neighbor happened to be on his boat and happened to hit her head and go over.

"How they gonna pin murder one on you?" asked B. C. incredulously.

"Well, there was the small matter of the anchor."

With the indictment, jurisdiction was transferred to Superior Court. Maimoni was arraigned once again in a crowded court-room with a full assembly of press and TV cameras on August 2, 1991. Two electric fans, strategically directed at the court officers, did little to dispel the oppressive August heat. The pre-1900 room, with its high ceiling and tall windows, was neither air-conditioned nor acoustically designed. Finally reporters in the press box, only five feet from the witness stand, complained that they couldn't hear anything. Other than cooling the court officers, the electric fans only served to drown out the proceedings.

The judge ordered the fans shut off. Maimoni's attorney Hugh Samson filed two motions. The first was to request $1,000 from the court for the services of a private investigator. The second request was that the names and addresses of prosecution witnesses be disclosed by the end of the day, particularly those of women who claimed they had been lured aboard *Counterpoint*. Samson told the press that the only thing his client was guilty of was panic and stupidity in "trying to cover up that someone died on his boat."

At his next court appearance on Friday, August 9, Thomas Maimoni's lawyer Hugh Samson—considered by his peers to be one of the finest defense attorneys in the county—stepped down as counsel for the defense. A newly retained criminal lawyer from Newton, Massachusetts, Jeffrey A. Denner, took over the case. Maimoni had contacted Denner from prison after obtaining his name from a fellow inmate. The new counsel requested the case be continued until September to give him time to prepare.

Afterward, on the courthouse steps, Denner told the press that although Maimoni now professed indigence, family and friends were coming forward with a defense fund in order to secure private counsel. The fund never materialized, however, and Denner ended up representing Maimoni on a pro bono basis.

Attorney Denner further informed reporters the thrust of his defense would be that a tragic accident had occurred on the night of July 12, and that his client might possibly have suffered post-traumatic stress disorder, causing him to panic during his sub-sequent actions. Describing the distress his client was experiencing over this "tragedy," Denner announced "life as he knew it no longer existed for Tom." When this showed up in the papers, readers responded by pointing out the same could be said for Martha Brailsford.

35

The job of the state was threefold: identify the murderer, catch the murderer, and finally put him behind bars. The first two having been accomplished, the most difficult part lay ahead. The state had now to prove Tom Maimoni's guilt to a jury. In the words of Assistant District Attorney Kevin Mitchell, assigned to try this one, "It's a whole different case in the courtroom."

It is an unfortunate fact that the guilty often go free. Just because a crime has been committed does not always mean that sufficient evidence has been left behind to prove it. This is not necessarily a reflection of the abilities of the investigators, the prosecution, the judge, or the jury. They could all be top-notch. The criminal simply may have left no traces.

Whatever happened aboard *Counterpoint* on July 12, 1991, it was clear that Tom Maimoni probably had spent the next twenty-four hours ensuring that no evidence remained. Since he was compulsive about his boat, the extraordinary amount of cleaning he did raised no eyebrows at the yacht club. The state essentially was left with two pieces of physical evidence: a few spatters of blood on the mainsail and a skeleton, which made very clear what happened *after* the event but shed no light on what had happened *during* the event. Kevin Mitchell worried that for lack of evidence Tom Maimoni just might get off.

And so in August 1991 and the months to follow, the investigation continued in earnest. Without knowing what would be stipulated in the trial, what would be Maimoni's final story and ultimate defense, the prosecution could leave nothing to chance. Every point they wanted to make to the jury had to be backed up by witnesses. Jennifer, the hitchhiker from Rhode Island, was interviewed. So, too, was every other woman who had called about an encounter with Tom.

Police talked to each of Maimoni's past wives. Prosniewski drove down to Rhode Island to visit Mary Cayer, whom Tom married fresh out of high school before joining the military. With Mary, Tom fathered two kids. After his discharge, however, the marriage fell apart.

Subsequently, Maimoni married Mary Ellen Bouchie. Although Tom later looked back at those years as some of his happiest, they were not long-lived. Mary Ellen left Tom after six months. Apparently, this was the breakup that had devastated him most.

It took a lot of digging and phone calls before Prosniewski managed to track down this wife. She had moved to Florida and was living under her new married name. Finally he was able to reach her by phone. The woman sounded scared but talked freely.

Mary Ellen was the wife who *did* in fact have cancer. However, she survived, no thanks to Tom. She told Prosniewski over the phone that Tom was remarkably unsupportive during her treatment. Their life together was not easy. He not only had bad credit, but also owed back taxes and child support. Mary Ellen had done some digging herself and had uncovered many of Tom's lies. She also described Tom as having a violent temper and a desperate need to control. Tom constantly told her she was worthless. He yelled at her when she disagreed with him in front of others. He twisted her arm as they were walking if she got a step ahead of him. During one argument, he threw a wrench at her. Had she not ducked, she'd now be dead. Mary Ellen feared Tom constantly.

During the conversation, Mary Ellen told Prosniewski that Tom had once beaten and raped her. However, when police later flew down to Florida to take a statement from her, she changed her mind about getting involved. Everything she had told him on the phone she now "forgot." Although a friend of hers corroborated everything in the original statement, the prosecution figured there was no point in trying to put an unwilling and scared witness on the stand.

Maimoni's third wife was Linda Lee Webb, who told police

their rocky marriage was due in part to her own bout with alcoholism. She, too, felt Tom had treated her like "shit." Tom had belittled her. Though she had paid for a boat for him, he wouldn't let her touch it.

The Salem detectives called the rest of the employers Maimoni had listed on his multiple résumés. Some indicated that the nature or level of his job with them was overstated. Maimoni had worked at GE Sylvania, but only as a contract employee, not as an aerospace engineer. Some told the police that Maimoni had been let go because he couldn't do the work for which he was hired.

"I always knew there was something about him. Some hole in his background," said one fellow employee to police, perhaps with the benefit of hindsight. "He'd usually end up getting the job done, but he'd go off to do it. Not in front of you. He never bounced ideas around with us."

Others said he was fired because of "contentious behavior" or due to arguments with other employees. At work some women found him to be condescending. Sources at Parker Brothers hinted that an argument with another female employee lay behind his firing. A neighbor offered a rumor, never verified, that a woman at one of Maimoni's previous jobs had ended up missing as well. Another source claimed it was his previous girlfriend who had disappeared and had never been found. It was the job of the police to wade through this churning of stories and to determine what was fact, what was outrage.

The police studied army records. They obtained copies of the harbormasters' log pages. They conducted more dives off Cat Island. A second weight belt was found. And a sock. Neither seemed to be connected.

Prosniewski went out with Hooper Goodwin and photographed a reenactment of the lobsterman hauling in the trap and anchor. They photographed the views from all points around Cat Island, including some from the air.

The detective constructed a timeline of every confirmed sighting of Martha and *Counterpoint* on Friday, July 12. He placed a pin representing each one on a nautical map mounted on the office wall. The last witness to positively ID Martha that afternoon was a man named Stephen Porter, a commercial diver for a marine construction company who had been working on a barge near the entrance of Manchester Harbor, six miles northeast of Salem. He also happened, coincidentally, to know Martha well. Porter noticed *Counterpoint* pass by between one and two-thirty, just thirty feet from his barge, close enough to clearly recognize Martha Brailsford on board. Porter said the day had been sunny and calm—a knot or two of wind, the sea as smooth as glass. When he spotted Martha, she was standing on the port side of the deck, holding onto one of the shrouds, the wires which secure the mast. The sails were down. The boat was motoring into the harbor. Porter called out to Martha, but she hadn't seen or heard him.

Another caller had spotted the boat in the Gloucester area later that Friday afternoon. Although he didn't remember how many people were on deck, he recalled the name of the boat clearly. Hillary Smart was a former Olympic gold medalist from the Star Class of 1948 and had enjoyed a fifty-year racing career. During the summer of 1991, he sailed his forty-four-foot Little Harbor sailboat out of Eastern Point Yacht Club in Gloucester. On the afternoon of July 12, Smart was powering his boat from Eastern Point to Manchester Harbor, approximately seven miles down the coast, sometime between four and six P.M. As he normally did when he sailed, he noted the names of boats he passed. He liked to see what sorts of things people called their boats and from where they hailed. As he neared House Island just outside Manchester Harbor, he passed a boat, also under power, with a name that intrigued him: *Counterpoint*. He felt it was an excellent name, referring to the "counteraction of work and play in sailing." He loved Bach, famous for using *counterpoint* in his music, the "action and reaction" also found in Dixieland jazz. Smart hadn't paid much attention to the occupants but felt there might have been two. He thought the other boat was going out to sea. It was near the "spindle", the rocks off House Island, maybe 50 to a 100 feet away. It probably had been close to five, to the best of his recollection, though it could have been a little earlier or a little later. Five days later he saw the boat on television and called the police.

Actually, there were three sailboats on the North Shore in 1991 with the name *Counterpoint*, two of them Cal 28s. Nevertheless, Prosniewski stuck another pin on his map.

36

Ray Mount had seen the news on TV. Initially, he had hesitated going to the police when he first heard the name *Counterpoint* broadcast. Speak up against a fellow sailor? A member of your own club? He wasn't sure he wanted to involve himself in the discomfort, inconvenience, and publicity of a police investigation. He wasn't sure he wanted to face Tom Maimoni in a courtroom. Many people would opt out under these circumstances.

But just before the body was found, the papers had printed Tom's story about being out all night searching for Martha. Ray Mount kept remembering the wet suit hanging in the cockpit. He remembered the day and the time. It didn't jibe with Tom's timeline. Just to be sure, Mount checked his appointment book for Friday, July 12. The afternoon had been clear of appointments so that he could sail. Then he called Charlene. Charlene was compulsive about logging her dives—dates, times, spots, conditions. She confirmed they had gone out Friday. The following day had been rainy and miserable. They wouldn't have gone out Saturday.

Mount finally decided to go to the police. A human life had been involved. Mount felt an obligation to help.

With a smile, Prosniewski reached for another pushpin. This one directly refuted Maimoni's last story to police. This one would be wonderful on the witness stand.

Police talked twice to the nurse who had reported the scream in the night. She stated that the screams she heard around sundown were from the same boat she had seen off and on that afternoon, until its disappearance around eight. From the deck of her patient's waterfront house, the nurse and her assistant had been watching boats through powerful binoculars during breaks in their three to eleven shift. The boat in question was a white sailboat, Boston clearly visible on the stern beneath the name. Shortly after four-thirty, the boat dropped anchor next to a channel marker about a half mile away, in full view of the nurse's location on Fuller Lane. Two people were visible on deck. The nurse heard an argument, escalating into yelling and screaming, which went on for nearly an hour. The sounds carried over the water.

During this time, the patient required constant attention. The nurse remained busy for the rest of the shift, interrupted only by the chilling screams just after eight. She beckoned for her partner to come and listen, but then there was only silence. In the waning light of evening, the boat turned on its running lights and headed northeast toward Cat Island, a mile out to sea. Her first opportunity to call police came only after her shift had ended.

Prosniewski listened to the nurse's story carefully. He added her name to the list of possible sightings, but since the identification of the boat was not as positive as Ray Mount's had been, he concluded that the nurse's boat could not have been *Counterpoint*.

Calls came in for months from people who had known Maimoni or had tidbits to offer the police. One woman called who had heard from her niece, who in turn had heard from a prison guard, that Tom planned to claim that Martha had been bitten by a mosquito on the boat, had suffered a severe reaction, and had died as a result. A fellow employee at one of his jobs came in with a fistful of Tom's résumés, job applications, and other paperwork. "I knew there was something funny going on," he told Prosniewski. "Maybe these will help you." It was a paper trail of Tom Maimoni's deceit.

Investigators also turned up people who spoke well of Maimoni. One coworker felt Tom had been a pretty good engineer. He also swore Tom had never lied to him. Many others, neighbors and acquaintances, said he was a nice guy. Some related how good he had been to Patti's handicapped students, who on occasion went out on the boat with them. At PCYC he was well known for an incident in which he had taken responsibility for saving a small hooded seal that crawled up on one of the docks one day. The animal appeared to be sick. Maimoni notified the Boston Aquarium, then watched over the seal until aquarium staff arrived to rescue it. Tom Maimoni's profile varied with each person the police interviewed.

Tom Maimoni kept himself busy in Middleton by reading the Bible, trimming his weight, and writing letters. From his cell he could see the stacks of the New England Power plant at Salem Willows, only eight miles away. The plant was one short block from his Collins Cove condo and just down the street from Salem Willows Park. The tall stacks with flashing red lights were visible for forty miles on a clear day, Beacons for planes landing at Logan Airport. Beacons for Maimoni's home and the life to which he could never return.

In a series of letters he wrote to his wife Patti, Tom attempted to lay out the truth. A bit more truth in each letter: his education, his past marriages, his motivations, and finally his undying love for her.

> *I am very lonesome and I cry all the time. The media has made a monster out of me. I know that you don't believe them. The mistakes and errors that I've made and secrets that I held from you, I am sorry. You saw the best in me at times and I believe you know my capabilities and strengths. In time I would have opened up and told you all these secrets after I let you see the good side of me. I just didn't want to be judged by those issues alone. I wanted you to love me, that's all I ever wanted.*

She did not reply. Each night the red lights of the Salem stacks blinked on and off quietly. On and off, on and off.

37

It was a Friday morning late in the summer of 1991. Dr. Benjamin Polan routinely took Fridays off from his dental practice in Salem. On this occasion, he headed up Route 62 from Danvers to the neighboring town of Middleton, home of the county's new jail. It was less than ten minutes from his own front door to the turnoff at the front gate. Dr. Polan pulled in to a stop. He read the sign three or four times: Essex County Correctional Facility and Sheriff's Headquarters.

Dr. Polan was two things. He was the former Essex County Dentist, meaning that while the jail was still located in Salem, he had the contract to do rudimentary dental work for the inmates. The Salem jail had no dental chair. So one by one, the shackled prisoners were taken in to Polan's Federal Street office, positioned in the dentist's chair, and tilted back. An armed state trooper stood guard by the door as the dentist readied his instruments. Since the county wouldn't authorize any other work if simple extraction was cheaper, Dr. Polan was normally expected to pull the inmates' teeth. Only the tiniest fillings were justified.

Front teeth were an issue. Knowing how hard it was for an inmate to get a job missing front teeth upon release, Dr. Polan took pity in these cases. He went ahead and filled the cavities, and just billed the county for an extraction. This man, who cast his vote during televised Miss America Pageants by how the contestants' teeth looked during the close-up singing shots, believed recidivism often came down to the quality of dental care an inmate received.

Dr. Polan scheduled the county cases only on his days off, preferring to keep the shackled patients separate from his unshackled ones. Though the scene on Fridays played out the worst dental chair nightmares, for most prisoners this was the only dental care they would know. Many seasoned criminals look on the bright side of their sentence: you get new shoes and you get your teeth fixed.

But the reason Ben Polan had come to Middleton that day was not to do dentistry. For the past three years or so, two of his patients had been Tom and Patti Maimoni. Polan had known them since the early days of their marriage, when the couple moved into an apartment complex on Federal Street next to his office. When they sought out a local dentist, Polan was convenient. The Maimonis were friendly, punctual, and conscientious. They also liked to chat and soon found much in common with their neighbor. All three liked to ski, and at one point Polan offered the Maimonis the use of his vacation condo near the slopes at Sunday River in Bethel, Maine. Tom talked about Vietnam, about his job at Parker Brothers, about engineering, about looking for a bigger house, and much more. Patti talked about special education and about the Carlton School. The two came to their dentist appointments together. Polan saw them hand in hand on the street or in the local stores. Patti told her dentist later that Tom had never laid a hand on her, never had so much as raised his voice.

The perfect couple—two decent, warm, caring folks. Ben Polan could not believe Tom Maimoni was in jail charged with murder one. Polan followed the events as they unfolded in the press and discussed every news item with his staff. He was obsessed with the case and with reconciling the man on the TV with the man he had known. With his engine running, Polan surveyed the ominous complex of white buildings, the high walls, the concertina wire. He read the sign once more: Essex County Correctional Facility and Sheriff's Headquarters. The dentist had come for one reason, to sit face to face with his friend and ask, "Tom, did you do it? Did you do it?"

But he couldn't bring himself to go in. What if Tom should refuse to see him? Or worse, what if he didn't refuse? Ben Polan couldn't face this gaunt, beaten, joyless man who would destroy his memory of the other Tom. His intended question was pointless, yet there was nothing else to talk about. Polan turned around in the parking lot and drove back home to Danvers. His impulse to visit never returned.

Maimoni and his cellmate were listening as Hurricane Bob roared outside their window, battering New England in its wake. Maimoni stared out through the glass at the driving rain. "I wonder if my boat's sunk," he murmured.

"Why do you care?" asked his roommate. "Don't you have insurance?"

Maimoni settled back on his bed and looked at the ceiling. "Anyway, it's the police's problem now. They're responsible for it." After a pause he added, "Maybe it would be the best thing if it did sink."

B. C. looked over at him. "Why?"

The anchorman closed his eyes. His words were nearly drowned out by the constant slap of water against the panes. "Because...then any evidence will wash away."

38

A couple of months into the investigation, Prosniewski sat down in the CID office to reorganize the boxes of evidence. Some of the stuff they had seized needed to be returned to Patti Maimoni, whose lawyer had requested the items be given back as soon as possible. Captain Paul Murphy had come to the office and sat nearby, chatting with the detective about the progress of the case.

As they talked, Prosniewski looked around for a map to illustrate a point he was making, any old map showing the Salem shoreline. Rolled up in front of him was Maimoni's chart book, sticking out of one of the boxes. That'll do, he thought, and reached over to yank it out. The detective opened it up to the page showing Salem and Marblehead waters. As they scanned the chart, their glances fell upon Cat Island, just off the shoreline. Simultaneously, the two looked at each other.

"You gotta be kidding me! Do you see what I see?" Prosniewski exclaimed.

To the right of the island was a small blue *X* in a circle, handwritten and totally missed during the initial perusal. Yet why would anyone have noticed it before? When the chart book was found, there was no significance to Cat Island, or even to that page, other than that the chart book had been open to that particular map at the time. What murderer would be nutty enough to mark an *X* on the spot where he had hidden the body?

Then leave his book open to that area? Then give police permission to have the boat searched?

Of course, what juror in their right mind would believe this evidence? The detective reached for his phone and dialed the DA's office. "Time to call Kevin," he said to Murphy. "He's sure not going to buy this one!"

Mitchell told the detective to bring the chart book over right away. Prosniewski rolled it up, tucked it under his arm, and set out the two short blocks to the district attorney's office.

By the time the detective arrived, a small crowd had gathered around Mitchell's desk and was waiting for him. Prosniewski rolled out the map so that all could see his great discovery.

"Yeah, right!" was the general response. "Three months afterward, Conrad happens to find an X on the spot." There was laughter all around. "Let's see your pen, Connie. So what color is it?"

Prosniewski swore up and down he hadn't touched it. "It was locked up! I swear!"

Mitchell just shook his head. Too bizarre, this case. "I can just hear Jeff Denner now."

39

One afternoon in mid-September, Jennifer Eccleston, the Rhode Island hitchhiker, found herself in South Providence badly needing drugs. Unfortunately, she had left her purse at home. So she decided to rob a liquor store. Unfortunately, she had no gun. What Jennifer lacked in arms she made up for in guts. It took guts to walk into a place, point a finger at the cashier, and demand money. And it was testimony to Jennifer's powers of persuasion that the woman behind the cash register opened up the drawer and proceeded to stuff bills into Jennifer's hands. "No, no," said Eccleston. "I didn't mean *that* much." She left most of it on the counter and ran out the door.

Once outside she stopped and began to sob. "Don't call the police! Please don't call the police!" Jennifer dropped the money on the sidewalk and sunk to her knees. She clutched her arms and felt the soft sleeves of the sumptuous sweater she was wearing. Her brother had just bought it for her a few hours earlier. They had been staggering around nearby Wakefield from dive to dive and he was just drunk enough to have become concerned about her attire. "Look at you!" he had said. So they had ducked into Kenyon's Department Store, where he bought her this $100 cashmere sweater, patterned with maple leaves in muted fall colors and adorned with silver buttons. Now she sought solace in its embrace. God, how she missed her mother. She looked around. She couldn't remember where she had left her brother.

Then the police arrived. Jennifer spent the night in the holding cell at the Providence police station. She was the only prisoner wearing cashmere.

Meanwhile, during the fall of 1991, the prosecution complied with defense requests for names and addresses of three female witnesses Tom had approached back in July. Jennifer Eccleston ended up serving a ninety-day jail term that ended in early December 1991. Thereafter she returned home to confront the fact that she was an addict and an alcoholic and to start her first attempt at recovery. Three days after her return, she received a letter from Tom Maimoni, written from Middleton. Full name spelled out, correct address. How had the man come by this information? It was just a chatty Christmas card. But Jennifer felt the unspoken message, brief and terrifying, might be to keep her from testifying. *I know who you are and where you live,* she sensed he was telling her. Horrified, Jennifer stuffed it into an envelope and forwarded it to Detective Conrad Prosniewski in Salem.

A short time later, Kevin Mitchell addressed the court in another trial. As he spoke, one of his state police investigators, Cpl. Jack Garvin, slipped into the courtroom and took a seat behind the prosecutor's table. Mitchell noticed him come in and fought to concentrate on his words to the judge. What the hell was Garvin doing here?

Finally, a break came in the proceedings. Mitchell turned around to see what Garvin wanted. The investigator smiled and said, "I got something for you." Garvin handed a photograph to the assistant district attorney. "Brian took this picture the night we searched the boat," said Garvin. Brian O'Hara had been the CPAC photographer. The photo was of Maimoni's chart book spread open in the cabin, just as they had found it. Garvin pointed to the spot that was Cat Island.

Mitchell let out a laugh of amazement, causing a few heads to turn in the courtroom. There, clear as day, was the X that Prosniewski had found written on the map. Proof it had existed on July 16, 1991, two days before the body was discovered at that location. If police had planted this mark, they were indeed clairvoyant.

Back at Middleton, Maimoni didn't have many visitors other than his parents and a couple of people working with Denner. But he did have B. C. One night they discussed the incident again, as Tom often did.

"So, were you guys doing drugs when it happened? Were you drinking?" asked his cellmate.

"No. I don't allow booze on my boat."

B. C. thought this over. "Too bad. That could have explained how she fell off."

Maimoni gave this point some consideration. After that, his story changed. Martha had taken care of herself during the sail, he would say. She had taken a drink, maybe two. With her small body weight, and the heat....

"What happened to her clothes?" B. C. continued. Tom's case was far more interesting than his own.

His cellmate answered, "I threw them overboard. They were all ripped up. I didn't want any evidence she had been on my boat."

40

Kitty Babakian, who had once declined to sail with Maimoni, was enduring the winter with growing depression. Winters were never happy times for this woman, who walked around Salem daily and who swam in Collins Cove five months of the year. Too little sunlight during this season. Her psyche withered as earlier and earlier sunsets robbed the northeast of its precious days, leaving behind numbing cold nights. After four years in Salem, she still felt adrift at sea. No anchors, no roots, no car.

The lack of light was only a part of her misery. The extensive publicity surrounding the upcoming Maimoni trial disturbed her. Life was now polarized. On one hand was Tom Maimoni, evil incarnate. On the other was everyone else, all the "good people." In part, she felt Tom had been a man in the wrong spot at the wrong moment in a situation he probably couldn't handle. He probably *had* done something very stupid. Yet who among them could know exactly what had transpired aboard *Counterpoint?* Who among them had earned the excessive self-righteousness that had rolled through Salem like sea fog?

Kitty later wrote: *In the winter, the god awful North Shore winter, battened down in my smelly two room apartment, watching the peculiar righteousness of the TV news, it struck me that my moral response did not mesh with that of society, and that I was in Hell.*

In counterpoint to the Maimoni case, Kitty was having a

difficult period with her parents this winter. Her small Irish mother was in the late stages of Alzheimer's. Kitty frequently took the train down to Winchester to be with her. Kitty could do nothing for her and felt increasingly helpless. The two sat together, each wondering who the other had become.

Meanwhile, Martha Brailsford's compassion and goodness were broadcast on the nightly news. In contrast, Kitty Babakian felt more like a "bad woman" and lamented that good women died while bad women lived on. More and more she felt mentally ill, just as Salem's citizens were scorning Maimoni's proposed defense that he himself suffered mental illness. The line between crazy and bad was becoming blurred. Kitty Babakian stopped walking through Salem, except to her work. She prayed no one would recognize her or greet her. She lost weight she didn't have. She brooded over her own perceived lack of compassion as the woman who wasn't caring enough to sail with a lonely widower:

I stayed shut up until Spring, mourning because I couldn't think of anyone to testify to the papers that I had been loving and good. I'd become a bad one in my thoughts. For months I measured myself by the hardening media view that the criminal and crazy were one.

41

And the justice of the holy court
Will show its terror of our sport,
And the powers of this world resort
To the whims of little girls.

I But a Little Girl
Bob Franke

Many in Salem still mourned the loss of Martha Brailsford. Each new season without her, however, took them further along in the cycle of healing. But as 1992 got underway, the city tried to heal another painful tragedy. This one had roots both deep and wide.

Church bells began to toll across Essex County at 3 P.M. on March 1, 1992, for the souls of the victims of Salem's darkest moment in history. Three minutes of continuous bell-ringing marked the official beginning of the county's tercentenary, 300-year anniversary, of the witchcraft hysteria of 1692. The events that had led to the deaths of twenty men and women on Salem's Gallows Hill continues to hold mystery, controversy, and fascination for curious tourists and scholars alike.

On March 1, 1692, the shocking accusations of a handful of adolescent girls culminated in the first of numerous witchcraft trials in Salem. Spectral evidence, fear, and intolerance constituted the burden of proof in such dark times. The accused were charged with consorting with the Devil. The accused allegedly had bitten, pinched, and inflicted mysterious maladies on the girls and had caused them to suffer fits.

Early on, both the accused and the accusers lived only in neighboring Danvers, then known as Salem Village. But as the months wore on, those charged with the crime of witchcraft hailed from twenty-two nearby communities. Salem Town, now modern-day Salem, was the capital of the Massachusetts Bay Colony until 1632, when it shifted to Boston, fifteen miles south. Salem was also the seat of Essex County and home to the county courthouse. In 1692, it was located on Washington Street, a short block from its present location. Nineteen good citizens were tried, convicted, and hanged. The twentieth, Giles Corey, was crushed to death after he refused to answer to the charges and loudly cursed both the sheriff and the town of Salem.

The trials and death sentences spanned some seven months, culminating in the last of the executions on September 22, 1692. Then eight men and women met their deaths. Of the 150 persons who still languished in the Salem jail charged with witchcraft, four had died in their cells. The exact site of Gallows Hill remains in dispute. So, too, does the location of the ravine where bodies of the condemned were tossed and denied the dignity of a Christian burial.'

Although the execution of accused witches was not unique to Salem (in fact the numbers were small compared to European witch hunts), historians have taken a particular interest in explaining the phenomenon here. There are at least three popular theories. One ascribes the behavior of the young accusers to the hallucinogenic side effects of a blighted crop of wheat that season. Another suggests the real problem was teenage boredom during a bleak winter in a stark, repressive community, precipitating in widespread clinical hysteria. Finally, some studies indicate that neighborhood feuds, estate disputes, power struggles, and sexism were at work in most every case. The condemned were often strong women, or eccentric, or very rich, or very poor, too independent for their own good, or too weak. They were usually without brothers or sons and in some cases stood to inherit property. Flirting on the fringes of normalcy and committing perceived offenses against femininity, they tended to lack defenses or the support of their communities when caught in the crossfire of village rivalries and "the whims of little girls." Most likely, all three played a part, though history still searches vainly for definitive answers. One aspect is clear. Being a strong-willed woman, unwilling to confess to lies, was a dangerous occupation. In fact, those who did confess were spared. In 1692, fear triumphed over courage.

The commemoration itself was not without controversy. During the initial planning, and then more publicly throughout 1992, the relationship (if any) between the events of the seventeenth century and Salem's current witch population was heatedly debated in the press. Each day the *Salem Evening News* printed a small box giving a bit of history from 300 years ago. "On the morning of Thursday, September 22, 1692, eight individuals were hanged for practicing witchcraft." And so on throughout the year. Next to the boxes were letters to the editor from local witches decrying twentieth century intolerance. Fundamentalist Christians warned of the dangers of Satanic worship. Reformed witches challenged the tenet that white magic is harmless.

At one point, Laurie Cabot publicly accused the tercentenary committee of persecution and bigotry for failing to use the commemoration as a means to educate the public about the true meaning of witchcraft, as distinguished from Satanism. Cabot claimed a strong affinity with the victims of 1692. She felt that some of the accused may in fact have practiced witchcraft or at least some facets of the religion. But even if they all had been devout Christians, they "died for our freedom" because they were executed for refusing to confess to committing a crime.

Helen Gifford, editor of the *North Shore Sunday*, took offense at what she regarded as Laurie Cabot's name-calling and attempts to rewrite both history and language. Like it or not, witchcraft in 1692 had meant consorting with the Devil, Gifford pointed out. Furthermore, the accused were in fact Christians, not "witches" of any kind. "She misses the point," Gifford stated in an editorial. "The Salem witchcraft trials were about superstition and fear and narrow-mindedness. They weren't about real witches. They were about us."

During March and April of 1992, Thomas Maimoni's own trial was still getting underway in four more pre-trial appearances at the courthouse in Salem. He would later decry his predicament as yet another example of Salem's witch hunt hysteria. On the contrary, the parallels could more accurately be drawn with his victims. Maimoni had sought out strong, independent women. In the case of Martha, stubborn refusal may have been her death warrant.

42

July 1992, a court officer assigned to the Essex County Superior Courthouse in Salem, went down to the basement to get Thomas Maimoni when his hearing came up. "Time to go, Tom," the officer announced, unlocking the cell. He gestured for the prisoner to follow.

Early each morning, sheriff's vans came from the various prisons and houses of correction to deliver inmates to the courthouse. There they waited their turns in the holding cells on the ground floor. Sandwiches and sodas were brought in for lunch, and in the afternoon the inmates were all taken back. It wasn't like anyone had plans. Many rather liked the chance to get outside the walls and concertina wire, maybe get a little glimpse of home on the way.

Tom Maimoni was usually quiet and polite throughout the day. Never impatient. He talked a bit with the officer while he waited—about his trip to Maine, how the police had treated him pretty decently. Not like an animal.

The prisoners were taken to the courtroom in groups of three or four at a time. Leg irons and handcuffs rattled as they shuffled in short baby steps. They sat shackled together in the dock. As each case was called, the defendant was unhooked from the rest. The defendant then stood up or approached the bench.

At the door of Tom's cell, the officer snapped handcuffs on Maimoni and bent down with a set of leg irons. Tom started to shake, then cry. The court officer paused and gave him a few moments to pull himself together. He didn't want to humiliate the man by dragging him into the courtroom sobbing. So he spoke quietly to him. "OK, Tom. Take it easy. You're going to go in there and be a man." When Tom regained control, the officer took him out and chained him to the others for the trek upstairs.

Today's hearing concerned the first of the defense motions to suppress evidence—in this case, the statements Maimoni had made to various police authorities. Jeffrey Denner contended that these statements, such as his "confession" in Maine and his lies to Salem police, had not been of Maimoni's own free will. Defense psychiatrists claimed: "Mr. Maimoni suffers psychological disorders which in stressful, confrontational moments render him unable to separate truth from the long-term falsification he has built up around him. Although it appears that Mr. Maimoni lied, in reality, he was retreating psychologically into old protected realms. His statements were therefore not voluntary, but were the product of inquisitorial activity interacting with his psychopathology."

To convince the judge to suppress, Denner called Dr. John Docherty, a psychiatrist from New Hampshire, to testify. As Tom Maimoni sat hunched with lowered eyes, the witness laid bare the inner workings of a sociopath's mind.

"Mr. Maimoni is suffering from a disorder called *pseudologia fantastica*, a condition in which the individual is disturbed by compulsive lying," Docherty told the court. "He is able to exercise some potential control over the form of the fabrication but not over the need to continue to fabricate." The doctor gave some well-known examples: Baron von Munchausen and another Massachusetts native—Ferdinand Waldo Demara—the "Great Impostor" from the 1950s, who was finally captured in Maine and was later immortalized in both a book and a movie.

Maimoni's disorder included avoidance and denial strategies when faced with problems he couldn't handle. His childhood was spent by hiding for hours in his room or running away into the woods instead of facing difficulties.

"With Mr. Maimoni was this paralleled, in his adult life," asked Denner, "by going out on his boat or running off to the woods in Maine?"

The doctor agreed.

Docherty's interviews with family members revealed that as a youngster Tom engaged in dissimulation as a way of handling problems or embarrassments such as bad report cards, a grandfather who didn't speak English, family social status, or lack of education. Tom created fantasies to replace them all.

This strategy then carried over into his adult life, lying on résumés and about former wives. But often the lies were little ones, like a dog he claimed to own but was only minding for a day. And later a boat he was borrowing, which he said was his. Then sailing and scuba licenses he didn't have. His own diving tanks had to be filled by someone else. Even the version of the "accident" Tom had given Docherty had self-aggrandizing components. Tom had described CPR and hypothermia treatment obviously far beyond his actual knowledge. Tom lived in a world of imagination and fiction. But the world he created for himself was ultimately self-defeating.

Prosecutor Kevin Mitchell, on cross-examination, pressed the doctor to cut to the heart of the matter: "Did Mr. Maimoni on the evening of July 15, 1991 understand the words of the *Miranda* rights read to him?"

"Yes, I am sure he understood the words," Docherty replied. "But Tom wasn't able to use reasonable judgment about the implications of waiving them and was compelled to talk and to lie."

The prosecutor pointed out that Tom Maimoni had fabricated stories, however, to conform to what facts the police knew and were confronting him with at any given moment.

"Sir, did Mr. Maimoni 'know' when he spoke to Bill Brailsford and Conrad Prosniewski on the morning of July 13 that Martha was weighted down on the bottom of the ocean?"

"I'm not sure that he did." The doctor explained that Maimoni's disorder fluctuated among fabrication, daydream, and delusion. At the time he was telling the stories he was believing them. Yet when confronted with reality, individuals with the disorder could comprehend at that moment *and* create a new fiction. With true delusional disorders, fixed ideas would be "totally unresponsive to external input."

"Not all of Mr. Maimoni's statements conformed to what the authorities knew," Docherty retorted. Tom blurted out to Maine troopers that "Massachusetts wanted him more." To Tom this fact made him "bigger" than the mere petty criminal they had apprehended for breaking and entering. His action typified his disorder. Tom had not made a calculated attempt to mislead the police. And Tom's fabrications were often silly and preposterous. He never seemed to fear being caught in a lie because he didn't think he was lying. If he were rational and truly attempting to hide something, why would he have made claims which clearly could be disproved? Like his wives and jobs, or not being seen with Martha on a busy dock in her own neighborhood.

Judge Charles Grabau ruled two months later that Maimoni's statements would be admissible, with the exception of "I killed my neighbor's wife," which he had made to police in Maine. *Pseudologia fantastica* had failed to fly. Seizing the opportunity to coin a new medicolegal term, Grabau concluded in his decision, "Maimoni's judgment as to whether to answer questions, what to say in response, and when to control the questioning was not impaired by *pseudologia fantastica* ... but was the result of *memoria falsa*."

43

Defense attorney Jeffrey Denner had his work cut out for him if he was going to get his client off. To track down every shred of evidence that could help, he hired a pair of New Hampshire private investigators, Paul Brochu and Zita Lamb of Accurate Information Consultants. They spent the months of June and July looking over the case files. On August 5, they met co-counsel Marie Saccoccio in Salem to familiarize themselves with the area. They videotaped Tom's house, Martha's house, the Willows, Collins Cove, Winter Island, and several related boat docks and piers.

At the Willows, Brochu, Lamb, and Saccoccio visited Dan Sweeney's Boat Livery. They rented a fourteen-foot runabout that guaranteed a top speed of three knots. In this they circumnavigated a couple of the islands, then chugged into Palmer's Cove Yacht Club.

For awhile they contented themselves with videotaping all the boats, the configuration and layout of the slips, docks, and moorings, plus the channel and the mouth of the harbor. They were looking for anything that could refute Raymond Mount's claim that *Counterpoint* was back in its slip by 6:30 that evening. As they puttered up and down the slip area, their eyes spotted a thirty-nine-foot boat called *Wings* out of Amherst, New Hampshire. On deck was a man in his early fifties. Having familiarized themselves with the case, the trio figured this man was Bob

Montague, Maimoni's friend from New Hampshire whom Tom had tried to reach from the cabin in Waite, Maine.

Zita Lamb was always ready to answer the door when opportunity knocked. Now squatting in a runabout, looking up at a potential witness for the prosecution, Zita did her best Mae West imitation, gesturing and shouting in a sultry voice, "Hey, Bob, how are you?"

Montague turned and peered down at them. The group looked like escapees from Gilligan's Island. He had no idea who these people were. After Zita's coaxing, the trio threw Montague a line. He caught it and engaged in a little flirtation with the two women as he hauled them up to the side of his boat.

"Hi, I'm Paul Brochu. We'd like to ask a few questions regarding Tom Maimoni," Zita's partner called up.

Montague grew suspicious and hesitated. "Well, you really shouldn't be talking to me because I have nothing good to say about the son of a bitch, basically."

Zita kept him going. "How long have you been friends with Tom?"

"I *used* to be friends with Tom. I'm not friends with him anymore."

"Bob, I read over the police report, about you and Tom on July 12," Brochu tried. "I was wondering, did you in fact run into Tom at all on that particular day?"

"No," Montague replied. "We were supposed to meet up in the morning. He never showed. I kept trying to raise him on the radio. Every twenty minutes I'd call him. He never answered."

Montague had brought his Corbin 39 up from Boston early on the morning of July 12, and had moored behind Cat Island until the afternoon. He and Tom had arranged to contact each other on channel 72, one of the accepted ship-to-ship frequencies. Palmer's Cove Yacht Club used channel 71 for ship-to-shore contact.

Montague had put out his anchor in a quiet, secluded cove on the backside of Cat Island and then had begun work on the refrigeration unit below. Periodically he had tried to raise Tom. He had moved his boat at one point, when staff from the Boy Scout camp on the island suggested he was moored too close to their swimming dock.

At about four-thirty on Friday afternoon, Montague motored into Marblehead Harbor for fuel, then to Palmer's Cove in Salem, where he picked up a mooring at the end of the channel. There, he fiddled with his refrigeration unit some more, until about nine. It had gotten dark. Montague motored in to the yacht club and backed the Corbin into his slip.

"What about that night? Later? Did you run into him then?"

"No, I didn't. I was moored right over there. All afternoon. He never showed up."

Brochu probed further. "You didn't see *Counterpoint* in its slip later? At any time that evening?"

Montague was adamant. "I was here till nine, nine-thirty that night. Right in that spot. I woulda seen him if he was in his slip. I woulda seen him if he came by. He was not there. I looked all night. He never showed up. I was really pissed at him."

"Bob, was there any way, any way at all, Tom could have slipped by you that evening?"

Montague's irritation was showing. "I said no. No way in hell." And then he added, "There's no way I'm going to help that son of a bitch."

Brochu wasn't fazed. "Did you tell the police what you told me?"

"Look, I don't want to get involved. I just told them I didn't see him, that's all. I don't want to answer any more questions."

"Wait," persevered Brochu, who was used to tough interviews. "Do you know where I can find Patti? You know if she's moved?"

"I haven't seen her."

"You know where she might be?"

"Try her family in Kansas. I'm done talking to you."

In fact, Montague *had* seen Patti. Three weeks earlier, almost a year after Maimoni's arrest, he had married her. On July 18, 1992, the anniversary of Hooper Goodwin's sad discovery, Montague had fulfilled Tom's last request, left on his answering machine when Tom called from his hideout in Waite, Maine: "*Take care of Patti.*"

44

During September 1992, both sides stepped up their preparations for the trial. Salem police investigators took the harbormaster's boat out to videotape Cat Island. Specifications and schematics of Maimoni's boat were obtained from the designer and were dry-mounted for use in the trial. All the weekend sailors on the prosecution team surveyed the results and drooled over the sleek design of the Cal 28, the only true eyewitness to the Brailsford murder. And the cradle of Martha's death? Tom Maimoni would have the court believe this exquisite boat was her murderer.

A Cal 28 similar to *Counterpoint* was located in nearby New Hampshire. Conrad Prosniewski, Mark Lynch, as well as members of the defense all went on a joint expedition to try raising and lowering the bloodied mainsail on its mast. Both wanted to prove or disprove possible scenarios which could be raised during the trial. The defense was searching for the least incriminating explanation for the pattern of dark splatters. When the sail was unfolded, they were surprised to find eight little holes where blood stains had been cut out for analysis by the state.

Fluid taken during Martha's autopsy had determined that her blood type was A. Coincidentally, blood samples taken from the defendant also showed type A. Tests on the sail were made to see if more detailed subgroupings could indicate whose blood it was. Unfortunately, the only subgroupings that could be checked were also identical. Further analysis was not possible due to the deterioration of the stains.

After the real *Counterpoint* was finally located in neighboring Connecticut, the defense team traveled down on a cold, rainy fall day to let their own forensic expert look over the crime scene. They all climbed aboard to search and videotape. Zita Lamb nearly fell off the boat as it rocked and twitched in the wind and rain. She was convinced Cal 28s had a dangerous design and were "death traps." An old chart book was found on board, plus two eerie spots near the mast where the fiberglass surface was embedded with hairline cracks. Slowly Zita knelt down upon the spidery imprints and noticed that her knees rested exactly in their centers. Her skin crawled. Martha must have fallen right here, she thought.

"How'd it go today?" B. C. asked his cellmate when he returned from a hearing later that month.

"Good. Good news. For some reason they can't do blood tests on the sail. I was really scared they'd be able to identify that blood."

Maimoni showed him a book he had found in the library. "I've got a book I'm reading on hypothermia. I'm working on that angle. If I can figure out how long it takes to die in the water from hypothermia, she could have died of hypothermia."

"How cold was the water?" asked B. C.

"I can find out. I can find out for that date."

B. C. remarked that he had been at the beach once in July 1991, between his sentences. "The water was cold. I'd guess fifty-five degrees," he offered. They looked through the book.

"Forty-five minutes," Maimoni announced.

Martha had to be in the water forty-five minutes to die of hypothermia for Tom's story.

45

With considerable justification Salem, Massachusetts, bills itself as the Halloween Capital of the World. October 1992 was a particularly successful Halloween, coming on the heels of the tercentenary. The days preceding the holiday constituted a decade-long tradition, a festival known as "Haunted Happenings." Merchants and witches alike promoted their wares and services. Tourism was at its heaviest, and each year saw the city offer more museums, haunted attractions, and intensive marketing of fright. There was something of a Mardi Gras atmosphere as thousands of people of all ages temporarily set aside semantics, religion, and Salem's past sins. Instead they wandered downtown dressed in rubber masks, capes, organdy dresses, and furry costumes with tails slung over their arms. The courageous waved swords and wands at the darkness and hooted with laughter to scare off fear. There was a sense of entitlement, of well-deserved fun, a brief respite from reality and the repression of craziness. Halloween was a time for letting go.

The other face of Halloween, recognized by a smaller group of celebrants, constituted the most significant holiday for practicing witches. As they did with most pagan festivals, seventh-century Christians associated this night with one of their own holidays, All Hallows Eve. But to witches it had been known for centuries as *Samhain* (pronounced Sa-wen), the beginning of the Celtic new year. The last night of October marked the transition from summer to winter as the earth passed into a period of transitory death, though with the promise of renewal the following spring. The veil between the worlds of the living and the dead was thinnest at this time. For witches, this was the time to consider their hopes and commitments for the coming year and to remember, honor, and communicate with their loved ones who had died. For witches, Halloween was a time for reflection and rebirth.

Meanwhile, another potential witness for the Commonwealth popped up—the young prison inmate, B. C., who had been Maimoni's cellmate for a time at Middleton while both awaited their trials. The guy had come forward on his own, with notes of conversations they had had together, "in order to see justice done" in Tom's case. B. C. claimed he was not a rat by nature. His initial proposal to come forward had included the possibility of a reduced sentence. When the assistant DA turned him down, B. C. said he'd turn over his information anyway. In B. C.'s estimation, Tom's crime was deplorable.

Mitchell hoped he wouldn't need B. C., knowing Jeff Denner would rip the kid apart on the stand. Mitchell anticipated having a tough time maintaining credibility while announcing to the jury, "My next witness is serving eight to ten years for armed robbery." Nevertheless, the assistant district attorney was holding on to the possibility of calling B. C. right up to the end of the trial. He would wait to see what Maimoni said if he indeed took the stand and would then decide whether B. C.'s rebuttal was necessary. In the meantime, B. C. was transferred out of Middleton for his own protection.

It was easy to picture the defense. Presuming B. C. was telling the truth, what about Tom Maimoni? The jury was going to be told that Tom couldn't tell the truth if his life depended on it. Whatever needs he had in Middleton, they might very well have dictated the picture he painted for his cellmate. A competent sailor didn't let a woman die in an accident on his boat. Behind these walls, better to have succeeded in a reprehensible plan than to have failed in a pathetic rescue attempt. Maimoni might have perceived that heroes were defined differently in the houses of correction. But to his cellmate B. C., the anchorman was no hero.

An acquaintance of Maimoni's delivered a videotape to the Salem police station, thinking it might be useful. It had been shot aboard *Counterpoint* on July 4, 1991. Much of it was devoted to the turnaround ceremonies of Old Ironsides in Boston Harbor that day. However, footage included the Maimonis and their passengers in various locations on the deck of Tom's boat. In view of the defense investigation's reports of cracks in the fiberglass by the mast, Kevin Mitchell took the Fourth of July video home. He played it all the way through, looking for glimpses of the deck, trying to detect damage, if any. He was curious about how much was present and whether it in fact predated Martha's death. To the bewilderment of his kids, Mitchell replayed the video again and again, looking but not finding. His children thought he was crazy.

All in all, Mitchell was still nervous about his evidence. There was precious little, to put it simply. On top of it, he had to endure the widespread public perception that Maimoni was clearly guilty and that the Commonwealth should have no problem convicting him. People kept saying to him all year long, "How can you possibly lose?"

Mitchell stared at them. "How can I lose? What do I have? How about—no cause of death!"

One of the local radio talk show hosts ranted one night about what a waste of time and money it was to have a jury trial in the Maimoni case. His guest suggested that the trial might get interesting and that it wasn't at all a sure win. The host replied, "You mean the prosecution could screw up?"

Mitchell, who was listening, cringed. "Jesus! My mother has to listen to this!"

46

Visiting hours were nearly over. B. C. rubbed his hands through his hair. He was nervous about the Maimoni thing. He hadn't heard from anyone about it. He hated being kept in the dark. Now he was explaining to a visiting friend why he was in this mess.

"I would never have done it, come forward. But he come up to me one day, and held out a picture of a girl posing with a mountain lion. She lived in Colorado. He was writing to her. 'Look at this dame,' he says to me. He called women 'dames.' She didn't know he was in prison. Then I realized that if he got out, he could go do to her what he did to this other woman. I may be spending the rest of my life here. But I figure, maybe I can do one small thing for society. I knew he had an expensive attorney. With his money he might get off."

Unlike B. C., his friend had read the papers. "I read the guy didn't have any money."

"You're shitting me!" B. C. said, genuinely surprised. "That can't be true. He worked for that game company, inventing new streets for *Monopoly*, I think. He always had plenty of money for the canteen. He had that boat, the condo, the plane."

"The what?"

"The plane. He kept it nearby. Beverly Airport, he said."

"Never read about any plane. He lost everything else."

"Tom told me the tail number and everything. He said it was

a Piper Cub. Me and the guys even kidded him. "'Hey, why'd you drive to Maine? You coulda flown your plane?'"

B. C. looked at his hands and searched his memory. "Tom did tell stories, though. Back in Middleton, we had a couple of guys who served in Vietnam. Tom told us all about the stuff that happened to him over there. But the guys who had been there, they said he was full of shit. You know, I joined the service in 1976. I was seventeen. The war had just ended, so I was sent to Germany. I met a lot of guys who had been in 'Nam. I always felt like I had missed out. Never really got to prove my manhood." He looked wistful. "Wanted to be a pilot, too."

Tom told B. C. every version of the *Counterpoint* story he had told everyone else. Tom also added a few more.

The "dame" was sunning nude on the foredeck. Tom went to lie beside her. He reached out to put his hand on her. She jumped right up. Startled, Tom grabbed her by the leg, and she fell, hitting her head on the mast. Tom described to B. C. the panic he felt as he stared down at her closed eyes and bleeding head. All he could think of, he told his cellmate, was what Patti would say. She'd divorce him for certain. Tom paced the deck for awhile, then decided to tie her up to the anchor and throw her overboard.

"Was she still breathing?" B. C. had asked.

Tom responded that all he saw was the blood. Blood getting all over everything. His mind went blank, just like the time he crashed in Vietnam, he said. Flashbacks. Big time.

In the months together as cellmates and later as friends on the same tier, Tom and B. C. did a lot of talking. In other versions, Tom slipped in the fact that someone stabbed in the stomach sinks right to the bottom. The body doesn't come back up. Tom also explained why he got scared when the police showed up at his door the next day: his hands were cut up.

"Maybe he was just telling you another story," ventured his visitor. "You believe all he told you?"

"He absolutely killed her," B. C. insisted. He added that he and the other inmates knew Tom made up some of the stuff. Things—details—changed each time. Sometimes Tom said something that didn't click with something else. "I'd say, 'But Tom, you said earlier...' and he'd go back and work on it some more. But he did kill her, no question."

"You two get along OK as cellmates?"

"Fine. We got along OK. We had the occasional spat. I'd get

mad at him sometimes when he paced up and down the cell all night like a caged animal. I'd yell at him, 'Tom, stop walkin' around!' When we were separated after three months, it was 'cause I smoke. He's a health nut. Afterward, we were still friends. I was pretty much the only one he'd talk to. Every time he came back from court, he'd come running to my cell to tell me about it.

"I got to know him better and better as time went by. He told me about all these women he used to pick up, you know. There was a real estate lady and some horny nuns. Well, Tom met a girl once through one of those lonelyhearts papers. He told us he got in touch with her and they arranged to meet up in, I think, Rockport. She was going to take the train up there, and he was gonna meet her. So her train pulls in. A woman gets off. He figures it must be her, he tells me. But she was a real dog. Not his type. So he doesn't get out of his car. Just starts it up and goes back home. I'm thinking, you know, jeez! Even if she was like real overweight or something, I still woulda taken her out for a cup of coffee. Not just leave her standing there."

"Visiting hours are over," intoned the lieutenant. He flicked off one of the overhead lights.

"Wonder if it was true about the nuns," B. C. said, as his friend rose to leave.

47

Jury selection for the trial of Thomas J. Maimoni began on January 28, 1993, and lasted two days. At the end of the first day, the court reporter Mary Hezekiah approached the bench. She recognized the defendant and felt she should let the court know. A young, attractive woman herself, she had once found herself on a boat with Tom Maimoni. Judge Patti Saris, the assigned trial judge, called a quick bench conference with the two attorneys.

"The court reporter has just told me that she was on a boat once with Mr. Maimoni."

Kevin Mitchell's jaw dropped. He turned to Hezekiah with a hopeful look. *Another witness!*

Jeff Denner asked what actually had happened. The attorneys and the judge were momentarily stymied by how to talk directly to Hezekiah while she softly chattered into her microphone. Unlike stenography, "voice recording" the proceedings required that the court reporter echo every spoken word into a two-track tape recorder and identify each speaker. Judge Saris frowned. "I don't have any way of letting her say it and getting it down at the same time." Of course, by virtue of Mary Hezekiah's speaking, it would be taped. Perhaps the unspoken quandary was, should she echo her own response?

"Could we have the court reporter's name?" Mitchell asked in this *Alice in Wonderland* dialogue.

"Mary Hezekiah," responded Mary Hezekiah.

The woman explained she was drinking with friends on their boat docked in Manchester Harbor one evening in the late summer of 1990. Tom Maimoni appeared out of nowhere. With a friendly "good evening, ladies," he invited himself on board. He got through the dead wife preamble and then explained he was in port for repairs. It seemed Tom had just completed his third trans-atlantic voyage, during which he sustained minor damage when a whale rammed his boat. They chatted for awhile. Eventually, Tom left. No one saw him again that night.

"Did he say what kind of whale it was?" asked Denner, who now took his client's tall stories in stride. He turned to cocounsel Richard Howard. "Richard, I think we should subpoena the whale."

To Kevin Mitchell's disappointment, it had been a harmless encounter. The defendant had been a perfect gentleman. No good for the prosecution. The judge ruled that another court reporter would be assigned for the remainder of the trial. Off the record, Jeff Denner leaned over and asked the woman, "Perhaps you'd like to be my witness?"

By the second day of jury selection, Judge Saris had impaneled a balanced jury. Miraculously, she had found at least five North Shore females who had never been on a boat with Tom Maimoni.

PART III

To this indictment the defendant at the bar has heretofore pleaded be is not guilty and for trial has placed himself upon his country, which country you are. You are now sworn to try the issue. If the defendant is guilty, you will say so. If the defendant is not guilty, you will say so and no more.

Members of the jury, hearken to your evidence.

Robert Murphy
Clerk Magistrate
February 1, 1993

48

"Good morning," Assistant District Attorney Kevin Mitchell said to the jury as he rose for his opening remarks. In a strong, clear voice he began by pointing to the wall. "As you look to your right, you'll see a calendar which reflects the days in July 1991. In this courtroom, you will hear Hooper Goodwin tell you that he is a lobsterman and that on the morning of July 18 he went out of Marblehead Harbor. Sometime around eleven o'clock, he found himself in the area of Cat Island. He will describe for you how he started to pick up one end of a six-pot trawl line, and as he came to the last pot—the sixth—he looked over the side of the lobster boat. As the pot started to come up he saw an anchor. That anchor had a rope, and that rope went down. And as that pot came through the water, he will tell you, he saw a foot...."

On Monday morning, February 1, 1993, the historic Newburyport Courthouse was packed. Snowdrifts and ridges of ice added to the challenge for this small seaport to absorb the demand for well over a hundred additional parking spots. The courthouse's own tiny lot was swallowed up by satellite trucks from each of the Boston news stations. Members of the press, onlookers, and jury members shuffled cautiously along frozen sidewalks. The temperature never rose above twenty degrees.

Upstairs, a single stationary camera was provided by the different local news stations that operated it in shifts each day. It was set up near a side window facing the witness stand. The cables snaked through the window of the second floor court-room, outside the building, and into a first floor window below. Inside, on the deacon's benches along the lobby walls, Boston television stations WBZ, WHDH, WCVB, and New England Cable News had set up their monitors and recording decks to share the video feed.

Throughout greater Boston, attention turned to the opening day of this high-profile trial with its promise of sex, lies, and video coverage. WBCN, a local radio station, greeted the morning with unquestionably bad taste by airing "Maimoni the Sailor Man" to the tune of "Popeye the Sailor Man."

Shortly after nine, the black van from the Essex County Sher-iff's Department pulled up to the side door. Court officers pushed back the crowd as Thomas Maimoni—dressed in a gray pin-striped suit, leg chains, and handcuffs—was brought out and was led up the courthouse steps. Cameramen hovered by the door to catch the "walk-in" shot.

In the courtroom family, friends, neighbors, and strangers filled the hard wooden benches. Bill Brailsford sat beside his mother in the front row behind the defense table. His father Paul Brailsford was seated close by, as was Sandy Clark, the vic-tim/witness advocate.

Mr. and Mrs. Maimoni, who shared unmistakable features with their son (though not his stature), helped each other slowly down the aisle and into two empty seats on the left. They looked lost and alone.

Mitchell spent the next half hour outlining the story of the investigation, the discovery, Tom Maimoni's flight to Maine, his lies to the police, how witnesses led Prosniewski in the right direction, how the experts reconstructed what had happened out at sea. The redheaded prosecutor rarely looked at notes, main-taining eye contact with the jury as he moved back and forth in front of them.

"The clerk this morning read you an indictment. It uses the archaic language of this system—*that he did assault and beat and by such assault and beating did kill and murder*. It is the lan-guage we use to present murder, no matter what the facts, be it shootings or stabbings. It is, members of the jury, the language we use when we accuse Thomas Maimoni on July 12, of 1991, of putting an anchor and a weight belt on Martha Brailsford and dropping her live and breathing body into the waters off Cat Island."

Those in the courtroom had waited more than a year and a half to hear these words. Heads now turned to see how the defense would explain away these apparently straightforward facts. Many of those heads felt there was nothing else to say in this matter.

Jeffrey Denner stood and faced the jury on behalf of the defendant. Tom Maimoni sat beside him, handcuffs and shackles removed while in view of the jurors. The attorney sketched for the court the defense's theory of the tragic accident and outlined the psychological factors in this case. He addressed Tom Maimoni's "lifelong pattern of pathetic, almost compulsive aggrandizement" and what happened to the man when his house of cards had begun to crumble. He suggested the police had been quick to judge his client guilty and had felt they had an open-and-shut case. Jeffrey Denner implored the jury not to make the same mistake. "All Tom Maimoni, Rick Howard, and I ask you to do is listen to this case with open hearts and open minds, use your God-given common sense, and we will be content."

49

Roxcy Platte of Marblehead was the Commonwealth's first witness. The judge had ruled earlier that the "prior bad acts" testimony of two of the women were admissible for the limited purpose of shedding light on Maimoni's state of mind on July 12.

Roxcy told the jury about her encounters with Maimoni in the late spring of 1991. She described how the sails had been friendly and platonic, until the last one, when Tom's behavior changed. "We sat in the cockpit eating lunch, and his conversation became suddenly very sexual." She related the story of the nun and Tom's sudden announcement that he wanted to sail naked. "As he said that, he dropped his pants." Back at the dock in Marblehead, Tom surprised her with his statement: "Let's not make a big deal of this. You don't have to tell anybody."

Denner asked, on cross-examination: "After you returned from that sail, it was your intention to have more such social engagements with Mr. Maimoni, wasn't it?"

Roxcy confirmed she in principle had been ready to sail with Tom again, to go out with him, and to possibly go on a cruise. However, she had been concerned that Tom might already be involved with someone. "Also, I wanted to make sure that he would not take his clothes off again."

Denner pointed out that after the "incident" the prosecution seemed to make such a big deal of, Roxcy again saw Tom on July

10, and was asked to go for a sail on July 12, though those plans were subsequently broken.

When Roxcy Platte called Salem police, it was not to report a crime or any wrongdoing, she admitted. She had read about the mystery boat in the newspaper and was anxious to learn if it was the same boat, the same man. Because the Commonwealth now needed to show a particular pattern of behavior, the details—sordid or not—of these rather inoffensive encounters were chronicled for the public record. Roxcy Platte now had to "kiss and tell." The public had to be cast as the voyeur. And, ultimately, both she and Patti Maimoni had been treated shabbily.

As Roxcy stepped off the stand, she noticed the defendant staring daggers at her. Quite a change from his inexplicable, flirtatious demeanor at the pre-trial hearing the previous week. Both made her shudder.

The Commonwealth subsequently called Rosemary Farmer. She had a different story.

Kevin Mitchell led the witness through the long July afternoon that stretched, involuntarily, into evening. The wine, the brownies, the dead wife, the bionic hand. The indecent and unwelcome exposure. And once again, the advances, this time rather more assaulting than bumbling.

When the assistant district attorney was through, Jeffrey Denner rose to cross-examine a potentially very damaging witness. Roxcy Platte could have experienced an isolated, momentary lapse in Tom's judgment and fidelity. Yet Rosemary Farmer's account showed not only a pattern, but an alarming tendency, toward increased aggression by Tom. The jury could connect these dots and could extrapolate what Maimoni's state of mind might have been three days later with Martha Brailsford. The courtroom was glued to Rosemary's testimony because her encounter might have been a dress rehearsal for Martha's assault. They looked to Rosemary more than to any other witness to tell them what Martha might have experienced.

Denner's approach, predictably, was to suggest that no assault had occurred. He began by revisiting the phony claims Tom made to this witness, in what must have been an effort to pull the defendant's deceit out of the prosecution's arsenal of weapons and into the defense's. Kevin Mitchell was demonstrating to the jury, wherever possible, that Thomas Maimoni consistently lied and that his explanation of what happened to Martha on the boat should not be believed. He lied because the truth would hurt his case. He had lied to police to avoid being caught. He would lie to the jury to avoid being convicted. Denner, too, was trying to demonstrate to the court that Thomas Maimoni's lies were compulsive and pathetic, not calculated, not evidence of "consciousness of guilt." So he drew particular attention to them, as if to humiliate his client.

"With respect to some of the stories Mr. Maimoni told you, you have since learned that most of those are not true, is that correct?" Denner asked the witness. At the defense table, his client fiddled with tortoiseshell reading glasses and looked uncomfortable.

Rosemary concurred.

"He told you about a lot of out-of-state clients he had as part of a big consulting practice? When he went to see your house, he told you that office would be wonderful for his clients?"

"I don't know whether it was with regard to consulting, but, yes, he was going to bring clients there, and there was room to put satellites and computers in my yard and in this room."

"For his big business?" Denner asked.

"For his business with NASA, yes."

"You testified that he told you he worked for NASA, the National Aeronautics and Space Administration?"

"Yes," the witness responded.

"And he told you that he, in fact, designed biomedical supplies for NASA?"

"He had told me he designed some kind of, something with blood, it was to work with blood on the moon."

"So he told you he had some relationship with the moon? Did he also talk to you on the boat about the bionic hand that you thought he had down below?" Denner asked these questions with a straight face. He managed to get the hand mentioned eight times for the benefit of the jury, to deliver the message that this man, his client, was a joke. And the joke demeaned the witness and threatened to eclipse the gravity of her painful testimony. *"Want to see my bionic hand?"* became the most memorable line of the trial. How could its author be considered dangerous if he couldn't be taken seriously? If Denner could reduce Maimoni in everyone's eyes, emasculate him, and bring him down, the image they had of a big, violent man would diminish as well.

The witness answered, "Yes."

The defense wanted the jury to infer from Rosemary's responses to Tom's outrageous lines that the situation could not have been terribly threatening if she had followed the defendant to see the hand. Surely, Rosemary must have known his true intentions, Denner implied.

The next defense tactic was to make the jury feel Tom's pain. Now that he'd been humiliated, show them his despondency as Rosemary had seen it and had responded to it. Denner led Rosemary once more through the sequence of events both above and below deck and through the discussions about Tom's dead wife.

"Did he appear as though he was ready to cry?" Denner asked.

"Yes," Rosemary answered.

"Very depressed?"

"Very."

"And you had conversations about that, about his despondency?"

"Yes."

"And whatever the source, it seemed very real to you?"

"Yes."

The more the jury believed in Rosemary and identified with her, the more her empathy with Tom would become theirs. The same empathy for which Martha Brailsford had been renowned.

Denner tried to dislodge the image of an indecent assault. He refocused on the instances of touching but highlighted the parts that involved Tom's head on her shoulder, a consensual hug, the clingy nature of Tom's grasp, and the force that counsel suggested was restrained. He also wanted the jury to hear about Rosemary's restraint as well. She had refrained from shouting for help, from screaming at Tom, and from forcefully resisting him.

Denner made her describe again in detail where Tom had touched her and where he had not.

"He was essentially fondling your arms and legs?"

"Yes."

"And you were screaming at him, saying, 'Stop that now!' Did you do that?"

"I wasn't screaming."

"You weren't screaming?" Denner emphasized, in mock disbelief.

"No."

"Tell me exactly how it was."

"I said, 'Tom, you have to stop it,' you know, and I'd take his hands out and I put my hands there. I would hold my pants, I'd hold my shirt wherever he was going."

"You kind of felt like you were in high school?" Denner asked with a smile, trying to win her over.

"I *never* had that happen to me in high school," she retorted. The women in the courtroom wanted to cheer.

The defense attorney cut his losses. "I went to the wrong high school," he remarked. "So for an hour and a half he's touching your arm and you're pushing him away and saying, 'Stop, Tom, you're irritating me'? You're not really deeply angry or scared, you're irritated?"

"I'm irritated, yes."

"And during this time Tom is telling you about NASA and biomedical supplies?"

"Right."

"And you're trying to be polite as you can be, but still be firm with him?"

"Yes."

"Is that because you still perhaps thought you'd be giving up a real estate deal if you were mean to him?"

"Yes. That was part of it, certainly, but also I was...I sympathized with him, I could feel his anguish. I had a brother that died. That doesn't mean it's right."

"So from wherever his anguish was coming, you felt that he was a very troubled man, very sad?"

"Sad, yes."

"With a great deal of loneliness?"

"Yes."

"And some hurt that you could feel?" Denner asked quietly.

"Yes."

Denner summed up the effect of Tom's behavior. After an hour and a half fighting off Tom's pathetic advances, Rosemary did not feel sufficiently fearful to shout to the crew of a nearby boat. After all his pawing, putting his hands in her shirt and pants, she nevertheless accepted an invitation to go below for brownies and wine. Then came the bionic hand, tricking her toward the berth.

"Would it be fair to say that given Tom's size, if he had wanted to pull you into that small bedding area, that cabin area, he could have done that?" Denner asked the witness.

"Yes, and that's why I stopped fighting him, because I realized the more I talked to him and tried to rationalize with him, he was easing up on pulling me. The more I pulled, the harder he pulled me."

"And when he was pulling you toward him, it was fairly clear to you that he just wanted someone to hug, is that it?"

"I don't—that's not—no, I don't think I could answer that and say that. He had said that's what he wanted to do."

"At some point he just lets go?"

"Yes."

"You start walking up the stairs, he comes up behind you, grabs you, turns you around and drops his pants?"

"Yes."

"And at that point, does he sexually assault you?" asked the attorney.

"No."

"Does he knock you down in any way, shape, or form or try to enter you or perform any sexual act on you?"

"No."

"He just talks to you?"

"No, he hung on me," Rosemary responded.

"Kind of a pathetic type of hanging?"

"Yes."

"He was pathetic at this point, wasn't he?"

"Yes, I would say so."

Denner next quoted from Rosemary's statement to the police to try to interpret her state of mind during trip back to Manchester: "'I was shattered, but I still asked him about the offer for the house.'" Rosemary confirmed that Tom did not restrain her at all when they docked. Denner read another passage: "'I left, and he didn't even walk me up the ramp.'" Rosemary agreed. Denner's implication was that Rosemary, like Roxcy, was more scorned than assaulted by Tom.

Walking an upset woman up the ramp to her car might instead have been an act of compassion, or of contrition, rather than simply commendable dating etiquette. Perhaps a solicitous gesture or acknowledgment that she had been wronged. But to Rosemary, her observation was an immense relief rather than a bitter complaint. She feared that Tom would find an excuse to follow her and that she would never get away from him. That he allowed her to walk away surprised her.

Whatever had transpired that afternoon, no one could now argue with her responses to the situation. The facts remained. Rosemary was here today. Martha was not.

50

"When I saw it reported that *Counterpoint* was supposed to be out sailing all night, I remembered that I'd seen it at 6:30, Friday. So I called the police." Dr. Raymond Mount's sighting was crucial for the Commonwealth. The family psychologist from Lynnfield, Massachusetts, testified that he had been back and forth to Palmer's Cove Yacht Club on July 12, sailing and diving with friends. Mount knew Tom Maimoni and his boat by sight. At 6:30, he told the jury, *Counterpoint* was in its slip. Maimoni's final statement to the police stated that the darkness he experienced a half hour after sunset added to the difficulty retrieving Martha. This claim put the alleged accident around 9 P.M. Raymond Mount's testimony now cast serious doubt on that possibility and on the defendant's credibility.

During cross-examination, Jeff Denner did everything he could to shake Mount. "Do you recall what you ate or drank that afternoon?" he asked the witness.

Mount did not.

"Did you notice any other boats?"

"Not that I recall."

"Were you looking for Tom's boat for any particular reason?"

"No."

"Were the ropes coiled? Was the sail cover on? The fenders down?"

The witness couldn't remember.

Denner also got Mount to admit he was at PCYC on Saturday,

July 13, installing a pump. The defense was suggesting to the jury that Mount's details were blurry and that his dates were probably off. However, the witness took out his appointment book to show that Friday had been clear for sailing. On Saturday he hadn't sailed. "It was a miserable day," he recalled. Ray Mount would not budge from the date and time stamped indelibly in his memory.

51

William Hooper Goodwin III was dressed in a suit and tie, his mass of curls now trimmed and tamed. A small, discrete earring replaced his scrimshaw. He was asked his occupation.

"I'm in the maritime profession. I fish commercially in the summertime, and I sail on my merchant marine documents in the winter."

"As a commercial fisherman, tell us what you do." Kevin Mitchell requested.

"I fish for lobsters. I also do a little commercial fishing for finfish as well. Cod, haddock. I hold a commercial Massachusetts lobsterman's permit."

"Would you describe to the jury what the trawl fishing technique is?"

"The way I fish my trawl is, I have two buoys. And onto each of those buoys there is an end line, which goes down to a trap. In between those traps is another line, ground line, which four to five other traps are connected to under the water. These buoys I use as end points, where my trawl starts and where my trawl ends."

"Would those traps be connected directly to the ground line itself?"

"No, they're each connected by a ganget—that's a small piece of line about a fathom long. Or six feet. When I haul my trap the ganget goes over an open block and then comes down to the hauler. I don't have to stop my operation to board the trap. I like to have about twelve to fifteen fathoms between each trap," explained Goodwin, drawing on a blackboard for the jury.

"What direction did you lay your trawls in July of 1991?"

"We set northwest by southeast. It would be approximately 315 degrees magnetic. I had five trawls set out on the back side of Cat Island at that particular time."

"Now, with reference to a particular trawl line, sir, that you worked on July 18, 1991, do you have a memory of that trawl line? How did you pull it in?"

"I haul the line up, it comes right down through the block, down around the hauler and stays right on the deck, right below my feet. The entire length of the trawl line."

"Are you pulling the trawl line along, too, as you bring it up?" asked Mitchell.

"As I'm moving toward the outside end, I kick my boat in gear, OK? So I'm moving forward, heading southeast, while my hydraulics are pulling my line and my gear up. So I try to pretty much keep an up-and-down tension."

"Now sir, at some point as you were trawling that line, did the first trap come through?"

"Fine, no problem." Same with the second trap.

"You got to a particular trap when you made an observation?"

"That's correct. That was the sixth trap," replied Goodwin. "That would have been the end trap on the outside."

"As you were standing on the boat, what did you see?"

"The trap was coming up by itself because I was fortunate enough to catch a couple of lobsters there. I was banding and gauging lobsters. The hydraulics were hauling the trap up at a slow pace. When it broke the surface and came up to the block, it wouldn't pull itself over and through...I had to turn the machinery off and look over."

"Did you see something?"

"I saw an anchor."

"Did you notice anything else?"

"Ah, yes I did. After I put the lobster down and gave it a second look, I noticed what appeared to be a human body attached to the anchor."

"Now, sir, what observation did you make as you looked down on it?"

"I made the observation that it could be the body of the

missing woman I had seen pictures of, both on boats and posted on Commercial Wharf."

As Hooper described his sad discovery, Mitchell introduced into evidence the multicolored weight belt, the anchor, and three pieces of green and white rope that were fastened to the body. The lobsterman identified each item. Two photographs taken on Hooper's boat that day showed the position of the belt around the waist of the skeleton and the manner in which the anchor was tied around the ankles. These photographs were also introduced, identified, and circulated among the members of the jury. Many faces mirrored the horror of the photos. One woman bowed her head and closed her eyes as she passed them on.

Hooper explained that the rope was about two fathoms in length (about twelve feet) and was tied haphazardly in a bunch of round turns and half hitches, not the standard bowlines or clove hitches a mariner would use. The line was secured around the "lower tibia/fibia area," which he pointed out to the jury on his own lower leg.

Kevin Mitchell used Hooper Goodwin for one other purpose: to tell the jury that the spot where he found Martha was uniquely secluded. Hooper related how he had written down his coordinates on his loran, which accurately placed his position in the water within fifty feet. A YMCA day camp was situated on Cat Island. Any number of people could have been crawling all over the island that day. However, a rock outcropping shielded the spot where Goodwin pulled up his sixth trap. Nearby Cormorant Rock also blocked any observations from Marblehead Neck. Only the top of Marblehead Lighthouse was visible. Moving only a hundred yards either way would have brought him into view, either from the camp or from the mainland.

Pulling out an aerial photograph of Cat Island, the assistant district attorney asked Hooper to mark an X on the spot where he made his discovery. The witness then did so. At that moment, the defense team objected. They had just realized what Mitchell was up to. Since Tom's own chart contained a handwritten X behind Cat Island, the use of an X on the current exhibit would "draw an unfair inference." The proximity in location would be exaggerated by the similarity in choice of mark. The judge found their objection hard to understand, then hard to believe.

At the sidebar, Howard explained why it was unfair the witness had used an *X*.

"Versus a *Y* or *Z*," added Jeff Denner, who seemed to appreciate the absurdity of this discussion.

"Versus a *dot*," said Howard, who did not.

"Excuse me," protested the judge. "This is too late. He said it. He put the *X* on. It's already on."

Rick Howard made a half-hearted attempt to get them to change the mark to a big *dot*. But the photograph was already being passed around the jury box.

"I don't understand the objection," shrugged Mitchell.

"Overruled," said the judge.

Mitchell then showed in succession the aerial photo with the witness's own mark and the chart book that was found on *Counterpoint*. He then asked Hooper to estimate the difference in distance. The witness said approximately 100 yards.

Defense attorney Rick Howard cross-examined, since he was the nautical expert on the team. He began by trying to shake Hooper's location. The loran measurements were done in decimals, but the latitude and longitude markings on the charts were in minutes and seconds. Hooper stood firm. He knew the area like the back of his hand.

Howard returned to the blackboard and reviewed Hooper's explanation of his hauling operation adding up lengths of the various segments of the trawl line. He put to the witness the hypothesis that Martha's body, on the last trap of six on a 450-foot line, would have been dragged along the rocky bottom at least 450 feet. He wanted to give the jury an explanation for the autopsy report yet to come.

Not at all, the witness explained patiently. As he had stated earlier, the remaining traps don't move during his operation—only the one being lifted, since the boat travels up the line at precisely the same slow speed as the winch pulls in the rope. The boat in effect pulls itself to each trap, rather than the converse.

Rick Howard didn't catch on. Long after the rest of the courtroom figured out what the lobsterman was saying, Howard continued to insist the body was dragged. He still believed Hooper must have stopped as each trap came up to band any lobsters and reload with bait.

"No, that's the whole purpose of having gangets. You don't

have to stop the hauler," the witness repeated. Anyway, on the day he set those traps, he noted the loran position of the end trap, just as he normally did. The position was exactly the same as when he retrieved it on July 18. No dragging, no drifting. And no damage to the body. Not by Hooper Goodwin.

Kevin Mitchell was relieved. He had worried the lobsterman might get carried away. But his witness had shined. He had demonstrated half hitches for the judge, had defined *gaffs*, *cleats*, and *gangets*, and had explained how the loran worked. By the time Hooper Goodwin III finished testifying, the audience had learned more than they had ever wanted about lobstering. They nevertheless were captivated by his self-assurance, his straightforward and conscientious manner, his competence, and his dignity. He was the perfect hero, a star in the courtroom.

52

Judge Saris requested the cameraman pan away as Bill Brailsford came up to testify. Kevin Mitchell asked the witness how long he had known Martha, how the two had met, and what sort of sailing experience she had gained. At Mitchell's request, Brailsford also explained to the jury that Martha's hobbies like windsurfing required both physical strength and coordination. Martha also walked daily for exercise. She was a certified scuba diver and a strong swimmer. She was in very good health prior to her death.

Mitchell had Brailsford tell the jury about Martha's watch, a Seiko sports watch she had worn for several years and had never removed. It was not found on her body and was never located in her home.

Finally, Mitchell asked the witness about the state of their marriage on July 12, 1991.

"It couldn't have been better," Brailsford answered, in a voice which never wavered during his testimony.

Jeff Denner cross-examined Brailsford to emphasize that Tom had invited both Martha and Bill. But the witness did not recall having that impression. The defense counsel also asked why Brailsford had not mentioned in his original statement to police that he was expected home at 7:30 that night. The defense hoped to show that his important piece of Brailsford's story had only appeared later, when his memory was not as fresh. Brailsford answered that he could well have overlooked it, given his state of mind when he talked to Sergeant Prosniewski. Denner's third line of questioning sought to plant seeds of doubt regarding Martha's state of mind during her many walks with Tom. They had been alone, they had talked a lot about personal things, they had gotten friendly. Martha had developed "warm feelings" toward Tom. But Denner didn't push it beyond that.

Mitchell stood for redirect examination. "Regarding Martha's frequent walks, do you have any reason to believe on July 12, 1991, that Martha wasn't as in love with you as you were with her?"

"No, no question."

Each night after court adjourned, Kevin Mitchell met with investigators to review the day and to follow up any little point the defense attorneys might have introduced during cross-examination. What was their case going to be? Who should be contacted now? Any new facts need corroborating? Mitchell had experts lined up on sailing, the military, the Vietnam War, boat design, weather, psychiatry. These nights were nothing compared to what they'd face when the defense put their own witnesses on the stand.

Julie Michaud saw less of Conrad Prosniewski during the trial than she had during the investigation. On top if it all, Britt, her eleven-year-old Yorkshire terrier, was critically ill and was scheduled for surgery that week.

The night before he was due to take the stand, Prosniewski got home late. After checking on the dog, he went over his notes, trying to remember which interview happened on which date. Fourteen pages of his affidavit and a file box full of interviews had to be committed to memory. One doesn't get to thumb through notes to answer every question on the stand. What day did they walk on Winter Island? What time did he read Tom his rights?

Before turning in, the detective opened his closet door wide. He started flipping through his shirts and thinking about justice. Would the jury be able to see beyond the paucity of evidence? No murder weapon, no cause of death, no eyewitnesses? He could only hope they'd use their common sense. Inside, the kid who had directed traffic at the age of five hoped and prayed that in the end good would still win out.

"Julie," he whispered since she was asleep, "what should I wear tomorrow?"

53

Dressed in a navy blue jacket, Detective Sergeant Conrad Prosniewski folded his hands in front of him and took the courtroom back to the morning of July 13, 1991, when he was first asked to investigate a missing person from the Willows. He recounted his first interviews with Bill Brailsford and with Tom Maimoni, the only sailing friend of Martha's the family could not rule out. Tom Maimoni, who then professed innocence, propriety, religion, and irresistibility all in one interrogation.

The detective led the audience back to the Willows, the neighbors, the beach, the pier, the boat livery. The jury followed in his footsteps as he visited Palmer's Cove Yacht Club and Baker's Island. Prosniewski talked to nearly a hundred people during the first three days of his investigation. Then, when he was confident he could discount Maimoni's story, he called the man in for a second interview.

The assistant district attorney had Prosniewski describe the location and size of the room, who else was present during the interview and why, the manner and tone of the entire interaction, and Maimoni's demeanor throughout. The jury's attention would be drawn by the defense to any use of harsh lights, confining or hostile space, intimidating posture, signs of coercion, instruments of torture. More than a dozen questions addressed Prosniewski's reading of the *Miranda* rights that night. Maimoni's signed blue *Miranda* card was introduced into evidence, as was his signed consent to search *Counterpoint*, and the nautical map on which Tom had drawn his circles, lines, angles, and vectors.

Prosniewski described the late-night search of *Counterpoint*, including his discovery of the chart book opened to Cat Island. The Commonwealth introduced as evidence the chart book and the state police photographs showing exactly how the book appeared inside the cabin prior to being touched or moved. Both the chart and the photo clearly showed a small blue *X* near the spot where the body was later found.

The detective related that his next appointment with Thomas Maimoni was to have been on July 18. They had planned to go out on a police launch to the location of the alleged accident.

"Sir, did you keep the appointment with Mr. Maimoni on July 18?"

"No, I did not."

"Something happen?" asked Mitchell.

"Martha Brailsford's body was found, and Mr. Maimoni fled."

When the defense had their turn, Jeffrey Denner grilled Prosniewski on his responsibility to ensure that all forensic tests that should have been done in fact were done. The implication was, of course, that they were not. He belabored for the jury the extensive pre-trial preparation and review of testimony the state was given the opportunity to perform. Witnesses were "prepared," their statements scrutinized for inconsistencies so that a cohesive story could be laid before the jury. This was Denner's recurring theme, a point he underscored with many of the prosecution's witnesses. These same witnesses had repeatedly slammed the door in the face of investigators for the defense during eighteen months of preparation for the trial.

Prosniewski's attention was next directed to Maimoni's chart book and the famous *X*, which Denner hoped to convince the jury had a less ominous purpose than to mark the victim's underwater tomb. Wasn't there in fact a second mark on the same page, Denner pointedly asked the witness. The detective agreed. The second mark noted the location off Graves Island east of Manchester of a submerged shipwreck called the *New Hampshire*, a contemporary of Old Ironsides, and a favorite spot for scuba divers. Next to the *X* were inscribed the letters *NH* in ballpoint pen.

Denner made one final point. Although there were a dozen, perhaps dozens of sightings of *Counterpoint* (or boats that looked very similar) on July 12, the police nevertheless had chosen only to follow up with those witnesses who validated their theory of the crime. Once the body was discovered wrapped with an anchor and a weight belt, once Ray Mount came forward and placed Maimoni back by 6:15P.M., the investigators had made up their minds that Tom Maimoni murdered Martha. They had proceeded to build their case around the scenario involving his early return.

54

Virginia McCarthy, who had shared her steak with Tom Maimoni three days before he went on the lam, took the oath in a voice taut with anger. There was no mistaking the emotions boiling inside her. Her body was tense. Her answers were emphatic. To Mitchell's question whether the person she knew by the name of Thomas Maimoni was in the courtroom, Mrs. McCarthy answered: "He most certainly is." She was asked to tell the court about Maimoni's visits the week after the incident and about his reaction to the news of the lobsterman. Her vivid rendition of the latter, including the shocked look in Maimoni's eyes, made an indelible impression on the jury.

Mrs. McCarthy described the shock she had felt during supper on the *Sarah B*, when Tom told them the Winter Island tale.

"How was Tom's demeanor?" Mitchell asked her.

"The way it is today—calm, cool, and collected," she responded curtly.

Jeff Denner immediately objected. The judge sustained.

Mrs. McCarthy's story seemed to tumble out determinably. She tripped over common courtroom land mines, like the "Just answer the question" trap. Mitchell asked whether she knew where Patti Maimoni had gone that week. Mrs. McCarthy responded, as would anyone, that Patti had gone to Wichita. When the defense objected and asked for a "responsive answer," Mrs. McCarthy was asked to simply tell the court if she knew where Patti was.

Answer: "Yes."

"Where was that?"

"She was in Wichita, Kansas."

Mrs. McCarthy described a subsequent conversation with Tom, when he told her about the accident. The prosecutor asked, "Did he tell you how it happened?"

"Yes, he did," said Mrs. McCarthy, who had learned this lesson.

"What did he say?"

"Only because I asked." Tom got no credit from Ginny McCarthy. She related Tom's story of the accident, which began with Martha's inappropriate shoes and her lack of knowledge about boats. Then the boom came into play, and Martha ended up in the water. At one point, Mrs. McCarthy asked Tom about Martha's missing duffel bag, which was mentioned on the news.

Tom answered in a cool, calm, and collected manner: "I threw it to her, hoping she could catch it."

Court then adjourned for lunch to digest this last, baffling explanation.

55

As an Essex County medical examiner who performed over 400 autopsies a year, Dr. Gerald Feigin knew death wasn't all it was cracked up to be. He disliked public fascination with violence, abhorred any attempts to romanticize or trivialize death. Every corpse he worked on "was a living, breathing person, once." Even the ones who were less than solid citizens had never deserved to die. And every one of them, "had a mother, once, a mother who loved them."

In class reunion group photos, Gerald Feigin was the guy who slapped on Groucho Marx glasses and a mustache just as the shutter snapped. He was proudly eccentric. He fervently believed most encounters between human beings would be vastly improved if people only "lightened up a bit." At the morgue the doctor displayed a small Visa/MasterCard sign on his desk in the hope that perhaps one day a client might have the grace to pay the bill on the way out.

But Feigin took his professional responsibilities seriously. In the autopsy room every mother's child, grown or not, sobered him. In the courtroom he became their only voice. In this courtroom he spoke for Martha Brailsford.

Dr. Feigin was asked to tell the jury the results of the autopsy performed in July 1991.

"I measured her height," Dr. Feigin began, "which was sixty-five and a half inches, and found that the body was almost completely skeletonized."

"Could you describe for the jury what you mean?"

"The skin, muscle, and internal organs were all missing, except for the upper face, the scalp, the fingers, the tops and soles of the feet, and a strip of skin on the upper back." He later offered that the extent of scavenging by marine animals suggested the body was unclothed while in the water. Nibbling usually "stopped at the cuffs," ceased where covering was encountered.

Dr. Feigin noted that the teeth were all present and natural. But he called in a forensic dentist to check for dental trauma. The dentist found a loose lower central tooth and a fractured lower left molar. The tooth damage was recent, occuring around the time of death.

Feigin retrieved a portion of heart tissue and found a tiny hole, a congenital defect in one of the ventricles, which in his opinion was clinically insignificant. He also found a piece of one of the lungs, soaked with water after submersion in the ocean. "It didn't tell me much of anything."

The pathologist found no evidence of injuries or fractures in the knees or bones, which he verified through X rays. The brain was intact and was checked for injuries or disease. Neither was found. However, when the scalp was examined, Dr. Feigin did find signs of trauma beneath the skin. Three distinct bruises appeared on three separate planes of Martha Brailsford's head.

Photographs of the bruises were marked as evidence and were shown to the jury. Dr. Feigin testified that none of the three had caused damage to the skull or brain, none had broken the skin, and none had been severe enough to be fatal. In fact, in all probability, none of the blows were sufficiently powerful to knock Martha out. Due to the location of the bruises, he presumed there had been three distinct blows, more likely from an object instead of a fall. Little could be inferred about the type of object, however, since there were no imprints in the skin itself. And a fall could not be ruled out.

At least one of the bruises had an irregular shape. "Irregularity indicates to me that it occurred before death," Dr. Feigin explained. The other two were smoother, suggesting they had formed shortly before, during, or shortly after death. Even after the heart stopped beating, a blow or fall could have resulted in a bruise if the victim were dead only a few hours. Broken veins beneath the skin allowed blood to pool into surrounding tissue, "unless the person forgot to pay their personal gravity bill," Feigin explained in a later interview.

In his cross-examination of lobsterman Hooper Goodwin, defense attorney Howard had suggested that Martha's bruises and the damage to her teeth might have resulted from being dragged along the bottom when the lobster trap was retrieved. Dr. Feigin now refuted this possibility when he described the area of skin remaining on the victim's back. Its very presence signified that she was lying on her back while, on the bottom. "If she had been turned over, the animals would have gotten to that." If she later had been dragged, scratches and abrasions would have shown up on that portion of skin. However, aside from one faint contusion in the middle of the back, the rest of the skin was clean.

Dr. Feigin had a few other reasons for listing the cause of death as a homicide. First, he knew that a person falling through water is unlikely to hit any object with enough force to cause a bruise. Second, by the time Hooper Goodwin pulled up his trap, Martha Brailsford no longer had sufficient blood to form a bruise. For Feigin, a third reason was the anchor rope and diving belt staring up at him from the autopsy table. Brailsford's death was ruled a drowning by exclusion. She could have been stabbed, suffocated, strangled, possibly even shot. None could be proved, none disproved. But in the last analysis, being thrown in the water shackled to an anchor and a diving belt would have ensured her death by drowning had she survived anything else. One way or another, somebody murdered Martha Brailsford—in Feigin's mind, beyond a reasonable doubt.

The defense attorney rose and asked the doctor about the possible causes of the bruises, which he reminded the jury were "minor" injuries. Could any have occurred by the victim being pulled up the swim ladder and being bumped against the rungs?

"It would be real difficult, but possible. Because you'd have to get your head all the way under a rung and pulled into it. It's not real likely to happen."

Jeff Denner then asked the doctor why tests were not performed that would prove or disprove drowning.

"There is no way of testing for that in any case," Feigin replied.

"There's none?" asked Jeffrey Denner.

"Not that I'm aware of."

"I see. You're familiar with the diatom test, of course?"

Diatoms are a type of algae that forms a silica shell. When a person drowns, diatoms present in the surrounding water are drawn through the lungs, pass into the bloodstream, and go immediately into the bones. By later dissolving the bones in lye, the silica shells of the diatoms can be seen under a microscope. Dr. Feigin did not believe in the validity of diatom tests. They were difficult to reproduce. They required a sample of water taken from the same spot and same time as the victim's drowning. Furthermore, the presence of diatoms in sea water fluctuates from season to season.

"Are you familiar with other experts in this country who feel that it's a legitimate test and use it?" Denner asked.

"I haven't met any, but I'm sure there's some people who believe that Santa Claus comes down the chimney, too."

"And you're not one of them?"

Feigin looked him straight in the eye. "About Santa, no. About the diatom test, no to that, too."

"I guess you don't want to hear about my other test that you think wouldn't be establishing anything, either?" Denner continued.

"Well, I'll listen to it," answered the doctor. "I'm always up for a laugh." Mentally, he readied his Groucho Marx glasses.

"What about the hemorrhaging in the mastoid?" the defense attorney quietly asked. Both the assistant district attorney and the court reporter complained to the judge that they couldn't hear Denner's words.

Dr. Feigin heard and understood. "That's a big problem," he answered. "Any body that goes below six feet of depth has been shown by the United States Navy, regardless if they've been dead a week or a month, once they go below six feet they get hemorrhage in that bone. So it, too, is worthless."

"I see," Denner said. "And are you aware of the fact that there are quite a few other experts in your position that disagree with you?"

"Well, there are some people in my position who don't have the knowledge or common sense that I do, who will testify to anything."

"In any event, with regard to Martha Brailsford in this particular case, there's absolutely no evidence to indicate whether her body was alive when it entered the water, is that correct?" Denner asked.

"That is correct," answered the pathologist.

In fact, if tests had proved drowning, neither side was particularly helped nor hurt. Denner's opening remarks had stated that Martha drowned earlier and that her floating body was retrieved. The converse, however, would have been damaging. If tests had ruled out drowning, they also would have ruled out the accident theory. The defense, therefore, was better off without the tests. Denner was merely trying to infer, once again, that the state had been sloppy.

When his job was done at the morgue and in the courtroom, Gerald Feigin went home to work in his backyard. In the springtime he made his garden grow with every kind of flower and vegetable he could coax out of the shady ground, including snap peas and fourteen varieties of tomatoes. He cultivated life with a vengeance. He kept his job at bay.

56

Robert Pino was a supervising chemist for the Massachusetts State Police Crime Laboratory's criminalistics division. Now he was called to the stand to describe his findings after searching *Counterpoint* and the Maimonis' condo in July 1991 and his subsequent tests on items taken into custody.

Pino described for the jury the numerous, visible red-brown spots he found on the mainsail. Later tested, they were found to be human blood. His job and expertise did not include typing the blood, a job left to the serologist. Pino had sketched the locations of the six separate groupings of blood spatters, some on both sides of the uppermost portion of the sail. He was not an expert in blood pattern analysis, so Kevin Mitchell did not ask his opinion of what could be inferred from the placement of those spatters.

The chemist described the subsequent search two days later of the boat and condo. This time, armed with a search warrant, they took a towel with blood stains from the cabin, a diving knife with scabbard, several pieces of rope and a fabric sample from the interior. Later given the piece of rope that was found tied to Martha's body, Pino visually matched it with the sample from *Counterpoint.* He also took apart a bit of each rope and counted the strands. The ropes matched.

Bob Pino had also been asked to weigh the anchor. It was thirteen and a half pounds.

Jeff Denner rose to cross-examine.

"You are now aware, are you not, that when the blood was deposited on the sail, the sail was actually down and draped over the mast, is that correct?" Denner asked the witness. The dramatic image of blood spatters stretching nearly thirty-two feet up the sail, and on both sides, nonetheless needed to be rectified. Pino's sketch appeared like a giant banner of violence.

Kevin Mitchell jumped up to object. He knew where this would lead. Pino was aching to tell the court his opinion of what happened. But he wasn't qualified, and his statements could be viewed as prejudicial in an appeal. "Objection, Your Honor!" shouted Mitchell.

Denner rephrased. "What is your understanding of the position of this sail when the blood was deposited on it?"

"*Objection,* Your Honor."

Judge Saris asked the chemist whether he had any personal knowledge of the position or whether his answer would be based on what someone else had told him. Pino answered the latter. The line then got a little muddied.

"So you have no personal understanding based on personal knowledge whether that sail was up or down when blood was deposited on it?" Denner asked.

"Are you asking my opinion on where, on how, I want that sail?"

"No, I'm asking from your personal knowledge." But then Denner abruptly backed off. Having made a thorough examination of *Counterpoint* on two separate occasions, the defense asked whether it were true that no other traces of blood or tissue residue were found on the boat aside from the spots on the sail and towel.

Pino replied, "That is correct, sir."

"Did you find anything—other than the anchor and the cut rope—did you find anything consistent with some kind of violent struggle? Any forensic signs or evidence consistent with what you as an expert would consider signs of a violent struggle?"

Pino had to agree there was nothing else on the boat.

Denner's last question, although he didn't say it, hearkened back to the "bad acts" testimony. "Did you do any tests for semen anywhere on the boat?"

"No, sir, I did not."

"Did you do any test for semen on any of the towels or any of the shirts or any of the clothing you found on the boat?"

"No, sir, I did not."

"I have no further questions, Your Honor."
Court was recessed for the day.

Three in the morning was Kevin Mitchell's busiest hour. He often woke involuntarily at that time during trials so that he could worry a little more about the next day in court. What evidence was he at risk of omitting? What critical question would he forget to ask? After sixteen-hour days the entire duration of the trial, he was physically and emotionally exhausted. In addition to the ongoing preparation after hours, there was the pressure of not letting down his investigators, who had been doing their job for a year and a half. But most of all, Martha's family now looked to him for justice.

57

atti Montague's voice made clear her reluctance to testify. Now a resident of New Hampshire, the former Patti Maimoni was anxious to get on with her new life. The murder trial of her previous husband was the last, painful obstacle.

In a soft, nervous tone, interrupted repeatedly by attorney and court requests for her to speak up, Patti told of their life together. She described some of their financial issues, starting with the purchase of *Counterpoint* before their marriage. Although they had agreed to split the down payment, the day it was due Tom suddenly claimed that his funds were tied up in "investments." So Patti paid his share.

After they married, Patti found herself helping Tom pay off $800 a month for what he claimed were medical bills related to his "dead" wife's illness. He told Patti that he had no medical insurance.

"Was Mr. Maimoni a scuba diver when you met him?"

"Yes he was," answered the witness, though Tom had little more than a wet suit at the time.

"How did he obtain all the rest of his equipment?" Meaning the expensive tanks, regulator, dive belt, and such.

"I bought it for him. For different holidays and occasions as gifts."

Despite Tom's numerous layoffs, they purchased their first home together, the condo on Settlers Way. With these debts they lived paycheck to paycheck. They were not in a financially secure position to hunt for a new house again in July 1991, Patti said in response to the assistant district attorney's questions. Certainly not in Beverly Farms.

On July 8, Patti left to visit her sister in Kansas, a trip that had been arranged months in advance. While she was away, Patti and Tom talked nearly every day by phone, but not on July 12. Patti could not remember whether she had tried contacting her husband that day or not. The defense very much wanted her to say that she had tried but that he hadn't been home that evening.

Assistant District Attorney Kevin Mitchell held up numerous items for Patti to identify. She recognized the road atlas found in Tom's car in Maine. The compass and knapsack were unfamiliar. The anchor was held up.

"Do you recognize this?"

"Yes. It was an anchor that my father had given to Tom. It was kept inside in the stern area. It was not the main anchor."

The diving belt was held up. Blue, red, and yellow swayed in the prosecutor's hand.

"Recognize it?"

"Yes, that was mine." Patti kept it on the boat under the sink.

"No further questions."

In his cross-examination, Jeffrey Denner wanted the jury to see both a sympathetic and a pathetic view of his client. "During the course of your marriage, Tom had a great deal of trouble holding a job, didn't he?" he asked Patti. "Did he seem to always be having difficulty at work, being laid off? It always seemed to be somebody else's fault, not his fault?"

"Yes," she answered.

"You came to find out that he wasn't an engineer by education or training at all? That at best he had a couple of adult education courses and a high school degree?"

"Yes."

"You found out that his abilities were far different than those which he projected to you?"

"That's correct."

"But in spite of all this, you loved Tom very much?"

"Yes," Patti answered.

"Because Tom essentially is a very kind and considerate man?"

"Yes he was."

"A very gentle man? Would it be fair to say that he never even remotely acted in any violent fashion toward you?"

"That's correct."

"Ever see him act violently toward anyone else? Did you ever see him even kick the dog?'"

"No, I did not."

"He was the kind of man who, apart from what he wasn't, was many good things as well?"

"Yes."

Actually, Tom's lies had begun to show before Patti's departure for Kansas. She had picked up signals earlier, she testified. Yet she still described their marriage at that time as being "great."

Denner held out the letters Tom had written to Patti during the first few months of his imprisonment. He asked if she recalled Tom writing:

Every day I wait for mail call hoping and praying that a letter from you will arrive. I hope our relationship is strong, that you know that all the things that were exposed in the papers about me were things that I would have shared with you, were it not that I feared losing you...Carrying the burden of not being honest with you and the fact that jobs were becoming harder to find, being laid off from Parker Brothers really drove me into the deepest of depressions. I felt that I had lost it all ...As to the boat and Martha, I can only say that it really was an accident, that I used every ounce of physical and emotional strength to save her life. I've suffered a complete emotional collapse as a result. It was important to me to try and save our relationship.

"Mrs. Montague, do you recall Tom writing these things?" Denner asked.

"Yes."

"Do you believe that Tom loved you that deeply, and many of the lies he told after this incident occurred because he could not face up to losing you?"

"Yes," she answered softly.

"No further questions."

Seated at the defense table, Tom Maimoni wept quietly into a handkerchief.

58

Kevin Mitchell implored his next witness to come to court in the full dress uniform of the Royal Canadian Mounted Police, the famous red jacket. Corporal Robert Teather from Vancouver, British Columbia, explained to Mitchell that they no longer wore those uniforms. Nevertheless, minus theatrics, Corporal Teather, was among the shining stars of Mitchell's lineup. Teather is one of the world's leading experts on the physiology of drowning victims, in particular, how bodies in saltwater and freshwater undergo decomposition and consumption. An esoteric specialty, to be sure.

Teather had studied the autopsy photographs and reports on Martha Brailsford and had several things to say to the jury, none of them pleasant. This case was perhaps the worst example of underwater consumption he had ever seen. The extent of scavenging from six days lying in the water did not surprise him. However, the skeletonized body convinced him, as it had Dr. Feigin, that Martha was nude when she came to rest on the bottom. The defense had also agreed to this fact. But Mitchell wanted the jury to infer that by removing Martha's clothes, Tom had increased the chances that his victim would be consumed beyond recognition and that any other wounds to her body would be obscured.

Corporal Teather confirmed that with rare exceptions people who drown sink within five seconds. Their final reflexive attempt to inhale air draws water into the lungs, creating "negative buoyancy." Teather further told the court that unweighted drowning victims typically come to rest in a "semi-fetal" position, making contact with the bottom only with their knees, forehead, nose, and the knuckles of their hands. Only these points of contact are subject to the feeding of bottom-dwelling crustaceans. As decomposition sets in and gases begin to form in the digestive track, the body slowly begins to rise. Within a few days, it reaches the surface. Even in the early stages, when the body barely lifts away from the bottom, the loss of contact puts an immediate halt to the feeding.

The weights on Martha's body, besides causing drowning if she had been alive, brought on two additional results. The belt around her waist pressed her horizontally against the sea floor, ensuring that all parts of her body were accessible to the crustaceans. Secondly, the combined weight of the anchor and the belt compensated for the buoyancy created during decomposition. The victim remained firmly on the bottom, where consumption would be complete. The body neither would have risen to the surface nor risked discovery. Mitchell pointed out that the weight of the anchor alone would not have been enough. Teather calculated the gases in Martha's body would have been sufficient to lift twenty or twenty-five pounds. The anchor itself weighed less than fourteen pounds. The diving belt added another twenty-five.

Kevin Mitchell wanted to make one more point with this witness. Normally, Teather explained, feeding begins on any accessible soft tissue areas of the body, such as the eyelids, nose, lips, and ears. However, any area where the "skin had been compromised," like an open wound, would attract the feeders first. The body in this case reflected such a pattern. The amount of remaining tissue on the face was highly unusual for this degree of overall consumption, Teather remarked. And, by the way, wounds in the abdominal wall would have prevented the buildup of gases needed to float the body to the surface.

One was left to wonder. If Maimoni's engineering degrees and diving certifications were fraudulent, if he were panicked and upset, would he indeed have had the knowledge and presence of mind to disrobe Martha, to calculate what was needed to weigh her down for all time, and then to slit her stomach, all with the specific intention of counteracting decomposition and guaranteeing total consumption by lobsters and crabs? And then to toss her in the one spot that was both rich in shellfish and hidden from any observation point on land?

Kevin Mitchell invited the jury to believe so.

59

On Friday morning the fifth day of the trial, the jury was taken on a view, to survey the Willows neighborhood where Tom Maimoni and Martha Brailsford had lived, and to take a close look at a Cal 28, similar to *Counterpoint*.

When they returned to the courthouse, the prosecution wrapped up their case with Mitchell's last witness, Bob Montague. The man who married Patti Maimoni a year after Tom's arrest had not been overjoyed at being subpoenaed.

Kevin Mitchell anticipated his witness might not be too cooperative. The ADA's intention had been to slip him in early in the week, sandwiched between powerful, compelling, memorable witnesses so that attention would be drawn away from him. But Montague had been laid up all week.

The prosecutor needed this witness to introduce the contents of Maimoni's telephone message from Maine, when Tom was on the run. "My life is over—take care of Patti" sure didn't sound like the last wish of an innocent man. Yet there was no other way to get this in front of the jury than through Bob Montague's unenthusiastic testimony.

Montague also described his failed rendezvous with Tom on July 12, 1991. The prosecutor had seen the defense investigators' report after their rowboat encounter with Montague at PCYC during the summer of 1992. Mitchell knew Denner wanted to use this witness to contradict Ray Mount's sighting. So the assistant district attorney asked Montague to explain that he had been working below deck for many hours on the day of the incident and therefore might not have seen *Counterpoint* returning that evening.

On cross-examination the defense attorney tried to establish that Montague was actively and angrily searching for Maimoni all day. Therefore, Montague would certainly have noticed if *Counterpoint* had passed by, or whether it was in its slip when he motored in later that night. The psychological underpinnings of Maimoni's rendition of the incident depended on his not returning until very late on the night of July 12.

However, Montague refused to give either side satisfaction. Over and over, he swore to the courtroom that he could not recall whether he saw Tom's boat that evening. Denner read to the witness from the investigators' report quoting Montague insisting *Counterpoint* had not been there. The witness responded under oath that the report was wrong.

Denner was visibly stunned. "If three people got up in court under oath, two investigators and a lawyer, and said you answered that way to them, they would be lying?"

"That's the way I feel about it, yes, sir."

Both sides were relieved to see this witness finally step down. The Commonwealth rested its case. Court recessed until Monday.

60

"Sir, have you ever seen any trawlers leave Gloucester Harbor and go out to the fishing bank?" Rick Howard opened the defense case as the second week of the trial got underway. One of his tasks was to find a source for the "rogue waves" Tom Maimoni gave as the reason an experienced sailor had fallen off his boat on a calm day into water smooth as glass.

"Yes. Very few people sleep on their boats there for that reason." His witness was Hillary Smart, the Olympic sailing medalist who had seen a boat named *Counterpoint* outside Manchester late on the afternoon of July 12.

"That reason is what?"

"There's so much wake. Big wake because they're heavy displacement fishing boats." The trawlers, some fifteen or so, left early each morning and returned to Gloucester in the late afternoon.

"And is it fair to say that the Annisquam River dumps into Gloucester Harbor, creating a rip and chop?"

The witness concurred.

The defense continued their case with an aggressive attack on Dr. Ray Mount's 6:15P.M. sighting. Not only did that early hour contradict Maimoni's own timeline, it left insufficient time for *Counterpoint* to have sailed the ten miles all the way to Gloucester Harbor, to have experienced the "accident," to have sailed to Cat Island and then back to Salem. And Gloucester was important to his story, the closest spot one could find any credible wave activity.

The defense used Smart's sighting, which occurred between four-thirty and five-thirty, to cast doubt on Ray Mount's story. They also called the former dockmaster of Palmer's Cove Yacht Club to the stand. His job had been to keep a record of the transient boats that came into the marina. The witness had brought his records of overnight charges from July 1991 to court. He showed that during the month of July 1991 Raymond Mount had been charged for fifteen days. These records did not, however, include Friday night, July 12.

Kevin Mitchell rose to cross-examine. "Sir, the way to determine if a boat was tied up overnight is you take a walk at 6:30 the next morning and see who's there, correct?"

"That's correct."

"Sir, if Mr. Mount were to testify that he had been out sailing Friday, came in to the dock to discharge passengers, picked up another group and went out for dinner, came back in to discharge them, then returned to his mooring late that night, and used his dinghy to come to shore, your records do not disagree with that at all, do they?"

"No, they don't."

"Common practice for those with moorings. And if an overnighter at the dock manages to slip out early in the morning before 6:30, they could also beat the three dollars?" asked Mitchell.

"Correct."

"No further questions." Mount's sighting had been salvaged.

61

The defense's next witness had come to Massachusetts to tell the jury that Martha Brailsford may have died from a congenital heart defect. Dr. Michael Baden, Director of Forensic Sciences with the New York State Police, had not examined the victim's remains but had looked at the autopsy report written by Dr. Feigin. The thrust of his testimony was that at the time of Martha's death, only one significant medical abnormality existed. A small hole in the septum of Martha's heart, under the right circumstances, could have been clinically significant, especially if she had been under great physical stress.

"Sir, did you take the opportunity to look at the heart before coming into this courtroom and testifying that it could possibly contribute to her death? With reasonable medical certainty?" Kevin Mitchell asked sarcastically on cross-examination. He was seething. The witness had also stated that none of the two-hundred-odd bones in Martha's body were fractured, that the bruises were insignificant, and that numerous tests which Feigin had failed to do Baden would certainly have done. Cavalier pronouncements from an expert witness who had not even taken the time to drive up to the morgue to see the tissue samples himself.

"No," answered the doctor.

"You could have, couldn't you. Dr. Feigin told you it still exists."

"I suppose so," Baden replied.

The prosecutor questioned him about the manner and degree

to which crustaceans had devoured the remains. "Isn't it true that crustaceans will attack a point of entry first, such as a bloody wound, rather than solid skin?"

Baden first tried to skirt the question, saying coyly, "Sir, we don't have lobsters in New York City."

Mitchell spun around angrily and stared at the witness. The prosecutor persisted, refusing to allow Baden to hide behind this flip remark.

The doctor finally agreed. "In general that would be true, yes."

"Well, her face was remarkably well intact after five days in the water, wasn't it? The head, ears, eyes," asked Mitchell, wanting the defense witness to concede that Martha might have had open wounds which were far more attractive to scavengers.

Again, Baden concurred.

Mitchell added, "Those tend to be soft tissue areas that go first, correct?"

Here Baden balked. "Not necessarily. Different animals attack different parts of bodies. Rats...."

The judge cut him off. Rats were too far afield.

"How about crabs?" tried the prosecutor.

"I don't know where crabs would go." No crabs in New York, either.

Baden also testified that the lack of abrasion marks on Martha's ankles suggested she was dead when tied up. Otherwise, she would have struggled against the ropes.

Mitchell held up one of the autopsy photos. "Fair to say there is nothing left of that leg, Doctor, above the ankle bone?" he asked with scorn.

The defense next brought out their own forensic expert, Stuart James, whose specialty was the interpretation of bloodstain splatters. James had examined the mainsail of *Counterpoint* when it was set up on a similar boat. Based on the distribution, shape, and large size of the droplets, he concluded the blood was the result of a "low velocity event" like a cut or a nosebleed instead of a blow or a gunshot wound.

"There was not a lot of activity involved," he added. Elongated drops that exhibit a clear direction suggest that the source had been above the sail. "Although most of the drops were from a dripping object, a few were transfer stains, as if a bloody finger had brushed against the surface."

To explain the location of the six or so blood groupings, James discovered in his field test in New Hampshire that he could drape and bunch the sail down sufficiently to create one large area of bleeding rather than six. To explain blood on both upper sides of the sail, he hypothesized that the top itself was flopping around freely. The wind, too, could have been a factor in the layout of the stains. Stuart James further estimated that the total quantity of blood found on the sail was a "few thimblefuls." Not much of a crime scene, the defense was implying.

On cross-examination, the witness admitted to Mitchell this was the first sail he had examined. He also admitted that his conclusions were based upon the assumption the sail was down. Had the sail been up, the elongations might suggest that the source was below the level of the drops. So which was presumption and which was fact? Mitchell showed the witness a photo of the stains and pointed to one near the top that had a forty-five-degree angle in an upward direction. Or forty-five degrees downward, argued James, if the top was upside down. As James observed, had the direction been upward, it would not likely have been due to "dropped" blood. "It takes considerable force to project blood upward like that," the witness offered. So, again, another conclusion. "Low velocity" was based on the sail being all the way down, the top slugs out of the channel.

"You set the sail up in a way that accommodates your theory, is that correct?" asked Mitchell.

"That's not correct at all," insisted the witness. "I set up the sail to show in fact that your prior analyst was quite incorrect in his assumption and conclusions that...."

"I don't believe we offered," interrupted Mitchell. He hadn't let Bob Pino give an opinion on the blood spatters because Pino lacked the qualifications.

"...that there were five to six different impact sites. That was my purpose," finished James.

"Sir, I don't think we offered any prior opinion," finished Mitchell. Nice of the defense to slip in that point for the prosecution, though.

62

Linda Beckley had been married to Tom Maimoni from 1984 to 1987. On Tuesday morning the tall, dark-haired woman described for the jury what had been a brief and tempestuous marriage. After Tom's later arrest and the disclosures about his private life had surfaced, Linda learned about his additional wife, the survival of the "dead" one, the lack of degrees. She also learned he was not in fact a ski instructor, nor a pilot. Yet she was in court to testify that during all the heated arguments and trying circumstances they had endured together, Tom had never exhibited any violent tendencies. Linda Beckley was currently a recovering alcoholic who was willing to announce this to the world to illustrate the volatile situation Tom had been in at the time. Drinking heavily during the marriage, Linda had been the violent one. When she hit Tom, his reaction had always been to run away. Twice he had run to the police, one time begging them to tell his wife to leave him alone. The other time he had sought a restraining order.

"He never fought back," she stated somewhat protectively.

Under cross-examination Linda admitted that she, like Patti, had purchased a boat for Tom, a twenty-five-foot Coronado, for $12,000. Even while she was making the loan payments, Tom had never let her touch his boat. Just a month after their wedding, the romance virtually ended. Two years later, they divorced. Linda Beckley retained the boat and the heavy debts incurred by her marriage.

The man who had told her he was a ski instructor, pilot, Ph.D., and widower somehow had managed to win her continuing loyalty even during the trial. Linda had been visiting Tom in jail, advising him, looking out for him. She was the only one of his ex-wives to stick by her man.

The prosecution's questions she answered defensively, and one might charitably guess, naively.

"Didn't you tell police that Tom was confrontational over your drinking?"

"I don't recall saying that," replied the witness.

"Didn't you tell the police that you never did anything good enough?" In fact, she had reported to authorities Tom had frequently told her that she was stupid, that her job was stupid.

"That's correct."

"Didn't you tell police you once slapped him, and he threw you against a wall?" Mitchell asked her.

"I hit Tom in the face with the phone, and Tom pushed the phone away from me. Tom didn't hit me. I tripped and hit the wall."

"Oh, they misunderstood?" the prosecutor asked dryly. "I have no further questions."

Tom Maimoni had tried to control Linda Beckley like he had tried to control his other wives. But Linda had managed to break him. With a temper that matched his own, she in some sense had grabbed the reins. She had taught him. She had helped improve his strategy. So when Patti Stochl later met Tom Maimoni, he was already a changed man.

Brown University in Providence, Rhode Island, yielded the next defense witness. Mr. Donald Avery was a nautical engineer. Avery testified about the handling characteristics of a Cal 28, which he described as "snappy and wet." He told the jury the hypothetical effects if such a boat were in the vicinity of Gloucester Harbor at 8:00 one summer night with the main sail down, the jib up, and two fifty-foot fishing trawlers were passing by at eight to ten knots a quarter to a half mile away. The waves generated in such a scenario would hit the boat hard. Avery performed numerous calculations for the courtroom. The calculations defied belief.

On cross-examination, Kevin Mitchell asked the witness about the trawlers passing a quarter mile away, allegedly obstructed by the jib of *Counterpoint*. "One of the nice things about trawlers is you tend to hear them long before you see them," offered Mitchell.

"I wouldn't say that," answered Avery.

"Well, a diesel engine lumping out of Gloucester at night?" Without waiting for an answer, the prosecutor added, "Isn't there in fact a five-knot speed limit until the end of the breakwater at Gloucester Harbor?" And if a trawler were forty feet rather than the hypothetical sixty-four, what effect would its wake have? Considerably less. "Didn't you say these waves come in sets, with the worst one in the middle, after at least one smaller warning wave? A warning any good sailor might recognize?"

Avery answered, "One doesn't really have that much warning. Innumerable times I've—the boat has been quite still, and all of a sudden it goes up and down and my thought is, 'Where in hell did that come from?'"

"As you stay on the boat?" pointed out the prosecutor with a smile. "The fact is, sir, as you tell us what might have occurred that Friday, July 12, you really haven't the slightest idea what really happened?"

"No," agreed Avery.

The next witness would make a quite different claim.

63

With long, quick strides and his head hunched forward, Thomas J. Maimoni came up to the stand to testify in his own defense. An overflowing crowd stood watching the tiny news monitor downstairs. After all the previews of the "pathological liar" defense, the entire courthouse now stared in wonder and anticipation as Maimoni raised his hand to affirm that he would tell the truth, the whole truth, and nothing but. The witness asserted, "I do."

"Other than a high school diploma, do you hold any other degrees?" Defense co-counsel Richard Howard handled the questioning and began by trying to clear up the fog surrounding Tom's background. The courtroom was dead quiet. After all the media references to Maimoni's fake degrees, what would he now say under oath?

"I claim to have an incomplete on those," the defendant answered dismissively.

Howard asked about his military career. The war in Vietnam had begun to escalate when Tom Maimoni graduated from high school. Maimoni was about to be drafted when he instead enlisted in the Air Force. After serving for a time at Tyndall Air Force Base in Florida, Tom got his overseas assignment. "Where were you shipped?"

Tom digressed by talking about his survival training in Florida. He took comfort in long, wordy answers to explain and impress. He moved about nervously on the witness stand. "Some of my classmates were shipped to Okinawa and Vietnam, and I got Clark—Clark Air Force Base in the Philippines," Tom finally explained. Tom's friends had all heard about his survival in the jungle after he was shot down while piloting a C-130 in Vietnam. Now, Maimoni told the crowded courtroom that he spent his tour in the Philippines without incident, without participating in or seeing any combat. In fact, he never set foot in Vietnam. At Clark, however, he helped unload corpses coming back from Vietnam. During the heavy fighting of the Tet Offensive, they ran out of body bags, he said. He attributed ten years of subsequent nightmares and his post-traumatic stress symptoms to this period of his life.

Maimoni married prior to shipping out. Unfortunately, his marriage to Mary Cayer, the girl he had taken to both the junior and senior proms at Pawtucket Vocational, deteriorated while he was overseas. When they divorced in 1971, Maimoni already had fathered a son, Michael Christopher, and a daughter, Christina Marie. Saying their names aloud in the courtroom choked him up. He had not seen his children for over twenty years. "My ex-wife remarried, and they were in a family unit. I made the decision not to interfere with that and not to be a part-time parent. I was estranged, with the exception of financial support." He struggled to regain his voice. "I can't explain in a word how I feel."

From his seat, Conrad Prosniewski stared at the defendant and felt anger welling up. A month after Tom's arrest in 1991, Prosniewski had gone to Pawtucket, Rhode Island, to interview Mary Cayer. Although she was not called to testify, her picture of Tom Maimoni was much different than that of the man Patti married.

The period before they separated had been a sad one. Tom was cheating on Mary. His girlfriends started calling him at the couple's house. At times his jobs paid good money, but it was never spent on the family. After returning from the Philippines, Tom seemed to resent being a husband and a father. Mary felt she had become an annoyance to him. At one point she found pictures in his bureau drawer he had taken of his genitals for one of his girlfriends. When he finally left, the family had no idea where he had gone. Tom rarely paid support until years later, when Rhode Island took him to court and worked out an $800 monthly payment schedule with him—coincidentally, the same amount he had gotten from Patti for the phantom hospital bills. Mary told Detective Prosniewski that Tom still owed over $10,000 in back child support.

Maimoni didn't quite leave the family in peace. Every few years he briefly resurfaced for reasons known only to himself. When his daughter Christina was sixteen, she became pregnant. On Tom's next visit, after learning of Christina's condition, he blew up at his former wife, claiming it was her fault. Mary had no morals. Tom threatened to kill the kids and burn down the house. Fortunately, he didn't stay long enough to accomplish this.

When Christina's baby was a year old, the seventeen-year-old decided it would be nice to try again to establish a relationship with her father. She located Tom and called him. Tom's response was short and to the point: he wanted nothing to do with her. He denied having a grandson. He asked her not to call him anymore.

As Prosniewski sat on the porch of their Pawtucket house listening to Mary's story, Tom's twenty-one-year-old son hung out in the doorway. Not speaking. Just listening. His stature and features were strikingly similar to those of his father. He also had Tom's voice. The kid was soft-spoken and polite. Prosniewski could see the kid was hurting. Hurt not so much by the incident that now brought the police but by his father's desertion. By all the years before 1991. Mike listened with sadness as his mother, in a low voice, talked about his father with little bitterness or anger. About their lives. "He just up and left. We never knew when he'd show up. Mostly he didn't. Never so much as a birthday card."

For Detective Sergeant Conrad Prosniewski, it all hit too close to home. "Me in my situation," he reflected. "Here I am dying 'cause my kids are in Florida. And this man could do this. I felt so bad for his kids." The image of Maimoni's fatherless son leaning in the doorway burned in his skull.

A year and a half later, sitting in the Newburyport courtroom for this man's trial, he listened to Maimoni gulp tears. Prosniewski wanted to choke the son of a bitch.

The defendant was asked about the ups and downs of his work history, why he was fired or laid off from company after company, starting with the construction jobs his father had gotten for him.

"None of those jobs lasted very long, did they?" asked Howard.

"The blue-collar jobs that I had? No, and it was by design. I was looking to find my career."

Maimoni placed the rest of the blame on companies experiencing trouble or reorganization. He launched into a brief lecture on the decline of the textile industry in the Northeast during that period. Nevertheless, with his high school courses in drafting and design and these short-term jobs, Tom Maimoni was able over time to build up some experience—or the illusion of experience—in engineering work.

In 1980, with increasingly creative résumés, he talked himself into a position with General Electric for a few years, then later with Arthur D. Little, although the company later declined to discuss the nature of his job responsibilities. Maimoni described it as aerospace hardware engineering. He loved the work, but the projects dried up after four or five years, as he told it. Arthur D. Little's records instead indicated that he was fired for contentious behavior.

Meanwhile, his marriages were following a similar course. While at GE, Tom met and married Mary Ellen Bouchie, a schoolteacher in Waltham, Massachusetts. Although it took four years to divorce him, Mary Ellen left six months after the wedding. Tom told the courtroom that they had purchased a boat together and that the boat had become the "other woman" in his life. Mary Ellen desperately wanted a child, but Tom was spending all their money and his time on his affair with the ocean. He resisted having kids. His career had not yet stabilized. The marriage was also saddled with Tom's prior debts.

So Mary Ellen Bouchie moved out. Tom returned home from work one day to find the apartment empty. Everything had been cleaned out. No note. "It was pretty dramatic. I was devastated, as I still am today."

"How did you deal with the pain?" asked his lawyer.

"I told my colleagues and friends...she had passed away. That was how I dealt with it. Death. That's how I dealt with the pain."

"Could you speak up so the members of the jury can hear you, Tom?" Howard asked gently. He wanted the jury to hear Tom's pain, not just his arrogance.

"I insulated myself," Maimoni continued in a husky voice. "I couldn't face the truth. I deeply cared for her. If anyone probed further, that's when I came up with the cancer routine."

The next wife was Linda Lee Webb (later to become Linda Beckley), who had already testified for the defense and who had also bought a boat with Tom. This marriage had failed, too.

Then came Patti, whose mother died of melanoma during the first year of their marriage. She, too, had helped Tom buy a boat. Patti had called Tom a superstar. Tom told the jury he had tried desperately to live up to it. He had lied to her about his marriages and his degrees.

"They were lies to build myself up in her eyes, not to question the reasons why I never completed the degrees. It was simply to say, yes, they were done, and be done with it. Get on with things." The numerous layoffs, however, gradually eroded both his image and the marriage.

In light of his financial hardship, Howard asked Tom why he had looked at property in Beverly Farms in July 1991. Tom claimed the Farmers' divorce had led him to believe that it was a "distressed property" and that he could have bought it for a song. The same house in western Massachusetts would have gone for less than a third of their asking price, he explained. "The financing for that house, I was told, could be done on a small business loan based on my contract's receivables. I also was indicating to some people that I would be selling the townhouse. I was sketching all of this up as counter-buying and selling." Tom wanted to find a single-family house for Patti, who seemed dissatisfied with their Salem condo. She needed a better "lifestyle."

Howard asked about the incident on the boat with Rosemary Farmer, to whom Tom was physically attracted. "I am a touch/hug kind of person," the defendant explained. When it had gotten out of hand and Rosemary had told him to stop, he "did." Tom conceded, though, that some sort of mistake had been made in her case. "My remorse is that I should never have been in that...put myself in that situation," he explained.

After an endless series of questions on how to operate a boat, defense attorney Richard Howard finally led Tom to the fateful sail with Martha Brailsford. He took the defendant through the afternoon in question to the point where Maimoni was motoring toward Marblehead Harbor. With the mainsail raised and trimmed, the boat was steadied and was more visible to other sailors at a distance. According to Maimoni, they talked about their families. Out past Great Misery Island, Tom shut down the engine and rolled out the jib. He then headed the sailboat toward Manchester Harbor. During this part of his testimony, Maimoni talked a lot about the winds spiking up ominously. Around five or six, he and Martha found themselves near an area known as the Spindle, where they paused for refreshments and "to enjoy the peace." Tom had a couple of Budweisers left from the Fourth of July cruise, which he drank. He told the court that Martha poured herself some pineapple-orange juice and "spiked it up" with Captain Morgan's Spiced Rum.

The court was transported onto the deck of *Counterpoint.* It was as if they could feel the summer sun on their skin, smell the wet nylon of the mainsail and hear the creak of the boom. The captain and the first mate, as he suddenly referred to his guest, "started to get hungry." The sun was sinking in the western sky. It was a little after eight-thirty when they decided to turn back. The boat was two or three miles outside Gloucester Harbor at this point. Tom wanted to lower the sail and motor back. He ordered his first mate to go below and take care of the galley. Martha did so, then offered to help with the transition. She jumped onto the deckhouse and "assumed the position" in what Maimoni described as the "restricted area" on *Counterpoint*—the area forward of the mast.

The winds were picking up, getting "squirrelly." There was a chop at the mouth of Gloucester Harbor. The water near the breakwater was "sloppy."

The underwhelmed courtroom was being primed for impending disaster. Maimoni, the Expert Sailor, was faced with a challenging set of circumstances here: choppy water, squirrelly winds, a boat described by defense expert Avery as "snappy and wet," and a woman who wouldn't stay down in the galley, wearing improper shoes.

At that moment, Judge Saris banged her gavel, bringing the courtroom back to land. The hour was getting late. Court adjourned for the day.

64

"Would you tell us now what Martha did and what you did for purposes of dropping the main and turning the boat around to head back toward Salem?" Defense attorney Rick Howard resumed questioning the defendant on Wednesday morning, February 10.

"There was a short discussion on where the crew would be and some warnings making sure she did not go forward of the mast." All references to Tom and Martha by name had disappeared. "As the boat was rounding up, the first mate's job would be to trim the mainsail in from the mainsail winch." The defendant hauled out a four-part diagram to illustrate the sequences that were about to unfold.

As he started to explain the little boats he had drawn, the sound of drilling out in the street suddenly drowned out his testimony. Judge Saris finally stopped him, lamented the noise, and asked him to speak up.

Tom continued in a high voice talking about rhumb lines, degrees, and "snubbing" the boom. "The maneuver is coordinated," again Tom named no subject in this sentence, "with the first mate, who is grinding the mainsail winch and trimming the main boom in."

Mr. Howard stopped him. "Please don't confuse the jury. Let's not talk about first mates or anything like that. Let's talk about Tom and Martha."

"Tom and Mrs. Brailsford, yes," answered Tom.

"Tell the jury what happened next."

"As...I was rounding the boat up into the wind, Mrs. Brailsford was in the position in the cockpit at the time."

"You called her Martha, didn't you?" Howard was not going to let him get away with even this amount of distancing.

"Occasionally, yes. I'm sorry."

"You can call her Martha today. I want to put the jury on this boat."

Tom agreed to cooperate. "Yes, Martha is fine."

At this point, Martha had finished trimming the mainsail and got ready to receive the sail as it was lowered. Tom locked the wheel and went to the port side to collect the halyard. He kept an eye on the jib, he said, to make sure the boat didn't go through the eye of the wind. He sat back down with tension on the halyard in his hand. By releasing it slowly, he allowed the mainsail to luff as it dropped down.

Martha started gathering up the yards of nylon as they cascaded over the boom and the coaming. But something was wrong. The gate was open at the bottom of the mast, and the sail was running out of the channel—or track—and all over the deck. Tom had to take his eyes off Martha and grope around for the sail ties. The mainsail was a distraction and a mess. Located off Gloucester Harbor, they were hitting sloppy water. The boat was beginning to ride up and down with the swells.

Maimoni explained the next problem. Martha, for unknown reasons, had gone forward and was standing on the foredeck. From the cockpit he yelled to her. She turned to face him and said something he did not hear. Gesturing toward the Boston skyline, she took a step toward him.

And then, said Tom, *the boat launched up over a wake*. Had Martha been "at her station" like she was supposed to have been, the wake would not have been a problem. Tom had other jobs he should have been concentrating on: keeping a keen eye out for other boat traffic, water conditions, and waves. Then there was that damn sail. Amidships, Martha would have been on the vortex of the pitching rather than "out of moment" out on the bow. She also had nothing to hold on to at that location.

As the bow pitched up sharply, "Martha came down the center line of the boat toward me, and coming down, struck the face of the mast. I didn't see the impact...all I could do was judge the trajectory. *I immediately went into emergency mode*."

Howard stopped him. "Describe what you saw."

Maimoni regrouped. "I saw her airborne, coming toward me. And I went into the emergency mode of doing the work I had to do to stop the boat from sailing. Cut sailing. Sailing is over."

Howard asked where the wave had come from. The so-called "rogue wave" the defense had been advertising for a year and a half.

Tom tried to describe the series of visions that had blurred his memory. One vision contained trawlers. He remembered seeing their white lights off to the right, perhaps a half mile, perhaps three-quarters of a mile. Partially obscured by the jib. Had he not suffered all these distractions and had been able to maintain his position in the cockpit, he might have seen their running lights. That was the job of the helmsman. Not clambering around after escaping mainsails or yelling at women who wander from their positions.

Martha had disappeared, obscured by the dodger. Tom's first priority was to get the boat under control before going to her aid. The boat was pitching, rolling, and yawing from the wake. The wind generated waves and tidal displacements. The area had a lot of crosscurrents and rips.

As he yelled to her to stay down, Tom then tried to finish the transition to auxiliary power. He threw off the jib sheet to luff the jib, then rolled up the jib from the cockpit.

Then he glimpsed Martha crawling up the mast, looking stunned and scared. She didn't utter a sound.

"'Get down! I want you down low on the deck, Martha. Just don't worry about it,' I yelled at her. I had several things to do...one of those was to stop the sheet, the halyard, because I didn't want the sail to run right out of the track." Tom then crossed the cockpit to reach the engine controls. He turned the key and hit the starter button to fire up the engine. He checked the RPM gauge and kept it at about a thousand so that he could use the transmission.

Martha, said Tom, seemed like she was diligently trying to get back to her station, where she was supposed to be, where he had told her to stay. "All this time I had been screaming for her to stay down. At this point, her safety was the primary concern." Tom finished starting the engine and went back to the steering wheel pedestal. The boat was veering off. Suddenly they took another wake broadside. The boat went into a sharp gunwale-to-gunwale rolling action.

"I had my hands full of work. I stood to my feet and was

searching the deck for Mrs. Brailsford," Maimoni said. "And I was alone on the boat."

The courtroom was quiet.

In later testimony, defense psychiatrist Dr. Harold Bursztajn provided a clinical backdrop to Tom Maimoni's story that gave it a kind of credibility. In a sense, his diagnosis and explanation connected the dots in Maimoni's bizarre rendition of events and allowed the jury to visualize a world of fear, apprehension, and overwhelming loneliness. A world where fantasy was essential for both self-esteem and self-preservation. Maimoni was afraid of being alone. His first reaction, which he spontaneously described to the jury, was not "She was gone," or "She was overboard," or even "Martha was nowhere to be found." His first gut reaction was, *"I was alone on the boat." He* had been compromised. *He* was the one deserving of compassion.

Rick Howard asked Maimoni, "What did you do to try to find Martha?"

"I looked at the...at the deck of the boat." Tom showed on the diagrams where he had searched. Then he looked into the water close by. "Over my right shoulder within the stern way, I could see Martha swimming toward the boat."

Martha was in the water. Rick Howard took Tom through his subsequent actions—what he did, when, and why.

"I was yelling, of course, as soon as I picked her up in the water at that angle. The boat is idling, I've got a mainsail that is screwed up, and I have a person overboard." The captain of *Counterpoint* explained the host of problems with which he was beset. "My job is to keep my eyes on Martha and to try to get her attention to me. But her head was...she was swimming with...I couldn't get her to...I was trying to yell to her to get eye contact with me so that I could do a flotation device type of thing. It would be a waste of time...time is of the essence here, to get the person back to the boat."

Although his "horseshoe person overboard device" (his life preserver) was handy to his position at the wheel, Tom explained that throwing it overboard would have been useless "without obtaining eye contact with the person in the water. That's the primary concern."

A harsh laugh punctured the stillness of the courtroom. Paul Brailsford, Bill's dad and Martha's father-in-law, had spent his entire lifetime on boats of every size. Thomas Maimoni's reasoning for not tossing the life preserver to the struggling Martha had outraged him.

Judge Saris interrupted to admonish and announce to the courtroom that such noises were totally inappropriate. She instructed the court officers to remove the next such offender.

In the meantime, Maimoni had stepped down from the stand. With his back to the audience, he sobbed quietly into a handkerchief. When the questioning was about to resume, Tom stepped back up and added a plea: "I need to get through this without interruptions. I can't...I can't break...."

Howard pulled him together: "In any event, Tom, you made a decision not to throw the 'horseshoe' to Martha. Why did you make that decision?"

Tom explained these were instinctive actions. With the sea and wind conditions, the device could have been lost, time could have been wasted. "Time is the element." He planned instead to take the boat to Martha, to attempt to present the swim ladder to her. Tom went into, as he put it, "recovery mode." He reached around to release the pair of metal clips holding the swim ladder. After kicking out the ladder, he went back to the wheel, threw the engine into reverse, and attempted to back the boat toward the woman in the water.

The waves were curled. Martha was swimming against a current, and handling the boat was difficult. Tom was backing into the wind, which collected in the errant mainsail. The sea conditions adversely affected stability control. The stern repeatedly rounded up in the wind. With each pitch of the boat, the transom rode over the chop and hit the water with a bang. The ladder itself posed a danger to Martha if he got it too close.

Tom kept his hands on the transmission lever to avoid oversteering or overrunning her. One foot too far and Martha Brailsford would be presented not with the rung of a ladder but with the blade of a churning propeller. After two attempts, Tom finally managed to position the bottom rung of the ladder right under Martha's outstretched hand. He waited at the top, one hand on the wheel, one hand reaching out to assist her.

But Martha didn't grab on. Her swimming motions, her hand motions, had slowed down completely. She was now just floating.

Tom knew from lifesaving classes that approaching a drowning person in the water could be risky if the victim panics. He also feared separating from the boat if he were to dive in. So his instincts told him to get into a flotation device and descend the ladder.

Two facts had come up in previous testimony that Tom now endeavored to explain. The first was that the seat cushions from the cockpit were missing when the boat was searched by police. Speculation abounded that perhaps they had been discarded somewhere. Perhaps they were stained with blood, stains which had not surrendered to Tom's frantic cleaning efforts.

The second fact was that Raymond Mount, who claimed to have seen *Counterpoint* later that night at the club, testified that a wet suit was hanging out to dry on deck.

"Tell us what you did at that point," Howard asked.

"All of these thoughts are instinctive...and in training. I reached down to the starboard side and threw cushions...." There went the cushions. "Whatever I had there, I reached...the unit that came out was my wet suit top. I threw that on right over whatever I had and zipped the zipper up." Maimoni explained that zipping was faster than buckling. He could zip up that zipper in a relatively short amount of time and still be at the wheel, still keep glancing over "for a person overboard." And it did, he rationalized, have some buoyancy. Not what one would expect from a dive top. But it conveniently explained why he got it wet that day and needed to hang it out to dry.

Tom brought the boat back for a third time. When he was about a foot away from Martha, he stepped onto the top rung of the ladder. "At that time, the boat came up over a wave as I was reaching with the other hand. I lost my footing and went right down the ladder. As I was falling, I reached for the swim ladder with this hand, and with the other I grabbed Martha by the back of her T-shirt, and I pulled her to me."

Half the courtroom believed this was a terrible, tall story. But many were transfixed and let out collective breaths. The audience was right there in the water. Sixty-three degrees, according to the experts, but a cold surprise nevertheless. Burning cold. Adrenaline pumps furiously when one falls unexpectedly into the ocean. Body heat is robbed even in sixty-three degrees. One's heart pounds, and one can hardly breathe from the shock. And many heads in the audience still ached from tangling with the mast. But Thomas Maimoni had grabbed Martha's T-shirt and, for a brief second, some who listened felt maybe she'd be saved. Maybe in the end it had come out differently after all. But this hope was fleeting.

However dark the path, hope is the fervent belief that if one keeps walking it will eventually lead back to the light. Though the sun may completely eclipse, within a few heartbeats it begins to reappear. "Whatever recedes will eternally return."

The listeners in the courtroom looked down at the arms of their chairs. They recalled where they were. Tom was telling about one hand on the ladder and one hand on the victim. One for the boat, one for Martha. If true, these hands were in vain, these hands that had promised rescue. The hard, dark arms of the courtroom seats already foretold the outcome.

"At this point, what did you notice about Martha?" asked Howard.

"I rolled her in to me, close to the ladder, and I noticed that she was unconscious. I was screaming all this time, screaming and yelling. Yelling and screaming. I probably drank a few gallons of salt water in the process, and I blew my voice right out screaming and yelling. Yelling into her ear and asking her to fight. Because if you were in the water," he leaned toward the jury, "looking up at the deck it looks like it's a long ways. It's probably three feet or so, from the water line to that transom. When you're in the water like that it's a long way up there." A long way, indeed.

Maimoni told the jury he clung to Martha as he did his calculations. Martha Brailsford, he told the court, was probably 30 percent heavier than the diving equipment he had routinely carried up that ladder. "Not a big *delta* from what I'm used to," he concluded. Hopefully, he would manage to get her attention, and she would lend a hand once he boosted her up. Somehow, under her own power, she would "go up the damn ladder."

Eighteen months later, in hindsight, Tom Maimoni told the court that probably "Mrs. Brailsford was dead at this time." But back then, still in the water with a person who was not going to assist him, a person possibly suffering from hypothermia, Tom struggled to get 105 pounds of dead weight up a narrow ladder that kept pitching up out of the water. Worse, the boat was rolling from side to side, changing the angle of the ladder.

Tom's hands and feet were numb. "In that area of Gloucester Harbor, there is upwelling and mixing. Colder water pushes up from the depths," he explained to the jury.

With his knowledge of wave mechanics and complex hydraulics, Tom managed to hook a foot on the bottom rung when the stern dipped. He maneuvered Martha so that she straddled his thigh. As the bow pitched down again, the rising stern lifted them hydraulically out of the water. Tom figured out there would be subsequent repeat waves and used them to gain one rung at a time. When he could rise no further, he reached under her backside, pushed her head first over the transom, and dumped her into the cockpit.

Tom looked around at this point. All the commercial vessels had departed the area. *Counterpoint* was drifting by itself, drifting toward the rocky shoreline between Magnolia and Gloucester. Tom could hear the breakers on the rocks less than a mile away.

There wasn't enough room in the cockpit to lay Martha flat. Besides, there were still one or two bruises on her head to explain. So Tom described how he half-dragged, half-carried her up the rolling, pitching deck to the foredeck. The path was narrow and strewn with protrusions. It was now dark. The foredeck had lights he could use. He positioned her belly down, head to one side, and gave her back a few pushes, hoping to clear her air passages. "Standard resuscitation for people just being taken out of the water," he said to the jury.

Rick Howard asked Tom to list some of the many lifesaving courses he had taken. They were numerous. He had kept current. Abreast. Tom took pains throughout his testimony to convince the jury that he was extremely knowledgeable. He justified every move he had made. Even the panicky moves he now described.

Martha had not responded to the air passage check. What was Tom Maimoni's next move? "I had to leave her to get back to the—to get the boat in—and—other things were on my mind. At this time I can safely say that my state of mind was terror and panic." Tom felt he had to secure *Counterpoint*. It was too deep to anchor there. The pitching was uncomfortable. He saw lights at Magnolia Harbor, put the boat in gear, and gunned the engine. He made a beeline for the lights. Ten, maybe fifteen minutes later, he was at a depth of twenty feet off Kettle Island. Tom spun the boat into the wind, moved forward, and dropped anchor. At last he could administer first aid to Martha.

The court heard about the endless checklist. First, bleeding. Tom checked her carefully. There was none. He concentrated on the victim and on his mental checklist. He grunted to her as he worked.

In what the psychiatrist would later describe as crisis-response based "magical thinking," Tom consoled himself with the certain belief that people ashore *knew* he and Martha were out there. Bill knew, people in the neighborhood knew. He could focus on his heroic first aid efforts secure in the knowledge that five harbormasters from the five jurisdictions surrounding his boat would soon be out to help him. "One call to any of them, and the whole area will be lit up with blue lights," he told the jury. Tom still believed this today, in the courtroom. He didn't even have to get on the radio. They had a float plan. Martha had told people they were going sailing. She was responsible for the float plan. And soon the cavalry would be called out. Bill himself had a 100-horsepower motor. If anyone should have been there, it should have been Bill Brailsford. At full speed, he could have been out in ten, maybe fifteen minutes.

So Tom concentrated on treating Martha and "reaching for vital signs." The next step was CPR. Although he had motored for some fifteen minutes with Martha on deck, not breathing, he nevertheless felt CPR would be a good thing. He turned her onto her back and "applied CPR in the central portion of her chest in units of ten." Between these repetitions, he "pitched back the head and blew air in mouth-to-mouth."

Tom's hands were numb. He used his nose and lips to try to detect a heartbeat or any breathing. But he could detect nothing.

Listening in the courtroom, Martha's husband winced at these images. This testimony was difficult for him to endure.

Tom gave up CPR for the moment and found the next item on his mental checklist: *hypothermia*. He explained the severity of this affliction to the courtroom. "Seawater is a monstrably dangerous conductor of heat." Martha's face was gray, her skin cold to the touch. Tom went below deck to fetch a pile of dry towels. Returning, he stripped off her shorts and T-shirt, just like the books tell him to do. He began to wipe her dry and wrap her in towels like a mummy. "I was working at breakneck speed." The wrapping was "combined with CPR."

Howard appeared swamped. "Now, at some time, did you stop these lifesaving efforts?"

Tom was having difficulty facing this moment of truth. "I kept at it a long time. I was getting—there was an anger component that was building—for a person that was in Kansas—that should have been here. I shouldn't have been out on this boat this day." Patti was to blame. "There was an anger toward family members, wondering if she told me the truth, that there were people ashore that knew where we were." Martha was to blame. "There was a component to damning myself. Wondering if I was doing the right sequence or following the right thing. There was a lot of frustration and anger, obviously. And I kept doing what I was doing."

Rick Howard asked about the radio. Tom explained that in order to go below and use the radio he would have lost sight of Martha in the water. When he was safely anchored in Magnolia, Tom talked about his dry mouth and his lack of voice control. He conceded that he could have croaked some sort of message, even keyed *SOS* on the buttons. The Coast Guard could have been alerted. Tom Maimoni was asked to tell the court why he decided not to call for help.

"I felt that I was in a compromising situation here. My—I have—my only witness—the only other person that knows what is going on here is laying at my feet. And that—I'm sure that had something to do with the component of fear, a driving fear—I'm alone and I was upset, and crying and trying at the same time to resuscitate this person."

Tom stayed as close as he could to Martha, talking to her, methodically, roboticly, checking for vital signs again and again, still trying to check his own mental checklist.

The sound of the wayward mainsail began to aggravate him. Yards of nylon scraped against the stays and flopped around the deck. Tom's boat was a disaster. The noise of the sail taunted him. It was the only sound at that moment. Tom left Martha and went to roll up the sail. He tied it off quickly. "Not a good job," just tied it off to quiet it, he said. In the courtroom, many were grateful. People were starting to trip on that sail.

The stress of his situation triggered a nosebleed, Tom added. He was prone to nosebleeds, due to his high blood pressure and varicose veins in both nostrils. "Never did get those cauterized—always meant to."

Kevin Mitchell turned around in his chair and caught Mark Lynch's eye. They were all wondering how the blood on the sail would be explained. Maimoni displayed no visible wounds when the police questioned him in July 1991. *Nosebleed! Aha!* Mitchell's glance to Mark suggested. *Pretty good!*

Maimoni made a pillow for Martha's head and spent a lot of time drying her hair. With the woman wrapped solidly in as many towels as he could muster, he turned his attention to cleaning up the deck. This included pitching her clothes and Seiko sports watch overboard.

"Why did you do that?" asked the defense counsel.

"I needed a reference point in Magnolia that I was there. I didn't have anything but myself to explain this situation to, and I wanted a reference that I was, indeed, out in this area. And that was—this is survival, this is a survival mode that you get yourself into thinking. It's not a conscious decision. I was robotic. It's part of survival training."

"Does that really make any sense, Tom, to have done that?"

"What's that?" Tom asked.

"To have thrown her Seiko watch over?"

"I believed at the time it did. I—looking back at it, it might look ridiculous—but to me—in the state of mind that I was in, it seemed like an important detail—as part of this whole thing. I mean, I had a life to protect. My sense was, I had a family, I had a new home, I had a life somewhere that I needed to protect."

Maimoni at this point pulled up anchor and motored back toward Salem. He wanted to intercept the cavalry. He wanted to go home. He kept his radio tuned to channel 16, ready to overhear any calls. He could see the lights of the Salem stacks, the power plant. Good. He could see his neighborhood. But he veered instead toward Cat Island to the south. Somehow he couldn't go home. From that spot, Tom explained, "I'm right in the middle of these harbormasters and I just felt that from this vantage point all I had to do was signal anyone that would come out."

By now it was early morning, Saturday. Tom was cold, wet, scared, and hungry. He reset the anchor and went forward to check on Martha. He still believed that somehow she had stabilized, that her hypothermic state suppressed her vital signs and mimicked death.

"At this time, did Martha show any signs of life?" asked Howard.

Tom stripped the big beach towel off her head and down to her waist. In spite of additional wrappings around her face, her mouth sagged open. He checked the towels and discovered they were soaked with urine.

"At that point, what did you think?"

"I lost it," answered Tom. He was losing it now, in the courtroom. His voice seized up. Between sobs, he managed to say, "I know what death is—I know what death looks—I know what dead is."

65

Defense attorney Richard Howard said softly, "Okay, Tom, I know it's a struggle, but we're going to get through this."

"I need to stop for a moment," Tom whispered.

Judge Saris asked Tom whether he wanted to take a morning break. The witness nodded, unable to speak.

After the brief recess, Rick Howard, began leading up to the single most important question of the trial. He asked Tom, "What thoughts went through your mind at Cat Island, at the time you realized finally that Martha was dead?"

"I was...I was waiting for someone to come and get me, and I had thoughts that I made a mistake coming in from Magnolia, that I should be back out there. I felt like I left the scene of an accident. And now that I've come in, I was feeling trapped."

Howard pushed him to continue.

"I wanted to go back out to Gloucester, and I wanted to get Martha off my boat."

"Please keep your voice up."

"I was waiting a long time, a long time, and I was scared."

Howard brought him to the question on everyone's mind: "What were you thinking when you made the decision to get rid of Martha's body?"

"What I was thinking?"

"Yes."

"That I was going to take it off my boat, take it off my boat and I was going to...I couldn't go in. I couldn't go home, unless somebody took it off my boat."

"Why was that? Why couldn't you go in?" Howard pressed carefully, fearing his client would break down.

"Because I had a naked, dead person on my boat." Tom's answer was barely audible. Tom told the courtroom he had promised Patti that he wouldn't sail alone with another woman anymore. She had requested that he not do so, despite his pleas that he could be trusted. He happened to prefer sailing with women. He didn't drink or carry on. He disliked talking sports. He just preferred women. "There is no way to measure the storm that would be directed toward me if I went straight in," he concluded.

Howard asked how he decided where to put the body. Maimoni answered that he was too physically and emotionally exhausted to return to the scene of the accident. He sat looking around for a long time from his vantage point behind Cat Island. "I decided to throw her away here."

"I'm sorry, Tom, I didn't hear that."

"I decided to throw her away here."

"Cat Island? How did you do that?"

"Weight, anchor. People put stuff on my boat. Junk. I had a junk anchor on the boat, belonging to Patti's father. And I had a junk weight belt that I was throwing away. They said it was Patti's. That was the old Patti's belt. I bought her a new one."

According to the police, two anchors were usually employed on *Counterpoint*. During the search, they only found one aboard. Patti Maimoni later identified the dive belt as her regular dive belt, the only one she used. A gift from a previous boyfriend. There was no "new" belt. There was no "new" Patti.

"So you went down below and you got an anchor and a weight belt?"

"Somewhere, yes." His voice contorted.

"And you put that on Martha?"

"Yes. Me." The word salad was gone. Tom's answer was simple, childlike, and was delivered on a sob.

Maimoni moved the boat from the north end of Cat Island to the southern tip, the spot where by day divers and artists sought inspiration. The defendant did not recall exactly why, other than the fact that the water wasn't very deep to the north.

Asked if he recalled where he had pushed her body over the side, Tom unraveled.

"I didn't—I didn't pick a spot. I went one way—it was somewhere, I just—I didn't plan on it—I didn't see what I did. I went out, and I didn't want that on my boat. I didn't want that mess on my boat." After dumping his passenger, Tom climbed back into the cockpit and turned the boat toward home.

The world over which Tom had control, over which he was Captain, was a mere twenty-eight feet. *Counterpoint*, and every boat before it, was Tom Maimoni's refuge. There he was the boss. He was the expert. Everyone aboard had to share his fantasy. No one fired him, doubted him, belittled him, divorced him. No one left him. Until Martha Brailsford. But somehow she had left him. Alone. The illusion was shattered. The fantasy was compromised. She was not just a "mess" on his boat. She was a leak in his balloon, in his inflatable psyche.

The boat was the only place where Tom had built a coherent sense of self. The only thing he could do to stop the leak and survive was to deny to himself and to the world that the event had taken place. For Tom, if he could hide the broken pieces, then nothing was broken. Accidents didn't happen on Tom's ship. Not while he was in charge. Not on his watch. Above all, he could not show panic, this man who was chronically panicked.

On this day, Tom was forced in this courtroom to face the "mess." He could not deny Martha's death. All he could do was try to deflect the responsibility.

"I needed Bill—I needed people—friends. I needed someone to help me. That's all I knew," he cried. Bill could take the responsibility. He had a bigger boat. He should be the bigger captain.

Martha's widower stared in outrage at the defendant. Around him, his friends scoffed more visibly.

Dr. Bursztajn later summed up Tom's motivation. "Mr. Maimoni would have been in such a state of panic and helplessness that his actions were dictated by a sense of self-preservation, a preservation of his identity, rather than an intent to harm or kill anyone." Given his state, the doctor concluded, Tom could not possibly have understood the consequences of his actions. If one were to understand this picture, Martha's downfall might have come not from being in the presence of a killer but from a companion's utter helplessness.

The psychiatrist believed the most probable explanation was that an accident had occurred and that Tom had disposed of the results. Yet there could have been a chilling flip side to his diagnosis. One was left to wonder. Though "nonviolent," was Tom indeed capable of causing death in the pursuit of his own self-preservation? Even if a person abhorred aggression, couldn't the apparent absence of conscience, empathy, or remorse place his companions in a dangerous and vulnerable position? Or, in the doctor's words, a loss of perspective in a time of crisis? It did not take great physical strength to tie an anchor around a stunned victim. It did not take violence to watch a person drown.

66

"*I felt I was in a compromising situation. My only witness is lying at my feet.*'" Assistant District Attorney Kevin Mitchell quoted slowly and deliberately from Tom's own testimony as he began his cross-examination of the defendant. "Then you took that witness and dropped her in the ocean with an anchor and a weight belt, and that body—that witness—is now destroyed and no one can see its condition. Is that correct?"

"That's correct," mumbled the defendant.

"Sir, you talked an awful lot about instinct. How do you develop instinct?"

Where Howard had drawn the jury near by using "Tom," Mitchell kept them away from the witness by addressing him as "sir."

"Training."

"Repetitive training?"

"Lifetime training."

"Over and over again? You don't even think, you just act, correct?"

"Correct."

"Sir, you have done the man-overboard drill often, haven't you?"

"Often."

"You *sight* first. What is next?"

"Recovery," answered Tom.

"No, sir. Exhibit twenty-three—the life preserver—is right next to the capstan, because number two is *throw something in*. Isn't that correct, sir?"

"Under orthodox conditions, ideal situations, yes."

"Instinct is repetition."

"No, I beg to differ with you."

"Sir, the life preserver never went in that water that night, isn't that correct?"

"That's correct."

"Because, sir, the alleged accident never occurred, isn't that correct?"

"You're wrong."

"Martha Brailsford never fell in the water until you dropped her in, isn't that correct?"

No one was objecting. Tom's lawyers were strangely silent.

"No," answered Tom, glancing at his attorneys.

"Sir," Mitchell's voice dropped, "could you see Martha Brailsford as she flailed for life?"

Tom could see her. One boat length away.

"Could you reach her with the flotation device, sir? Could you throw it a boat length?"

"Yes."

"You didn't, did you?"

"No, I did not," came the quiet reply.

"What is the worst that would have happened if you did?"

"I would have thrown away a life preserver."

"*Fifty dollars!*" Mitchell exclaimed scornfully and turned away.

The prosecutor took two paces toward the rear. Facing him in the front row of reserved seats were all the "lieutenants" from the DA's office, Mitchell's five peers. They had come today to hear his cross. His own little jury. He spun around toward the witness box. "Sir, did you apply for Koch Services, telling them you were an engineer, and they couldn't verify it?"

"You're squeezing time together."

"As you started getting jobs, you were losing them, correct?"

"That's correct."

"Now, sir, at some point in the process you created a history of jobs, did you not? A fictionalized history?"

"Yes."

"Somewhere in the process you started to add degrees, correct?"

"Somewhere in the process, you're correct."

"At Parker Brothers you tell us they hired you, but then they abandoned you, is that correct?"

"I think if you look at the company, yes, that is correct. They're no longer in existence," Maimoni said defensively.

"Did you receive a notice you just couldn't do the job?"

"I don't recall that, no, I don't."

"You don't recall? Is that something you might have forgotten?" the assistant district attorney asked sarcastically.

"I may have overlooked it, yes."

"In fact, A.D. Little is a consulting firm that does military work, and, again, you didn't stay with them? Was it to get a better job, or did the company leave you again?"

"It was to get a better job."

"So, you quit?"

"It was a mutual severance. They gave me a handsome severance package, yes."

Unusual for someone to get severance when they quit. Mitchell intimated that each time Maimoni's work got to a point where he might need security clearance, he somehow found himself out of a job.

Tom Maimoni was a master of language. As Mitchell went through the defendant's failed marriages, he asked about Linda Beckley: "She got you a boat?"

"*We* got a boat," was Tom's answer.

"She paid for it?"

"We got the boat together."

Mitchell repeated in a louder voice, "She paid for it?"

"We're arguing about semantics," replied Tom.

At one point, Tom described the cancer pickup line as though it had evolved on its own. "Somewhere along this...it became a cancer routine, and the sickness—it's been blown into a little more proportion than it was actually said, but somewhere along that line the subject of cancer came into it."

Back to Vietnam and the impact of the Tet Offensive on Tom's life in the Philippines. "Mr. Maimoni, you were attached to the 6400th Supply Company. The supply company handled the uniforms and the tomato soup and all the rest, correct, sir?"

Maimoni suggested that during the intense fighting he had handled bodies, too. He had volunteered.

Mitchell handed the defendant a form. "Is this your military record?"

"Not in detail," answered Tom.

"It says you arrived at Clark Air Force Base on February 14, 1968?"

"I don't recall."

"The Tet Offensive took place in January 1968. You were in Florida when that occurred," Mitchell reminded him. "And how about those body bags? Isn't it true, Mr. Maimoni, that bodies never left Vietnam unless they were in transport boxes? Did you ever actually see a body bag at Clark Air Force Base?"

"When they ran out of transfer cases."

"They loaded them in Vietnam? What did you do with those?"

"I was only a passenger on the aircraft."

Mitchell tried to dig out the terrible Vietnam experience that had allegedly precipitated Tom's post-traumatic stress disorder and his years of nightmares.

"Military personnel were coming through Clark all the time. They would talk about what they went through. What they saw. It was being exposed to those conversations," Tom explained.

The prosecutor gave him a mock-sympathetic look.

Kevin Mitchell punched into every aspect of Tom's testimony. Tom's responses could barely be heard. Often the prosecutor steamed right over them with his next question, signaling to the jury that the answers weren't particularly important. Certainly not to be believed, at any rate. The defense rarely objected. Denner and Howard would have cheered if Tom had broken down on the stand. The prosecutor knew this and tread carefully the invisible edge. He was scared Tom would break. Not the picture he wanted to paint.

"July 12, 1991. Did Martha Brailsford know you were married?"

"In the first meeting, no," Tom replied.

"You told Martha Brailsford when you first met her you were a widower?"

"It was a thirty-second conversation."

"You talked to her about the pain and anguish of the loss of your wife?"

"I don't know."

"When did you finally tell her the truth?"

"Aboard *Counterpoint*."

"So up until being aboard *Counterpoint*, she believed you to be a widower?"

"There was no relationship, there was no friendship, there was…it was a person on the street."

"She believed you to be a widower."

"Yes, she did, apparently. Apparently, she did."

"You told Roxcy Platte that?"

"Yes."

"You told Rosemary Farmer that?"

"Yes, I did."

"Why?"

"I believe I explained that sufficiently. That was a fence."

"Where did Rosemary Farmer try to cross over into your territory?"

"I...I didn't want to talk about my personal life to her or anyone else, any other strangers."

Mitchell jumped back to Roxcy Platte. Tom had begun sailing with her while Patti was still in town. As justification perhaps, Tom remarked that he had been against Patti's trip. Mitchell asked whether on their final sail Tom had behaved like a gentleman with Roxcy.

"Yes," assured Tom.

"Did you keep your pants on?"

"I was on my boat."

"You walked around naked?"

"Yes."

"For how long?"

"I don't know."

"Did you ask her permission?"

"Yes." And she gave it, he added. "She turned her back while I changed."

"While you changed? Changed into what?"

"From whatever clothes I had on."

"Into your birthday suit?"

"From birthday suit into sailing shorts." Tom was safely back in his pants.

When Mitchell returned to the incident with Rosemary Farmer, Maimoni shifted to the passive voice, letting English syntax displace his responsibility for anything unheroic that might have happened.

"Is it true you gave your name as Thomas *Mahoney* to Mrs. Farmer?"

"The name 'Mahoney' was spoken," Tom explained.

Mitchell asked, "Did Mrs. Farmer describe accurately what happened on *Counterpoint?* Everything you did to her she described accurately?"

"Yes. Yes."

"You took your clothes off?"

"Took whose clothes off?" Tom looked miserable.

"You took your clothes off?"

"There was a change of clothes, yes. I apologized for that."

Mitchell responded, "I didn't ask for an apology, Tom."

"Not to you, to Rosemary. It was inappropriate."

"Sir, did she describe it accurately? Were you in a sexual state of mind?"

"I've been in a sexual state of mind all my life," the defendant responded with the barest grin.

The prosecutor repeated this amazing declaration.

"I like—I enjoy being in the company of women," Tom clarified.

Then back to Martha, to whom Tom admitted being attracted. "When Martha Brailsford arrived at the dock, it was by her selection, correct?"

"Yes. She suggested the Willows."

"Did you invite her to PCYC?"

"I don't remember. I...we may have had a conversation to that, but immediately the focus shifted to the Willows pier."

"Whose idea was the Willows?"

"I don't know how that exchange went, but it may have, in fact, been Martha's. I'm not...I have taken my boat to that Willows pier."

"Of course, your wife Patti is known at PCYC?"

"The whole club would know. Yes, I was discreet with bringing, bringing women down to Palmer's Cove, I was discreet, I would use discretion."

Mitchell revisited the events leading up to the alleged accident, including Tom's turning the boat around and transitioning to power. Considering the wind direction at the time, some of Tom's maneuvers even before he had reason to panic had the sailors in the courtroom scratching their heads. Many, like the neighbor Jim Brown, questioned Tom's skills at sea.

"Martha was an excellent sailor," the prosecutor clarified. Tom had denigrated her sailing abilities in his statements to the police and his friends back in 1991, before he had heard Bill's testimony about her crewing in the Caribbean.

"She was following my directions."

"She was an excellent sailor," repeated Mitchell.

"She was a good sailor. I...."

"A good sailor!"

"Platitudes. We have a difference in platitudes," Tom said.

"Was she better than you?"

"Some people call me the world's greatest sailor," Tom offered, "but I wouldn't agree to that." Neither would the courtroom sailors. "We were a team."

The thrust of Kevin Mitchell's attacks was not just to expose Tom's lies and deceit but also, more importantly, to show that his lies were calculated and conforming. Tom lied, Mitchell was saying, not because he was crazy but because he was crazy like a fox. The lies were designed to gain something, to preserve something. Jobs. Women. Status. Condo. A slip at the yacht club. Police off your back. That wasn't sick. That was just manipulative.

Rick Howard attempted rehabilitation on redirect examination of his client. He got a little more explanation about the life preserver, how it might have blown away on the wind. He had Tom explain that the Tet Offensive had lasted nearly a year. He gave Tom a chance to suggest that he had done and seen more than appeared on his summary military record. "We've searched the records looking for details," Tom told the court. "With secret clearance, I assume that my military records were destroyed. There's a lot of controversy during that period. And a lot of things were covered up."

The prosecutor at the end of his cross-examination asked in a voice laced with disgust, "Sir, did you get your bloody nose when Martha Brailsford hit you?"

It was almost too easy, this bullying game. Tom Maimoni was a great, bottomless bag of words. Poke him and more would come flying out, filling the room with a protective cloud of obfuscation.

Tom denied the accusation. "No. No one hit me. Martha and I had no...not one foul word between us the whole day. She was a sailor and my friend. She invited me into her friendship. She came to me, not through sympathy and not through any sexual encounter of any way. She was a friend. I felt that she was truly fond of me in some way, not romantically. She was welcoming me into the neighborhood. I had hoped to extend that over. And that day, the whole premise was to extend a friendship or to begin a friendship, not a relationship or sexual relationship. It was a friendship.

"And I risked my life. Thomas Maimoni died on that day, too.

I don't...that person does not exist anymore. And I resent having that turned into a sexual mess. It was not that. I'm sorry."

67

After Tom Maimoni's testimony, the community waited with a mixture of skepticism, outrage, and curiosity to hear what his shrinks would say. Broadcast news reporters scurried to their trucks to glean sound bites from the morning's session in time for the noon deadline. Restaurants near the courthouse were packed beyond capacity at lunchtime, with patrons dissecting and deliberating. "What do you think really happened on the boat?" reverberated from table to table.

Bob Pino, the Commonwealth's forensic chemist, had fulfilled his role in this case and was on his way to work in Boston. He and a coworker stopped at the Boston Sail Loft for a quick lunch before their shift. After they decided to risk the Cajun scrod special, his companion leaned forward and echoed the question of the day: "So what do you think really happened on the boat?"

The popular restaurant overlooked the Charles River. Its nautical motif and dark wooden tables gave it a yacht club atmosphere. At noontime the closely packed tables filled up with vice presidents in Italian suits and computer geeks in L.L.Bean grunge wear. Two people in his/her business suits were being seated at the next table. Pino looked like he had just gotten out of bed, which he had. His week had included days in courtrooms, nights at the forensic lab. In between he had been processing yet another homicide scene. "I'm getting a little old for these hours," had been his initial greeting.

Now Pino smiled and put down his fork. He folded his paper

napkin into the shape of a sail, then bunched most of it down. "I pretty much agree that the sail was down. But where the defense presumes the top was unattached and flopping around, I gotta disagree with that." He kept the top of the napkin rigid, extending it above the bunched part. It was assumed most of the sail was draped over the boom at the time of the incident. But the position of the top was a critical question. Blood was found on both sides of the sail, including within a few inches of the top, where an attached rope, or "sheet," drew it up the length of the mast.

The people at the next table glanced at his mashed sail, then returned to their menus. A waitress came by and offered more coffee. The disheveled chemist rubbed his eyes as he held out his cup.

During his testimony (perhaps to explain the pattern of blood drops), Maimoni had claimed that as he lowered the sail, Martha—merely an "inexperienced day sailor"—somehow managed to open the gate at the bottom of the channel in the mast. This allowed the slugs to spill out. The slugs along the vertical edge of the mainsail normally fit into the channel and kept the sail attached to the mast. When the whole sail allegedly came down, it continued to fall out onto the deck. Maimoni had implied that this added to the confusion and distracted his attention. This explanation also positioned everything conveniently for his later claim that his nosebleed was the only source of blood. Droplets were found on both sides of the sail. This could have occurred, for example, if wind and boat movement had caused the top of the sail to flop back and forth.

So with one sentence, Maimoni had set up his nosebleed scenario, had cast aspersions on Martha's seamanship, had earned sympathy for the difficult job he had faced, and had stressed his own expertise and heroic competence. "Martha!" he claimed to have yelled at her when he saw the slugs coming out.

But 320 square feet of white nylon had allegedly kept coming at him, gaskets landing on the coaming, the mainsail spilling out all over. Like blood gushing from a wound. The end of his control over the situation. The start of his nightmare.

"You don't think it happened that way?" the coworker asked Pino.

"I'm telling you, the top of that sail never left the channel. And that means the top couple of feet of sail were rigid. One little nosebleed wouldn't have been able to land on *both* sides of that sail. The source of that blood had to purposely move from one side of the boom to the other. Maybe by being chased. Like she ran around the bow, but he coulda ducked under the boom and caught up with her again."

In one of Maimoni's early stories, the boom was swinging wildly and hit Martha on the head a couple of times. Perhaps one way and then back again.

"Wouldn't that account for the blood on both sides?" the coworker asked.

Pino grinned again. He loved this. The trial must have really frustrated him. "All the blood was on the edge of the sail closest to the mast." He pointed to the fold in his napkin which he was dotting with blood from a Bic pen. The people at the next table declined dessert. Pino continued. "If a boom was going to knock you over or do any damage, it would have to be farther away from where it attached to the mast. Not enough momentum where they join. Doesn't travel much distance."

His visual aids were convincing. It appeared that getting one's nose to drip onto a vertical surface—and onto both sides at that—was a pretty awkward maneuver. A crucial question remained: "How can you be so sure the top of the mainsail was still attached to the mast? That it was still in that channel?"

Pino cradled his coffee and leaned forward. "Two reasons. After it happened, the guy scrubbed that boat spotless. He didn't clean the sail. If the top were loose like he had said, he could have let it hang over into the water. Seawater would have done the trick. But he didn't. Scrubbed the entire deck. Didn't touch the sail."

Even a nosebleed would have spattered the deck. Maimoni had removed every trace. And seawater could destroy even the invisible blood traces that a Polylite was supposed to pick up.

"Second reason. The top of that sail is real hard to get out of the channel the way the sheet is attached. Three of us tried it the night we took it as evidence. I finally gave up, and we just cut the rope. Believe me—just opening up the gate—no way could it fall out."

"So what happened, Bob?"

Pino sat back. "He beat her up. The blood on the sail was Martha's blood. Six groups of droplets, six blows." Then he continued: "She may have been unconscious. Maybe dead. Maybe he weighted her down, slit her up a little, and threw her in the water."

The couple at their elbow loudly demanded their bill. While they calculated the tip, Pino and his colleague calculated the chances that two people would both have type A blood. About one in five. Their tip came to about three dollars.

"Tough break about the blood types. Any chance that technology will improve and you can go back and subgroup those stains some day?"

Pino shook his head. "Not after that long in a salty environment. Sail's full of it. Salt breaks down all the proteins. The defense attorney managed to delay the blood tests for over a year, rendering them absolutely useless." The tests required cutting small squares out of the sail, which Denner had argued was destructive of the evidence. By the time a judge's ruling allowed the tests, it was too late to prove or disprove Maimoni's claim that the blood was his own. Obviously the defense had its reasons.

The waitress came by to scoop up their plates and paper mainsails. Pino and his companion picked up the bill and worked their way up to the cashier. As they waited to pay, they joked a bit about how many of the sailing witnesses in the trial were being asked about the length of their boats. Somehow this established their credibility—the measure of the man. "Well, *I* myself have a *thirty*-eight-foot boat..." they would answer. If one had looked carefully, one might have detected a slightly crushed look on the defendant's face. As if this were the final insult, putting down his mere twenty-eight-foot boat.

Bob Pino pushed open the front door. As they stepped outside, he laughed and said, "You know what the old salts standing around the waterfront were saying while we worked on *Counterpoint* that night? 'That's a lot of sail for such a small boat!'"

68

The crux of the defense's argument at this point was to give the jury a credible alternative explanation why Tom did the things he did and said the things he said. Jeff Denner was about to call both a psychologist and psychiatrist, although there was no insanity plea. The defense was not claiming that Tom Maimoni committed murder because he was crazy. Rather they claimed that no murder was committed. Because of his personality disorders and dysfunctional coping strategies, Tom's handling of the accident made it appear that a crime had occurred. A unique defense.

Dr. Steven Shapse, a psychologist from Lincoln, Massachusetts, had administered a battery of tests to the defendant: an IQ test (Wechsler), a test for neurological functioning (Bender Visual Motor Gestalt), a storytelling test (Thematic Apperception test), the Rorschach inkblot test, and the Minnesota Multiphasic Personality Inventory (MMPI). Dr. Shapse had conducted these tests in a marathon session at the jail a year before the trial.

Dr. Shapse began with the intelligence test results. Overall, the scores suggested that Thomas Maimoni functioned intellectually in the 37th percentile nationwide. Fifty percent is considered average. Specifically, Tom's IQ measured about ninety-three on the Wechsler, 7 points below the norm. Tom, according to his defense team, was of below average intelligence.

The defendant sat uncomfortably next to his attorney without looking at the witness. The painful testimony continued.

The Bender Gestalt indicated no neurological impairment, said Dr. Shapse. No physiological injury to the brain. However, in the inkblot test, Tom had found "unusual" images. This suggested he suffered from "distorted reality," which could affect his judgment abilities, the doctor explained. He also had exhibited diminished coping styles in unfamiliar or stressful situations. For example, facing aggression, Tom had withdrawn into himself. The storytelling test indicated that Tom's "life themes" centered around loss, death, pain, and sorrow.

The MMPI results, according to Dr. Shapse, indicated "Mr. Maimoni's profile was a valid profile. The validity scales were within a normal range." This meant Tom had not faked the other test results, he said.

Based on these tests, his interviews with Tom's family, and his consultation with a psychiatrist who would testify next, Dr. Shapse had come up with a list of personality disorders from which Tom suffered.

When Kevin Mitchell rose to cross-examine, he tore into the witness. The assistant district attorney scoffed at the IQ score and the conclusion that the defendant had subnormal intelligence. "Tom Maimoni was hired by Arthur D. Little as an engineer, did you know that?"

"Yes I did," answered Dr. Shapse.

"He was hired by Parker Brothers as an engineer. General Electric, four years as an engineer." And all that time he was not in fact trained as one. "A 93 IQ? Does that sound right to you?"

"Based on my tools, my testing which I have given hundreds of times, I believe that that is his IQ within a few points."

"Well, sir, if an engineer is 93, what is there about 80? Judges would be about 150, of course." Mitchell gave Judge Saris a smile.

"Mr. Mitchell, you're a little low there," answered the judge.

The prosecutor pulled out an answer sheet from Tom's vocabulary test and read off some word definitions for which Dr. Shapse had given Tom only half-credit: *Sentence* Tom had defined as a "group of words put together to make a meaning." His answer for *evasive* was "trying to avoid." For *enormous* Tom had "large." Mitchell clearly thought those answers were pretty good. "In fact, Tom's low IQ of 37th percentile turned out to be rather important in your ultimate decisions, didn't it?"

"Could you clarify, sir?" asked the witness.

Kevin Mitchell held up the printed analysis from the company that had processed Tom's MMPI answer sheet. The MMPI evaluated the validity of all the other test results. The results which suggested Tom had impaired judgment and "life themes" of sorrow and pain.

"You told us that he had a valid score?"

"Yes, sir."

"What is the first thing they said to you, sir? Number one, first line."

Dr. Shapse began to read from the analysis: "'The client responded to the MMPI items in an unusual manner.'"

"Keep going," urged Mitchell, whenever the witness paused.

"'He claimed an unrealistic amount of virtue while also endorsing a great number of psychological difficulties. This infrequent response pattern reflects some unconventional and possibly bizarre beliefs. Careful evaluation of the individual response attitudes should be undertaken to explain this highly unusual validity scale pattern. The following hypotheses might be explored.'" He stopped.

"Keep going," Mitchell said again loudly.

"'He may have consciously distorted the test responses to create a particular impression.'"

Mitchell jumped in. "That says, might be a problem here, right?"

"'Or he may be generally unsophisticated,'" Dr. Shapse continued.

"Meaning, not too bright?" asked Mitchell. Tom had to be "not too bright" because the alternative meant he would have "consciously distorted the test results."

Mitchell strongly disagreed with the psychologist's conclusions. Not only did he clearly suspect bias but he also took considerable offense at Dr. Shapse's lack of candor in trying to convince the jury that the MMPI "showed" Tom Maimoni's profile to be "valid."

Dr. Bursztajn from Harvard Medical School's department of psychiatry had interviewed Maimoni in jail. He now came forward to explain the man to the jury.

"Sir, is it your understanding that Mr. Maimoni is a pathological liar?" Denner began.

"Yes," the doctor answered. "Part of his mental illness is that he can't tell the truth even if his life depends on it."

Dr. Bursztajn kept each interview short, he explained, because long sessions with people who lie tend to encourage them to lie even more to "fill in the gaps." He explained that this tendency is a way of covering up a lack of knowledge or the ability to remember, particularly in crisis situations. People like Tom, who are so frightened, so ashamed of not knowing or not recalling something, who feel so badly about themselves, will feign that they are indeed knowledgeable and credentialed. They make up the missing details. Their fear, Dr. Bursztajn continued, "is that if they don't make these things up, you won't want to have anything to do with them. They'll be all alone—profoundly anxious or profoundly depressed. They have to make something up to be in a relationship with you, but they can't tell the truth because the truth, they feel, is just something which won't allow you to be in that relationship with them." The relationship they construct on lies is a "pseudo-relationship." "Lying is a way of, not really relating to people, but pseudo-relating to them."

Tom Maimoni lied, explained the doctor, because he was wrapped up in his long-standing need to ward off immense anxiety and depression. "Making believe" not only was an anxiety-reducing mechanism for Tom but also a self-preservation mechanism.

Tom's lying differed from that of the well-known Walter Mitty, who lived in a world of daydreams. Walter didn't depend on others to feed his fantasies. Tom Maimoni needed other people to keep his daydreams alive, to provide the mirror in which he could see himself clothed in the make-believe identity he had created. "He needs other people, and he's afraid of other people at the same time."

Tom's need to retreat into fantasy increased with stress, particularly in situations that threatened his self-esteem or that involved the loss of an individual on whom his self-esteem depended. For Tom, more than self-esteem was at stake. His self-identity, or "self-coherence," lay behind the fragile walls of his fantasyland. To this end, Tom's version of the events of July 12, 1991, exaggerated his role as a rescuer and the degree to which he was in control. In terms of what had actually happened, Dr. Bursztajn didn't believe Tom Maimoni really knew what the "truth" was.

When Tom had begun to attach the anchor and weight belt to Martha, his "self-coherence" had begun to crumble. His failure to be the heroic rescuer and to be the big captain of his big ship had forced him to depersonalize what was happening at that moment. Forced him into delusional, magical thinking, in which he had found solace only in the irrational belief that Martha's husband Bill would appear any moment to rescue *him*. If Bill would only show up, Tom could somehow claim to Patti that Bill had been with them on board, and that therefore everything had been OK.

Dr. Bursztajn clarified for the jury that this diagnosis did *not* depend on actually believing Tom's story. Dr. Bursztajn was absolutely clear, however, that Tom Maimoni had lapsed into psychosis when he affixed the anchor to Martha's body. Even during the doctor's interviews a year or more afterward, Tom had exhibited physical signs of psychosis whenever he was asked to relive that moment. Widened eyes, dilated pupils, sweating, wringing his hands. Tom couldn't talk about it directly or without panic.

Dr. Bursztajn presented his primary diagnosis to the jury. Tom Maimoni suffered from a schizotypal personality disorder, a response to his underlying feelings of overwhelming anxiety and depression. The disorder not only produced the Walter Mitty personality but also Tom's grandiose and histrionic style. Tom believed far beyond normal limits that people talked about him behind his back, that people stole from him, that he himself had special powers, that he had exceptional knowledge and abilities even with no education, that he had heightened or unusual perceptual experiences. For instance, Tom could sense a funny smell when he concentrated. This was a disorder of Tom's thinking, feeling, and communicating. Furthermore, these characteristics rendered an individual more vulnerable to becoming psychotic and delusional under stress.

Dr. Bursztajn listed his secondary diagnoses. Tom suffered from brief reactive psychosis, the profound disturbance in judgment and consciousness that Tom had experienced in response to the events on *Counterpoint* on the night of July 12, 1991. Tom Maimoni also suffered from dysthymia: chronic depression, a lack of self-esteem, a sense of hopelessness. This sort of depression, the doctor pointed out, was not always apparent. One might not appear particularly gloomy, especially if one were ashamed of feeling sad. Dr. Bursztajn's final secondary diagnosis was post-traumatic stress disorder (PTSD). For someone with schizotypal personality disorder who hid his suffering from other people, the risk of PTSD increased after a traumatic event.

Defense attorney Jeff Denner asked the doctor about Tom's

sexual advances toward the other women, including his inclination to sail naked.

"For Mr. Maimoni," answered Dr. Bursztajn, "the only thing that he has of value to show people is his body. He doesn't value himself, so he can't imagine the possibility that other people might value him unless he exhibits himself in some very childlike, obnoxious, and offensive way."

Denner then asked the doctor's opinion whether Tom was capable of acting in a violent or aggressive manner, whether such action was consistent with his diagnosis. This was one of the primary questions in this "very complex case."

"It's my opinion that Mr. Maimoni avoids violence at all possible costs." There had been no history of violence. He had endured Linda Beckley's violence by running rather than fighting back. Tom's psychological tests indicated withdrawal from physical violence. As a child, even with his size, he had avoided fights and had been known as "shy and timid."

Finally, defense counsel asked: "Sir, assuming solely for the sake of hypothesis that an accident did not happen in this case, do you have an opinion...whether Mr. Maimoni by reason of any mental disease, defect, or the foregoing impairments you have just shared with us, would have the ability, or did have the ability, on July 12, 1991, to form a conscious and fixed purpose to kill, or to cause grievous bodily harm, or to premeditate?"

"Given his state of mind, given his magical thinking, given his panic, he would not have the conscious intent to kill, nor was he able to have a fixed purpose to cause grievous bodily harm."

Denner asked Dr. Bursztajn whether Tom had the capacity to appreciate premeditation. The doctor wouldn't go so far, however, as to say Tom didn't have the capacity in an abstract sense. But he did suggest that in a worst-case scenario (Tom makes a sexual advance toward Martha, Martha rejects), Tom would not have been able to think, "Okay, I'm going to go ahead and kill her." He also would not have been able to think, "Well, let me see, what are the consequences of what I'm going to do as far as Martha Brailsford is concerned?" At that point, the doctor explained, Tom's focus was totally on preserving himself and his identity.

Denner concluded by asking Dr. Bursztajn to reiterate that he was not assuming the worst-case scenario in fact happened. "You don't know what happened on that boat?" he asked.

"I don't know what happened on that boat," replied the doctor.

Kevin Mitchell immediately went on the attack. "Sir, did you tell this jury that as you come into this case you make no assumptions whether or not the event occurred?"

"I try to consider the worst- and best-case scenarios without assuming either is true," was the doctor's answer.

"But sir, you have explained all of Mr. Maimoni's actions subsequent to the assumption of the 'tragic death' of Martha Brailsford, have you not?" the prosecutor asked in a loud voice, his arms folded.

"That's not an assumption. That is a fact—that her death was a tragedy."

Mitchell spared no hostility. "No, I don't want to talk about a tragedy. I want to talk about *accident versus murder*. It makes a big difference in the personality of Tom Maimoni if she died by accident or if he murdered her, does it not, sir?"

Unable to get a yes or no answer on the accident assumption, the assistant district attorney hammered Dr. Bursztajn. Each time the response was a frustrating step to one side. Mitchell finally barked, "Let me go back again. We'll stay there until we get an answer!"

Kevin Mitchell led the doctor through the prosecutor's hypothetical worse-case scenario—murder—and asked at each step whether Tom's actions seemed rational or irrational.

Getting rid of the body. Especially if it had bruises and marks. Putting it in a place with lots of lobsters and crabs. "A rational response to murder, correct?"

"Yes and no. It can be rational if you put the body someplace where it has no chance of being discovered." A 'rational' person would have dumped her much further out to sea, in hundreds of feet of water, not fifty.

"But if you happen to know of a location where there are a lot of lobsters and crabs, that's a good place to put it. Isn't that a rational act?"

"It can be. And I did consider this as a possibility."

"Then, what's his next move," asked the prosecutor, "after the body was found?"

"What he does is, he drops off his wife and takes off driving north so that he can be out of radio range of the reports," said the doctor.

"How about, *he just takes off?* Is that fair?" asked Mitchell. And then there was the compass, the map, the proximity to the Canadian border. This from a man who "didn't do anything, but just in case he did do it, didn't understand what he did?"

Dr. Bursztajn objected to Mitchell's rewording of his analysis.

The assistant district attorney asked the witness whether Tom had the ability to form a malicious intent. Bursztajn would only say that in this instance Tom had not. The reason was that he had no proclivity toward violence.

"How about," asked Mitchell, "putting a weight belt and an anchor around a woman and dropping her alive into the ocean, is that a proclivity to violence?"

"If he believed she was alive when he did, then it would," answered the doctor. But Tom had consistently expressed his belief that Martha was dead at the time. It may not have been a nice thing to do, but disposing of something that was dead and "anxiety provoking" wasn't evidence of intended violence.

"Excuse me, sir, even in the assumption that he killed her, aren't you going back to the assumption there was an accident? I'm talking about, *he kills her*. If she's on the boat, she's alive, he puts an anchor and a weight belt around her, and he drops her in the water. Isn't that a proclivity toward violence?"

"I don't understand your question."

"Did he understand that when you put a live person in water with an anchor and weight belt that they die?"

"That's not the kind of decision making that Tom would have been exercising, especially in a crisis situation, one where his self-identity was at risk," Dr. Bursztajn replied.

"Why was Tom in danger of losing his identity?"

"If there were an accident and he as boat captain should have prevented it, or if he did go ahead and strike her, that he shouldn't have done that."

"In other words, if Martha was going to complain about something when he got back, his fear of getting caught? And he didn't understand what he was doing?"

Bursztajn had considered this possibility. However, he countered, "Tom's basic experience at that point had been that Martha was dead."

"Sir, you believed some of the things he told you?"

"I don't necessarily believe the content of it," the doctor responded. "I do believe the feelings of helplessness, panic, and disordered thinking which were exhibited."

The prosecutor switched to Tom's inappropriate sexual behavior on the boat, which the doctor had termed a "desire to exhibit himself." Couldn't this, Mitchell asked, also be consistent with "heightened sexual feeling?"

"Considering the ineptitude, the childish offensiveness, it was more likely a means of medicating his anxiety and depression and acting out his image of himself as a very sexual man," Bursztajn insisted. "The sexuality was probably secondary."

The doctor summarized: "One of the easiest ways of misunderstanding Mr. Maimoni is to assume that he feels and he reacts the way you or I would under certain circumstances."

69

"The life of Thomas Maimoni is a great confirmation of the saying that the two worst things in life are, first, not to get what you want, and second, to actually get what you want." Attorney Jeffrey Denner stepped forward to persuade the jury with his closing arguments to set his client free. "Thomas Maimoni is someone who always wanted to be somebody, more desperately than most. So much that he was willing to create himself out of whole cloth. Ironically, Mr. Maimoni got his wish. He did, in fact, become a somebody. He never dreamt that the somebody he would become would be so universally hated and scorned." Denner implored the jury to separate any passion, anger, or distaste for his client from their impartial determination of the facts. "You are the only judges of the facts in this case."

What were the facts? From all the Commonwealth's experts? All their forensic evidence? Martha Brailsford had drowned. But even that was a "diagnosis by exclusion." The tests that would have established more conclusive answers, "that could have really told us what happened here, were simply not done."

Why? Because, Denner stressed, "when the investigators found the body at the bottom of the ocean with the weight belt and an anchor, when they found Tom Maimoni making up a new story every day or two, they figured they had an open-and-shut case. There was a real rush to judgment."

Denner took them through the experts' testimony, one by one. Baden, who had told them the apparent absence of hemorrhaging tissue around the ankles suggested that Martha had been dead when the rope pulled her downward. Again, microscopic tests by the medical examiner would have been more definitive, had they been done.

All the doctors who had taken the stand agreed that the bruises were not associated with external bleeding, cortical brain injury, or skull fractures. Both sides had agreed that none of these bruises would have caused death. The most likely result would have been some degree of confusion, with only a slim likelihood of unconsciousness. Peri mortem, antemortem, or postmortem—all were consistent with Tom's story and the effects on Martha's head.

The blood on the sails. No prosecution witness had disputed the defense's own witness who testified that the blood stains were "low velocity" drops, not spatters. In other words, blood had "dripped" onto the sail, most likely from above. It had not been hurled there as the result of a stabbing or a punching. It was consistent with a bloody nose or a "cut on the hand." There was no other blood on the boat consistent with any kind of violent interaction. No blood had been found, even in the tiniest cracks, despite two thorough searches with special lights designed to pick up traces of blood even after the most vigorous of cleaning efforts.

And no semen. Where was the evidence of this big sexual assault the Commonwealth inferred had happened?

The dental injuries. Consistent with a blow on the chin, possibly the result of slipping on the deck. As much a likelihood—if not more—than any malicious act.

Denner reviewed for them Avery's testimony about what it might have been like to stand on a convex deck with no handrail and to be hit unexpectedly from behind by a wake. He recalled for the jury the timing issues—Hillary Smart's uncontroverted sighting and Ray Mount's, which, he said, was disputed by the dockmaster's records. Denner mentioned Robert Montague—the "friend" who had wasted no time courting Tom's wife and who had come to court and under oath contradicted his own previous statements and the observations of three witnesses. Denner asked the jury whether it was credible that on a summer evening in July there had been not one other person at the busy Palmer's Cove Yacht Club besides Ray Mount who could have reported seeing Tom's boat in its slip. All this, despite the media coverage and the utter willingness of people down at the club to do all they could to help the police make their case against Tom Maimoni.

"That's not true!" a young woman cried out as she watched the monitor in the lobby below the courtroom with the reporters and the overflow crowd. Charlene Colella, Ray Mount's companion on the day in question, couldn't believe her ears. Although she and Ray had obtained seats for the closing remarks, Kevin Mitchell had asked them to leave. Her reaction now to Denner's comments probably had been anticipated by the prosecutor. Charlene could not contain herself. Charlene had been there. Charlene had seen, had remembered. How could this man be allowed to lie outright to the jury? Tears of frustration and anger filled her eyes, and her voice bordered on hysteria. One of the news reporters turned to Ray Mount, who was standing with Charlene. "Maybe you'd better take her out of here, try to calm her down," the man suggested.

Denner continued. The testimony of the two women, the Commonwealth's evidence of the "sexual depravity" of the defendant—hadn't impressed the defense counsel very much. "Roxcy Platte had a horrible experience," Denner stated, with mock outrage. "Kissed nicely, still willing to go out with him, but thought she ought to report it to the police. Rosemary Farmer. *Horrible* experience. 'Why didn't he walk me up the dock?' It's clear she was raped within an inch or two of her life. *'Why didn't he walk me up the dock?'*"

Jeff Denner reminded the jury that Dr. Bursztajn had felt the most likely possibility was an accident, given Tom's absolute lack of any history of violence. "When people are violent with him, he runs, he cries, he hides, he denies, he lies, he dissimulates. This is not the profile of a murderer. This is not the profile of someone who's even sexually aggressive. He's pathetic. He drops his pants. He tells everybody, 'Look at me!' He's a child in a man's body. This is what he's all about.

"If this horrible accident hadn't happened, he would still be taking women out there, telling them he has a Ph.D., a masters in this, a bachelor in this, the most terrific guy that ever came down the road or down the waterway, and he would be doing it for the rest of his life, and it wouldn't be true. And it doesn't mean that he doesn't love Patti, and didn't mean that he didn't love Linda Beckley, or any of them.

"What it means is, he can't make it alone as a human being. For whatever reason, he's screwed up. He has a deep hole in the middle of his soul that requires constant esteem, the constant admiration of other people, because he feels so little, despite how tall he is, so little that everybody has always got to fill it up with admiration and praise for him and he's got to build a fantasy life to reflect off of those people so they'll like him. 'Gee, Tom, you're great. You've got a Ph.D. You're the world's greatest sailor. You're sexual all the time.'"

The worst thing the defendant could have said in a case like this, Denner offered, was to admit to being in a "sexual state of mind all his life." But Tom Maimoni was so weak he couldn't stop himself from standing up and saying that to the jury. "He hurts so much that his own sense of himself is still so tied up in these images. Even when trying to save himself, he says things that hurt him, things that are still tied to the macho, wonderful, 'ain't I great' type of mentality. 'Don't you love me, and therefore shouldn't I have some right to love myself?' But it ain't so, and you know it's not so.

"He didn't start lying on July 12. This is the way he is. You can understand how credible it is that Tom Maimoni would have reacted the way he did that night. 'Oh my God, what am I going to do now? Somebody better come out and save me. Maybe Bill will come out. Where is that Bill? Where is that magical intervention that is going to get me out of this?' Because that is how he lived his life—exactly that way.

"If he's charged with being a jerk and a liar and pathetic and of disposing of a body, he's guilty. He's charged with murder. I ask you to look into your hearts and your minds and understand what the psychiatrists have told you, understand it from the top to the bottom who this man is.

"There is no evidence to support anything other than the theory of accident in this case. When you deliberate, you must remember these are not just words: it is the Commonwealth's obligation to persuade you of the absence of accident beyond a reasonable doubt. And after you have thought about this case and have reviewed the evidence, if you come back and you think, 'Gee, I just don't know,' then they have not satisfied that burden. You must come back with a verdict of Not Guilty."

Now it was the Commonwealth's turn. Assistant District Attorney Kevin Mitchell strode up to the jury box for his last shot.

"You almost got the sense that to decide this case you need

the experts to tell you what to do, and Dr. Harold Bursztajn was certainly ready and available to do that. But most cases for most of the time since the court system has existed have simply said, give us twelve men and women who apply common sense, common experience, and ask to hear the witnesses who were there, the witnesses who saw, the witnesses who listened, the witnesses who knew, not the witnesses who come in later and opine what could have been."

Mitchell reviewed the Commonwealth's case, starting with the doubts raised by the defense regarding Ray Mount's sighting of *Counterpoint* at 6:15 on the evening of Friday, July 12. Mitchell stressed that whether Mount was right or wrong, the evidence was overwhelming and didn't depend on this timing.

The prosecutor argued that the defendant—the man supposedly compelled to lie, compelled to spill out admissions to the police—nevertheless managed to control his lies very effectively, conforming to known facts at every step. And his compulsion to confess to the authority figures he so loved? He seemed to have no problem telling the Maine police that he wouldn't talk about Massachusetts. He had, in fact, never to this day "confessed" to anything, to anyone. Tom Maimoni was very much in control of what he said. The jury should hold him accountable for his own sworn statements on the stand.

The experts. Some you like, some you don't. "I suggest to you when you look at all the witnesses, Mr. Maimoni included, possibly you may find the most offensive, in your opinion, Dr. Michael Baden." Clearly, assistant district attorney Kevin Mitchell had. Dr. Baden had tried to convince the jury that from a photograph of the body he had been able to infer that Martha was dead when tied up, despite the fact that the tissue in which he had "found no hemorrhaging " wasn't even present. The drowning test arguments? Both sides claimed drowning, so what was the difference?

Mitchell checked off the other defense experts. Most had said nothing. Stuart James was interesting, said the prosecutor. A great toxicologist, yet not so experienced in crime scene analysis. Never had done a sail before. A blood-splattered surface with no fixed planes, countless possible positions. James had not worked with the sail to discover what its position most likely had been. Rather, James had constructed the position that best accommodated his theory of the blood spatters. To comply with his hypothesis, James had concluded that the top of the sail came off the mast and was flopping around. He had reasoned that the slugs had come out of the groove. Tom Maimoni in all his accident stories for more than a year—to the police, to his friends, to neighbor Jim Brown—had never mentioned the slugs nor the sail coming out, until James had done his research a few months before the trial. The first time Maimoni had ever brought up slugs and flopping sails was on the witness stand earlier that week.

Mitchell went through all the outrageous "mistakes" Tom had claimed Martha made for the "accident" scenario to work. This woman, whom only yesterday Tom had finally conceded on the stand was a "good sailor," since his testimony came immediately after Bill's description of Martha's expertise. For the preceding year and a half, Tom had dubbed Martha a "lousy" sailor.

The Herculean recovery—interesting details—putting on the wet suit, taking off Martha's clothes. Banging her head around a bit during the rescue. Why include these details? Because the prosecution has already shown these to be facts, incriminating facts.

What about Dr. Avery's precise calculations on the dynamics of this boat, with those unknown trawlers of unknown speed and size? "This is not a courtroom of possibilities," Mitchell said to the jury. "It's a courtroom of probabilities." But even Avery's mathematical formula had come up with what? An effect much like an elevator ride. This was no tidal wave. This was no "gunwale-to-gunwale" roll. Not with a recreational boat like the Cal 28.

Why hadn't Tom thrown the life preserver to Martha the moment he spotted her struggling in the water a few yards away? Because, said the prosecutor, *the "accident" never happened.* Closing arguments were the only time in a trial when each side could suggest its own theory to the jury. Tom Maimoni may not have taken Martha out on the boat to kill her. He had other purposes, and "things" happened. "And sure, he panicked, but it's the same panic that any person would feel after what had just occurred between him and Martha."

Why had Tom told the jury the weight belt was a "junk weight belt?" "Did any of you really believe that Tom bought a second weight belt? We may each need a couple pairs of shoes. Does anyone need two weight belts? And why describe it as 'junk?'" Because Tom wouldn't have had to answer the next question, explained Mitchell. The prosecutor had put it to him: "What were you going to tell your wife when she came back and she asked, 'Tom, where did my weight belt go?'" Tom had one more week before Patti's return. The chart with his *X* and only fifty foot of clear water in a familiar diving spot would have made it possible to retrieve the belt in time. And also offer the opportunity to rid the body, once its identity and injuries had been obscured by crustacean activity, of the only evidence of murder—the anchor and belt. But no, Tom would say. No need to retrieve those. It was a "junk" belt. And a "junk" anchor.

"Not every crime occurs in public. But this case does have the benefit of circumstantial evidence and common sense, and Tom's activities afterward that tell you what occurred. You know the facts. You know it was a 'quick sail.' You know she believed him a 'widower.' You know what was in Tom's mind. You know she was out on that boat."

The jury also knew, said the prosecutor, that the spot where she was found was uniquely protected from prying eyes. Only important if it had still been daylight, of course.

Here was a man who had married four times, who took from every one of his wives and never gave back. "Mr. Denner was telling you exactly the truth when he said in his opening statement that Tom was in a panic because he couldn't afford to lose this marriage. Tom couldn't afford it, not because of his love for Patti but because of his love for himself. His desire to protect himself. On that boat when Martha Brailsford reacted and the event occurred, Tom had said: 'I'm taking care of myself.'

"Ladies and gentlemen, I submit to you, we haven't replaced the jury system with psychiatrists yet. You've got the injuries, you've got blood on the sail, the mouth…Think about knocking a tooth out, what that takes."

Kevin Mitchell told the jury to think also about Tom's testifying, "Bill should have been there," then remember how on the morning after dumping Martha's body Tom had patted Bill calmly on the back and had promised to say a prayer. "Magical thinking? Tom Maimoni *is taking care of himself*. Members of the jury, the evidence is there."

70

Judge Patti Saris stood up and asked the members of the jury to do the same. The judge's job was now to give them instructions of law, three years of law school crammed into an hour or two. "You must follow these instructions, whether you agree with them or not." These charges included basic constitutional principles that governed the case and elements of the alleged crime that the Commonwealth had to prove beyond a reasonable doubt. Finally, Judge Saris reviewed the choosing of the jury's foreperson, the selection of alternates, and the mechanics of deliberations.

The jury's job was the hardest one. They would have to decide which witnesses were credible, which weren't, "which ones remembered, which ones forgot, who told the truth, and who didn't." The jury would have to determine which evidence to accept, how important it was, and what conclusions to draw from it. Occasionally, Saris told them, a defendant waived the right to a jury trial. In that event, the judge would have to make these same decisions. At such times, "I would give anything to have eleven other members of my community from different corners and from different walks of life to help me make that decision. There is a certain beauty and significance to the fact that there has to be a unanimous verdict—twelve out of twelve of you." From jurors who were agreeable to both sides.

The jury was reseated. The judge read her charges. "All parties, whether they be the prosecutor or the defendant, stand as equals at the bar of justice. So when you go out to deliberate, the question before you can never be, 'Will the Commonwealth win or lose a case?' The Commonwealth is *you.* You are the Commonwealth of Massachusetts, and the Commonwealth always wins when justice is done, whether the verdict is 'guilty' or 'not guilty.'"

There were four possible verdicts in this case. Murder in the first degree required proof of malice aforethought, combined with either deliberate premeditation or extreme atrocity. Second-degree murder required only malice aforethought—the specific, conscious intent to kill. If malice had not been proved, yet the death had not been an accident, the jury must find Mr. Maimoni guilty of manslaughter. If accidental death could not be ruled out beyond a reasonable doubt, the defendant must be found not guilty.

Everyone stood as the jurors filed out.

The jury in the Maimoni case consisted of nine men and three women spanning a broad band of the occupational spectrum. They included landscapers, painters, scientists, social workers, truck drivers, Ph.D.s, and the unemployed. The Maimoni jurors had spent two weeks together, sequestered only on the night they began their deliberations. In 1993, two weeks seemed like a long time. Nevertheless, they had gotten along nicely and had suffered no scandals. A few had gone to work after court adjourned each afternoon, further lengthening the long, cold days marked by early sunsets and treacherous commutes.

When they were finally given the case on February 11, 1993, they quickly came to a nearly unanimous consensus. However, at least one juror felt uncomfortable with the timing of the events on the boat. Could Tom have murdered Martha, weighted her down, dropped the body, and returned to PCYC within two and a quarter hours? Both Hillary Smart and Ray Mount were convincing, credible witnesses. If the timing were off, it wasn't clear any other theory was plausible, either. Nevertheless, it stuck in the juror's mind and would nag him for a long time to come.

The jury deliberated for two hours after dinner, taking the opportunity to carefully look over the boxes of evidence. Many of them reached out to touch the cold, hard surface of the anchor and to heft the diving belt. Some looked through the graphic photographs. A few wanted to see the bruises again. Most still could not believe how much damage crustaceans could do in a week. Around 9 P.M. the jurors agreed that after such a long trial and an exhausting day, they had better sleep on it before rendering any decision.

The next morning, on Friday, February 12, the jury returned to Newburyport Courthouse to finish their deliberations.

71

Seen through Palladian windows in the second floor courtroom, a predicted snowstorm arrived on Friday morning. It intensified during the noon break. Witnesses, observers, faithful Willows neighbors, the press—all trudged across a sloppy street to the Mall Restaurant for lunch. Shoulders slumped, leaning into blowing snow. Judge, prosecutor, police, and defense attorneys ordered in. As did the jury.

Eyes were glued to the courthouse door for any sign of activity. Weariness was kept at bay by raging anticipation. By one o'clock, everyone had eaten lunch. They watched snow accumulate and waited for the axe to fall. Now, this large group of people, who had spent their days together for two and a half weeks, put on coats and crossed the familiar street, returning to the courthouse one last time. Overlooking an icy pond in the center of town, the Bullfinch exterior of the oldest continually operating courthouse in the country seemed to promise justice. Daniel Webster had argued his first cases here.

With pulses quickening, the spectators filed heavily into the large hall, snow-covered, shaking from the cold, adding slushy water and road salt to the polished wood floors. Cold wind off the ocean rushed in, an unwelcome companion, to chill those sitting on the long church pew benches. The press read its own words from city and town newspapers. TV crews stood about, internal motors idling. Soggy, wet, wool coats steamed over old-fashioned radiators.

On the walls of this courthouse, rich in history, candle lamps glowed in sparkling glass chimneys. These added the softness of yesteryear, a time when formal dress and ball gowns would have more appropriately filled the room. A Christmas ball. A New England tradition.

The audience waited. And then they waited some more. They waited for the electric pulse that would signal the jury had come to a decision. At one point a court officer exited the jury room and headed up the stairs to the judge's chamber. A flurry of excitement. All for nothing. The court officer returned to the jury room. It was simply a question the jury had on a point of law. The sea of stoic New England faces settled into disappointment. Amid the smell of steaming wool coats, people moved about the hall nervously.

And then the moment arrived. The long-awaited signal moved like a wave through the lobby. With a burst of energy, the court officer threw open the door to the jury room, then closed it with equal firmness. She rushed up the stairs to the judge's chambers. This time she averted her glance. The pleasing personality and warm smile this dark-haired woman had worn for two and a half weeks was now on hold. The moment had come.

The crowd surged and mobilized into a thick line. New rules were put into place. Electronic body searches for all.

Newsmen stationed in the lobby slapped on their headphones. Kevin Mitchell rounded up the Brailsford family and took them into his office to preview for them how things would proceed. Members of the media shoved their way up the stairs to the front of the line. Court officers started the search process. When the victim's family came back out, they were allowed to ascend the stairs with the press, to the annoyance of last-minute curiosity seekers who jockeyed for position, who had not learned the procedure, and who did not know the players.

Upstairs, in the unevenly heated courtroom, reporters resumed their seats under the huge windows, their backs to the excessively toasty radiators. Everyone chitchatted furiously, responding with meaningless noises to the dictates of their nerves. They sat and waited.

When the family of Martha Brailsford were all inside the courtroom, they were removed as a group. Each was searched a second time, as a precaution. It was eerie to see them finally singled out. The overt recognition that they had been wronged, measured by the danger they might now pose toward the defendant. This gentle, quiet family. Bill's silver-haired parents. Martha's delicate-boned twin sister and teary-eyed brother.

Everyone rose with pounding hearts as the jury was led in. None of the twelve faces surrendered to the stares of the audience. Denner's and Maimoni's mouths went dry, and they chewed furiously on wads of gum.

The clerk straightened up. "May I inquire of the jury, your honor?"

"You may," answered the judge.

"Mr. Foreman, has your jury agreed upon a verdict?"

"Yes," answered the foreman.

"May I have the papers, please? Mr. Foreman, what say you to Indictment 19432, charging the defendant, Thomas Maimoni, of murder? How do you find the defendant, guilty or not guilty?" The courtroom froze.

"Guilty."

"Guilty of what, Mr. Foreman?"

"Murder in the second degree."

"Mr. Foreman and members of the jury, hearken to your verdict as the court has recorded it. You upon your oaths do say the defendant Thomas Maimoni is guilty of Indictment 19432, charging with murder in the second degree, so say you Mr. Foreman and members of the jury, you all say?"

To a silent courtroom, the jurors chorused: "Guilty."

The defendant and his attorneys kept firm hold on their emotions. Their jaws worked nervously on their gum. Tom's eyes grew small and focused inwardly. Martha's family reached out to one another with both a mixture of relief at the guilty verdict and shock at the lack of its severity. Bill reached over and shook his brother-in-law's hand. Second degree was a disappointment. Bill Brailsford maintained the composure that had seen him through this arduous trial. The dignity without obscured the insult within.

72

Muriel Conant Garvey bore a strong resemblance to her fraternal twin sister Martha. Muriel's hair was darker, but her features echoed her sister's beauty, depth, and sensitivity. The elegant design of Muriel's blue jacket indicated she also shared with her sister an appreciation for artistic creativity. Reading a statement from the stand in a voice that conveyed both her earnestness and her grief, Muriel Conant Garvey spoke for her sister.

"Never has this world, fallen under the shadow of so much senseless and brutal crime, needed caring and compassionate individuals more than it does now. The loss of even one voice speaking out for kindness, helpfulness, and respect for all life diminishes the fragile humanity upon which a meaningful existence is built." Although sentencing was predetermined, the family was given the opportunity to address the court first.

She spoke of Martha's artistry, her style, her generosity, her reaching out to strays. Broken wings. Broken hearts. Broken souls.

"How sad to think it was this very compassion in the end which proved itself a vulnerability to be exploited and violated. How ironic that a ready willingness to reach out the hand of friendship to someone she believed distressed and grieving for a loved one became the very act of her undoing. How tragic that a response to that, which she felt to be a human cry for sympathy and understanding, became the very means through which her voice was silenced forever."

Paul Brailsford, Bill's father, came up to the front of the courtroom and made a plea for tougher laws against those who stalked and murdered women, those who were never rehabilitated but who were released to stalk and kill again. He thanked the jury in this sad case and the women who had mustered the courage to come forward to testify.

As family members read their statements, those listening couldn't help thinking of the multitude of hidden effects this tragedy had on all who had known Martha. Favors no longer done, support no longer given, voices no longer heard. T-shirts drying on the balcony, a dog tied up outside. Someone else now had to bring them all inside.

Thomas Maimoni declined to make a statement. As one news reporter put it, when the "con artist was offered the opportunity to speak," he chose not to. "In the end, Maimoni apparently had no more performances to give."

Sentencing was predetermined. Second degree murder in the Commonwealth of Massachusetts brought life imprisonment with the possibility of parole after fifteen years. One and a half of those years had already been served. Tom could come before the parole board in 2006 and be out before he reached the golden years of retirement.

This time Tom Maimoni was handcuffed before exiting the courtroom. As he was led up the aisle, he passed by his parents, seated in the back.

"There goes my boy," his father said softly.

73

A s dusk descended outside, schools all over the county were breaking for February vacation. But here, inside the court-house, family and friends hugged each other in subdued comfort. Newsmen and newswomen chattered at their cameras in the lobby. Mitchell and Denner were interviewed. Members of the jury made a run for the front door through a human obstacle course. Reporters were lined up at the single pay phone, calling in their stories.

Once again shackled and cuffed, Thomas Maimoni, too, had to run the gauntlet when the Essex County Sheriff's Department van arrived to take him to his new home at the maximum-secu-rity Cedar Junction Prison. Camera lights blinded him as he was led out the side door. Mark Wile, a well-known reporter from WHDH-TV news was waiting at the top of the stairs. "Tom, how do you feel about the verdict? Do you see a second degree conviction as at least a partial victory?"

As the guards cleared a path down the steps, Tom turned politely and addressed the reporter on the first-name basis ac-corded the newsmakers of the world. "I can't comment on that now, Mark."

While the jury was deliberating, the predominant feeling among them had been that Tom's testimony simply was not credible. As a result, little relevance was placed on the psychiatric testimony, since it seemed to apply only if they could have believed Tom's story. Jeff Denner's closing argument that being a pathetic jerk didn't make a murderer out of Tom had made a powerful impression on some. And for others, there was still the issue of timing. But in the end, the burden of proof weighed in. The image of the weight belt, the memory of Virginia McCarthy's eyes as she described Tom's reaction to the news of the lobster-man's discovery, the diving suit hanging out on the boat Friday night in readiness for a possible return trip. The testimony of Roxcy and Rosemary, setting the tone, and Tom's likely state of mind—all critical, critical testimony for the jury. Then the testi-mony of Bill Brailsford regarding his marriage and Martha's pre-dictable habits. During the night, one juror couldn't help thinking about how happily married the Brailsfords seemed to have been. Tom's story of Martha's afternoon and evening just did not fit. What did fit—and what seemed most likely to the jury—was that Tom Maimoni had made a pass at Martha and that she had absolutely and angrily refused him. A struggle might have en-sued, resulting in the bruises, and possibly an accidental death. If Tom had used that story—admitting his spurned advances—the jury might have found that very credible. They quite possibly could have found her death to be accidental and could have considered Dr. Bursztajn's testimony more seriously as an expla-nation for the attempted cover-up.

Instead, Tom's version seemed a far-fetched attempt to por-tray himself in the best possible light. In doing so, he had stretched the jury's acceptance beyond the breaking point. The mountain of little improbabilities piled up into an almost laugh-able fiction. The psychologist had explained away Tom's behav-iors and statements too neatly, too conveniently. Professor Avery, with two sets of glasses and a calculator, had punched out G forces with six-digit degrees of accuracy. The "rogue wave" had rolled around the jury box like a joke.

Judge Saris met with the jury in private to answer any ques-tions they might have, informally, openly, without robes. As human beings. It was her way of thanking them personally after a long, emotional trial. It was cathartic for her as well.

Onlookers were hesitant to leave the intimacy of Newbury-port Courthouse. Once out the door, this small moment in Salem's history would be behind them, replaced by the driving snow now assaulting their faces. They scraped off their cars and cranked their engines for the long, treacherous ride home.

Bill Brailsford sought out Patti Maimoni to express his sympathy for her as a victim as well. Then he and his family stepped out into the snowy evening and disappeared through a curtain of white.

74

A week or so after the verdict, the other members of the Criminal Investigation Division arranged a surprise party for Conrad Prosniewski at the Pig's Eye. Julie Michaud, co-conspirator, agreed to bring him to the restaurant on the pretext of, "Let's go out for Mexican food," the specialty at the Pig's Eye on Monday nights. When the two arrived, the gang did their surprise thing, and Dick Urbanowicz made a little speech.

After dinner, Julie drove back to the house. Prosniewski and the rest of the division elected to roll downtown to Jonathan's for "one more drink." There they relived the highlights of the past year and a half and toasted one of the best examples of teamwork the department had ever known. They reminisced about what the prosecution team had dubbed the "Maimoni moments" in the case. And they reminisced about everything else.

As closing time approached, Prosniewski's friends peeled off one by one, took their leaves with a final congratulations, and disappeared. When the last one left, Prosniewski pulled on his coat and looked around. Somehow he had been left with no car and no ride. He stepped outside and took another hopeful look around. Nobody there. "Shit," he sighed, and trudged across Salem to his home.

It wasn't until he received a thank-you note from Bill Brailsford a short time later that Prosniewski finally felt satisfied with the verdict. He shared the family's disappointment with the failure to get a first-degree conviction. But the detective initially wondered how the outcome would sit with Bill. When Brailsford indicated it was enough of a resolution to try to start putting the events behind him, to begin rebuilding his own life, Prosniewski felt the case had begun to close.

Meanwhile, the media wasn't ready to let go of this compelling case. *Hard Copy* did a segment for national television soon after the verdict was in, during which the camera cut frequently to ominous images of waves slapping against the side of a sailboat (a stand-in boat, of course). A few local papers mentioned the case in their year-end retrospectives. The *Beverly-Peabody Times* wrote about the "Maimoni moments" in a December 31, 1993, article. One of those moments was Tom sending Assistant District Attorney Kevin Mitchell a bloody pillowcase from his prison cell a few weeks after the trial, along with a note explaining he had suffered a nosebleed. He had just wanted Mitchell to know he had not been lying when he announced on the stand that the blood on the sail was from his own nose. Tom was offended that Mitchell had doubted this claim.

For a number of weeks after the trial there was some sporadic poking around by writers from the West Coast. Conrad Prosniewski received a faxed letter from Los Angeles with a document entitled "Free Option and Purchase Agreement for Free Option and Purchase of Biographical Material," proposing to buy his story for $5,000. A short treatment was included. Prosniewski knew he could not accept but let it hang around on top of his In box for awhile as a topic of conversation, perhaps hoping to garner a little more respect from his department.

A made-for-TV movie popped up in the fall, clearly inspired by the Maimoni case. The *Disappearance of Christina* borrowed only the most sensational aspects of this case. In the movie, a glamorous woman disappears from the deck of a sailboat, and some guy onboard (her husband) is suspected of throwing her into the drink. After a lengthy search, a skeletonized female body is recovered in a commercial fisherman's net. The subtlety takes a nosedive after that.

Later, in March, Salem Police Chief St. Pierre sent Detective Sergeant Conrad Prosniewski a letter of commendation, thanking him for his superb investigation, his professionalism, and for making the department look like a million bucks. "You're a great cop," he wrote.

"Personally, I don't believe in commendations," growled Prosniewski's supervisor Dick Urbanowicz. He called Prosniewski at home about the same time. Something he never, never did. "But if I did, I guess this might be as good a time as any for one. You did OK."

That was the best part, Prosniewski told Julie. Dick calling.

75

Four days after the trial ended, it was snowing again. After the long President's Day weekend, Sandy Clark, the victim/witness advocate, needed a day off to do all the errands she couldn't do during office hours. She first called in and got a vacation day. Then she took care of her errands.

There was still, however, unfinished business. The trial was over. The Brailsford family now had to begin the healing process. The prosecution team could pat each other on the back. The media could go find the next front page story. The defense team could go to work on the appeal. Tom Maimoni could settle in to his new home at the Cedar Junction Prison. Safe, structured. But for Sandy, there had been no closure. Everybody's "mother," the victim/witness advocate was facing an empty nest. The good-byes had been too sudden. Endings had passed too fast.

So Sandy turned north and drove to Salem Willows. Pulling up beside the beach on Cove Avenue, Sandy shut off the engine and stepped out into the snow. There beside the seawall, was a tiny garden ringed with stones—the monument to Martha just where Sandy had heard it would be. She stood there, unsure of what to do or say, or why she had come. No, she knew why she had come.

The plants were dead, of course. The flowers gone. Little sticks thrusting up through the snow. Memories of last summer, promises of next spring.

"Martha," she began. "I thought we should meet." All the

people whose needs she had attended to these past eighteen months. She had gotten to know Bill, Roxcy, Rosemary, Jennifer, and numerous others. She had not gotten to know Martha. How could she say good-bye, when she'd never said hello?

The sound of a car threatened the mood. Sandy turned around, conscious that she had been speaking aloud, though curtained by the falling snow from eavesdroppers. The car slowed. A man waved from within. As he pulled to a stop, she recognized the driver.

It was Bill Brailsford. He stepped out, crossed the snowy street, and joined her at the seawall. His face told Sandy there was no need to explain why she was standing here in the middle of a February blizzard. She, in turn, had grown accustomed to the countless crossings of paths in the Brailsford case.

Bill pointed out the various parts of the garden and where the original plaque had stood before it was lost in October 1991, during a storm locally known as NoName. He showed her the water fountain nearby, encrusted with bits of broken pottery and pieces of Martha's jewelry, lovingly inlaid by the neighborhood kids in her memory. Martha and the kids used to work with pottery together.

In the cement at the base were a set of paw prints. "Those are Rudy's," he explained. Then it so happened a neighbor chanced to come along, as if on cue, walking Rudy. Martha's dog had been adopted by the entire street. Bill turned. "Come and meet Rudy." He introduced Sandy to the dog. The famous Rudy. Prime witness. Sandy smiled. Rudy smiled back. Bill Brailsford had come out of nowhere with a gift for Sandy—closure.

They looked back toward the garden. Bill said, "Want me to tell you about Martha?"

Sandy nodded. "Please, do."

And so he did.

PART IV

And it's under the willows, come walk with me, love,
The sea at our feet and the sky up above,
The children at play know there's nothing to fear,
In the sweet Salem breezes, come walk with me, dear.

Under the Willows
Bob Franke

EPILOGUE

Within the thirty days allotted by law, Denner and Associates filed a routine notice of appeal. Shortly thereafter, Tom Maimoni and Jeff Denner severed their relationship, and all the attorney's files were turned over to a new court-appointed lawyer, Stephen Weymouth of Boston.

Now sitting in his cell at the Norfolk prison fifteen miles south of Boston, Maimoni is convinced that Denner "screwed" him. By the time they had gone to trial, the defense strategy had shifted all over the place, he contends. The ultimate picture that was presented was not at all what Maimoni had expected. IQ of 92? "I have a measured IQ of 160. The psychologist Denner sent spent fifteen minutes with me. That says it all," he now counters. Pathological liar? Maimoni insists he is not. Under stress, or to avoid conflict, he prefers the words "incurably dishonest."

He also bristles at being called a stalker of women. "I've always been called a 'Tomcat'," he says with thinly disguised pride. "But people don't understand. It's just that I prefer the company of women. I'm a feminist. I've always promoted equality in the workplace." People also call him a chameleon, he complains. "I get along with everyone, that's all."

All in all, Maimoni claims, the defense team sold him out. During the trial they told him to sit quietly and to take all the names the prosecution was calling him, assuring him that everything would "fall into place" in the end. In fact, during summation Denner himself had called Tom a pathetic jerk. Not only was his defense "incompetent," it was humiliating. Next time there would be an "even playing field." Next time the "facts" would all come out.

Maimoni also believes the justice system itself failed in his case. Not much improvement over the Court of Oyer and Terminer that conducted the witchcraft trials of 1692.

In May 1995, Tom Maimoni's new defense team submitted a motion to appeal based on a number of legal issues. The defense contends that the "bad acts" testimony of Rosemary Farmer and Roxcy Platte should not have been allowed. From the time he was convicted until the time of his appeal, Maimoni had cautioned everyone not to prejudge him guilty just because he had been found guilty in one court of law. "Wait for the appeal. Wait for all the facts to come out," he had said. What were the new "facts" in the appeal? None. Only old facts which should not have come out.

In the months and years since his trial, Maimoni has spent much of his time reviewing the "tapes" in his mind of the events of July 12, 1991. He has thought a lot about what he had meant to say, or wished he had said, and about everyone who "perjured" themselves, who participated in the conspiracy to sell him out. Like viewing countless reruns of the same old movie, Tom's life in prison affords little in the way of distraction. And as he views, he edits.

Take for example, Martha's belief that Tom had lost his wife to cancer. He never told Martha that, he now says. Perhaps he had once mentioned that Patti's mother had passed away, about a year earlier. He may have talked about Patti's father and the grief he felt. Martha must have put one and one together and jumped to the wrong conclusion, Tom explains.

Although he accepts responsibility for mistakes he made, he believes "many others shared in the responsibility" for the course of events on July 12, 1991. One is his wife Patti, whom he feels "should never have left me alone that week." Her "moral obligation was to be by my side." In hindsight, he would say for years to come that had he known his wife's true feelings at the time, he would have brought Martha's body home. Everything he did that night was to save his marriage, the marriage he thought he had.

For Tom, freedom was just another word for loneliness.

Tom's identity was stripped by the removal of the comfortable structure of his daily life, the expectation of self-sufficiency, in the absence of an adoring and supportive audience. Devoid of both wife and job that week in July 1991, Tom Maimoni's terror, his utter panic, had begun long before the "rogue waves" hit him broadside.

Bill Brailsford also shares the blame, Maimoni says. Bill was supposed to be with them that afternoon but had never showed. And he should have contacted the Coast Guard when Martha failed to return at 6:30. Had it been Tom Maimoni who had returned to an empty house, he would have "torn Salem apart" looking for his wife. Every harbormaster would have been called.

Lastly, the community is to blame—all the neighbors whom Martha had told of her plans. Everyone who lives on the water, Maimoni explains, has a responsibility to all those who venture out to sea, to keep an eye out for them should they be late in returning. But in Salem in 1991, no one cared, he says bitterly.

Everyone else was guilty of "hysteria," the same hysteria that plagued Salem 300 years ago during the witch trials. The same rush to judgment. No one can know how they'll behave in a situation like that until they're in one. Tom says he panicked. *That* was his only crime. With all his emergency training, he had learned to handle all kinds of situations, but they had never taught him how to handle those situations *alone*. He was alone, he explains. He was alone then, and he's alone now.

It was so stupid, Tom says. So stupid. "They have an expression—when your life is reduced to its lowest common denominator. Well, that's what my life is now—reduced to its lowest common denominator."

Tom is alternately the hero or the victim of every story he tells, every thought he forms. He is the subject of every sentence. In every solar system, he is the sun. And to this day he maintains his innocence.

Jennifer Eccleston should have been particularly paranoid from her drug use at the time she met Tom. Mistrustful by nature, a shrewd expert on manipulation, she wondered later at her total abandonment of caution that afternoon. Family car, tiny dog, retractable leash. How tame can you get? And Tom had been totally at ease. All the hallmarks of safety and comfort. "He was as good as me," she said later, comparing his manipulative skills to her own. That made her mad. She has begun to conclude that perhaps it wasn't so much that she didn't sense risk. Instead, at that point in her life, she simply didn't care. Today she's starting to care. Jennifer has been clean and sober since 1994 and is currently taking college courses in Rhode Island.

Rosemary Farmer has moved to a new town on the North Shore and continues to teach. She still asks herself, now and then, "What did I do?" People around her—friends and strangers—have hounded her with the same questions, and not always kindly. A sad but common aftermath for victims of assault. But when she's asked which was hardest, dealing with friends or dealing with strangers. She responds: "Dealing with myself."

Roxcy Platte has become more cautious as a result of her experience, but not to the point of refusing to crew again. There is a feeling of community and trust in the boating world that is hard to give up. Sailing with people one doesn't know well is common. People who on land might be strangers on the water are practically kin. "Anyway," she observes, "your own husband of twenty years could be capable of doing this. The ordinary person just doesn't know how to detect psychopathic behavior."

A psychiatric social worker who spent more hours with Tom than the defense psychiatrists did, Roxcy can now look back on the incident with a clinical eye. It also means she is harder on herself. Her questions, "*Why didn't I see?*" and "*Why is this still not resolved for me?*" are particularly acute in her case.

When Tom had asked Roxcy to go dancing two days before his fateful sail, Roxcy went out and bought a dress. But then he had stood her up, calling it off at the last possible moment as she was heading out the door. Her response was casual, hiding her disappointment, where it stayed for years hanging in the closet with the dress. Admitting to herself or to others that she had held any expectations in this now regrettable association was more painful than the canceled date and more costly than the price of the dress.

Although many of these women had found support and compassion from their male acquaintances and from the police, they had often found it lacking in their female friends. Women can be hard on women who have been victimized, they discovered. Women don't like to think they are so powerless. Until it happens to them, women often believe they themselves would have been in more control. They look at those dresses hanging in their own closets and say, "I let myself be fooled!" instead of saying, "*He* fooled *me.*"

As for Tom, Roxcy still struggles to resolve what might never be fully resolvable: how to reconcile the vulnerable aspects Tom Maimoni presented in 1991 with the deed he committed on July 12 of that year. She realizes Tom actually has two vulnerable selves, one fake, one real. The fake one was used as bait, the "pickup line" so effective with the women he seemed to single out. The "dead" wife. The abandonment, through no fault of his own. This was a metaphor for his other and real vulnerable self: the man who was deeply lonely despite his living, breathing wives at home.

Tom's attempted seduction wasn't about sex, of course. It was about his feeling powerless and emasculated, the classic characteristics of a batterer, even one who has not necessarily battered before. Roxcy's theory is that when Tom met the resistance of a strong-willed, independent woman, his "helpless little boy" most likely flew into a rage. Martha's "denying" him was a distorted but unbearable assault on his ego. Tom would have wanted— needed—to overpower her. In the process, somehow, Martha was killed. Tom may have utterly panicked at the time. Roxcy has a hard time believing otherwise but realizes her belief probably exists for her own emotional protection.

Most of the women who encountered Tom Maimoni also recall how during that period their lives were at a low ebb. Tough circumstances had depleted their own emotional arsenals—losses of very close relationships, even deaths of beloved pets. Tom's pain and vulnerability echoed so strongly their own that they felt safe with him. Tom wasn't primarily looking for sympathy with his stories. That crass an approach wouldn't have worked with the intellectual caliber of these particular women, all bright, creative, empathetic. Tom was looking for connection. For the empathetic, it was hard to turn one's back on.

Ray Mount, too, is still trying to bring closure to the case. After his experience, Mount, a family therapist has grown disillusioned at the use and misuse of psychological data in the courtroom. Experts unwittingly become pawns when their data is used in ways it was never intended. "The science and art of psychology is too vulnerable to distortion when people use it for a selfish purpose," Mount believes. It disturbs him to see the noble and pure purpose of his revered field tarnished and distorted.

As an indirect result of his exposure to the judicial system, Mount has since become an activist and champion for the confidentiality of psychotherapy records in cases involving victims of domestic violence. Women who are attacked are currently told they can either prosecute or get counseling. If they try to do both, their attacker can get access to all their therapy records. Dr. Mount is working to see that this is changed.

The prosecution scenario disturbed and haunted Mount for a long time. He spent many sleepless nights working out in his own mind a plausible story that fit the Tom he knew. Tom didn't go to Cat Island to dump a dead body in Ray's favorite dive spot, he decided. That would have been sheer lunacy. Instead, he took a live woman there to show off his great lobster-catching skills. Whatever happened had occurred while Tom and Martha were anchored there. Rather than sail around with her body, it made more sense to weight her, to take her down the anchor line, to tie her to it, to cut loose, and leave her there.

In the end, Ray Mount feels robbed. He cannot bring himself to go back to his favorite Cat Island dive spot. Of all the disillusionment Mount has experienced from this event, Tom's violation of human life and his use of the sea to cover it up has been the hardest to accept. Sea people tend to be caring, responsible, and respectful of Mother Nature. "We're a family," Mount explains, echoing the words of Roxcy and so many others who share his sense of betrayal that a sailor—a *sailor*—could do this.

Four years after the tragedy, Mount tried returning to Cat Island. "It wasn't the same," he says. Spoiled forever by Tom Maimoni's violation of that special place, it now feels like a grave.

On September 8, 1995, Judge Robert A. Barton, Justice of the Superior Court of the Commonwealth of Massachusetts, denied a motion by the defendant that requested a new trial on grounds of ineffective assistance from counsel. One year later the State Appeals Court upheld Maimoni's conviction, turning down his second appeal for a retrial. Meanwhile, Maimoni continues to be a model prisoner at the Norfolk correctional institution. He has promised to keep sending bloody pillowcases to Kevin Mitchell in the DA's office.

Judge Patti B. Saris is now a federal judge in the U.S. District Court in Boston. She has recently taken on an active role talking to teens about the rising tide of domestic abuse and violence among the young.

Hooper Goodwin and his boat *Nadine S* have appeared since 1992 on a Boston commercial for WBZ-TV's coastal stormy weather reports. He later managed, sang, and wrote for a local rock band, Jones Port Transit. In 1993, as his own way of finding closure, Hooper composed a ballad about Martha Brailsford. He still fishes commercially and has served as shellfish constable and assistant harbormaster for the Town of Marblehead.

Patti Montague resigned her position with the Salem schools in March 1993 and now works in New Hampshire, where she lives with her new husband.

Captain Paul Murphy was given the Excaliber Award by Laurie Cabot on behalf of Salem witches for his efforts in protecting the civil rights of witches during the summer of 1992. Their immense gratitude embarrassed him at first. He claimed he was just doing his job. But it made him realize just how little support they normally got.

In November 1994, Maine State Trooper Jeffrey Parola, who had kept Maimoni company after his capture in Maine, died in the line of duty at age twenty-seven, one month after receiving a state police award for bravery in an unrelated incident.

Bill Brailsford continues to live and work in the area, hopeful that he can put this event behind him and rebuild his life without any recurrence of the intense public scrutiny to which he was subjected in 1991.

Kevin Mitchell is still trying cases for the Essex County District Attorney's Office. He looks back on this case as the most intriguing one he's seen in his eighteen years as a prosecutor in the Superior Court. More than any other, "this one was a mystery." Asked what he would have done differently, had he been the defense attorney rather than the prosecutor, he answers: "I would never have put Tom on the stand." Asked how the jury was to imagine his explanation on their own, he replies: "The defendant doesn't have to explain. That's the whole point. When he does, when he gets on that stand, it shifts the burden of proof."

Detective Sergeant Prosniewski is still an investigator with the Salem Police Department, and now serves as media spokesman as well. The Maimoni case has been his biggest so far. On November 13, 1993, Conrad and Julie were married in Hamilton Hall, Salem, Massachusetts. To commemorate the night at Jonathan's when Julie's red dress won Conrad's heart, the last dance at their reception was "Lady in Red."

Salem witch Laurie Cabot still walks the streets of Salem in the black robes that signify her craft. It wasn't until long after the trial that she learned with surprise and relief how accurate her predictions were during the fateful summer of 1991. Subsequently, Captain Murphy has called her for help on another case of a missing Salem woman.

Laurie continues to write and lecture on witchcraft in her efforts to counter the deep-seated misunderstandings of her religion. She officiates at ceremonies and rituals, especially those which mark the changing of the seasons. One of the roles of a witch is to assist in turning the Wheel of the Year as life continues its unending cycle. During each ceremony she casts spells for protection and to neutralize harm. She ends each one by asking that the spell be "correct and for the good of all."

For six terror-filled years, he couldn't be stopped—
until one journalist ingeniously cracked his twisted code...

SLEEP MY LITTLE DEAD

*The True Story of the
Zodiac Killer*

Kieran Crowley

The award-winning *New York Post* reporter whose brilliant work helped crack the Zodiac Killer's secret code
reveals the inside story—as only he can tell it—of the
man who terrorized the streets of New York City for six
years, stalking, savagely attacking, and often killing his
unsuspecting victims in cold blood.

SLEEP MY LITTLE DEAD
Kieran Crowley
___96339-4 $6.50 U.S./$8.50 CAN.

AVAILABLE WHEREVER BOOKS ARE SOLD
FROM ST. MARTIN'S PAPERBACKS